Intellectual Property Management
in R&D Collaborations

Contributions to Management Science

Martin A. Bader

Intellectual Property Management in R&D Collaborations

The Case of the Service Industry Sector

Foreword by Oliver Gassmann,
University of St.Gallen, Switzerland

With 50 Figures and 21 Tables

Physica-Verlag

A Springer Company

Series Editors
Werner A. Müller
Martina Bihn

Author
Dr. Martin A. Bader
BGW AG
Thurgauerstrasse 4
9400 Rorschach am Bodensee
Switzerland
martin.bader@bgw-sg.com

Diss., Univ. St. Gallen 2006, No. 3150

ISSN 1431-1941
ISBN-10 3-7980-1702-3 Physica-Verlag Heidelberg New York
ISBN-13 978-3-7908-1702-7 Physica-Verlag Heidelberg New York

Physica-Verlag is a part of Springer Science+Business Media
springer.com

© Physica-Verlag Heidelberg 2006
Printed in Germany

Cover-Design: Erich Kirchner, Heidelberg

SPIN 11676034   88/3100/YL 5 4 3 2 1 0 – Printed on acid-free and non-aging paper

For Zwanet Hermien, Henri Constantin and Julie Anastasia

Foreword

With this work, Martin Bader examines how companies can take an intellectual property lead during the early stages of inter-firm research and development (R&D) collaborations. Previously, little research has investigated the management of patents in the early phases of the innovation process. Furthermore, there is a dearth of research on patent management in the service industry sector, in which intellectual property management remains a new concept. Bader offers a detailed examination of the process by considering the service industry sector and analyzes a current, relevant, complex problem prominent in management research.

The research at hand stems from two phenomena, both of which are based on knowledge gains achieved in the area of intellectual property management in recent years. First, the number of announced patent applications has increased by 20–30% per year — even without considering multiple patent registrations in several countries. Second, the number of collaborative agreements in the innovation process has simultaneously increased. However, many R&D collaborations eventually turn out to be unsuccessful, so the question arises: To whom does the intellectual property generated by a collaboration belong? This ownership often is decided and specified during the early phases of the R&D process.

The author has conducted a series of interviews with companies in a variety of industries, as well as a detailed examination of IBM, SAP, Swisscom, and SwissRe. According to four identified determinants (broad, narrow, in-bound, out-bound), he identifies four archetypes of intellectual property management: Absorber, Multiplicator, Filtrator, and Leverager. Bader investigates each of these archetypes further to determine their respective and relative strengths and weaknesses.

Although patents often serve as indicators in the innovation research process, the management of intellectual property has not been examined sufficiently. In the service industry sector, patents have begun to be filed offensively only recently and European companies fall far behind their American counterparts; however, the current state of research on intellectual property management offers only little substance so far.

Martin Bader's elaboration distinguishes itself by introducing new findings gleaned through solid research. The goal of the work is reached through clear examples and empirical results and aided by both science and practice.

In his recommendations, Bader does not provide solely experience-based advice, as might have been expected given his extensive industry background, but also thoughtful organizational recommendations based on his previously developed hypotheses. Both the depth and content of the recommendations are convincing and thoughtful.

I wish for this work a wide distribution and for the companies employing this new concept the best of success.

Prof. Dr. Oliver Gassmann

Director
Institute of Technology Management
University of St.Gallen

Acknowledgements

«*La vocation de l'homme est de
dominer et d'ordonner le réel*»

Georges Bernanos

This book emanates from my thesis "*Managing Intellectual Property in Inter-firm R&D Collaborations – The Case of the Service Industry Sector*", which was accepted by the Institute of Technology Management at the University of St.Gallen in Switzerland. This document has only been slightly adapted and altered for the purposes of this publication.

During the writing of my thesis, I had the opportunity to broaden my professional and academic experience. My great respect and gratitude therefore goes to Prof. Dr. Oliver Gassmann, Director of the aforementioned Institute, for supervising my thesis, providing me with the freedom of action while supporting convergence at the same time. Furthermore, I would like to thank Prof. Dr. Beat Schmid, also from University of St.Gallen, for the co-supervision.

As a basis for the thesis I conducted around 450 interviews and discussions with experts from practice and academia. In this context, I am especially grateful to Markus Bedenbecker, Donat Bischof, Peter Bittner, David Brown, Daniela de Capitani, Tim Crean, Dr. Fank Cuypers, Dr. Gary M. Einhaus, Prof. Dr. Holger Ernst, Dr. Stephan Fischer, Benoît Gilligmann, Prof. Dr. John Hagedoorn, Alexander Harte, Nadine Heitmann, Prof. Dr. Lutz Heuser, Daniel Huber, Daniel L. Kapp, Eric Lauper, Dr. Thomas Müller-Kirschbaum, Dr. Erich Rütsche, Guenther Schmalz, Philippe Therias, Fritz Teufel, Sinan Tumer, Harald Ulrich, Dr. Christoph Wilk and Dr. Juan-Carlos Wuhrmann. Furthermore, I appreciated the support of Dr. Werner Müller and Barbara Feß during the publication process.

I would also like to thank my colleagues from the Institute of Technology Management, and from its spin-off Kuehne-Institute for Logistics and from the Institute of European and International Business Law at the University of St.Gallen. We had a very good time together. Moreover, I would like to thank my diploma and bachelor students at the University of St.Gallen, the University of Karlsruhe, Germany, and at the Ecole Nationale Supérieure de Génie Industriel INP Grenoble, France; comprising Karim Askar, Lukas Müller, Roger Sutter and Angela Beckenbauer. Angela will be succeeding my research activities at the University of St.Gallen, I would like to thank her for the fruitful discussions and the work on our collaborative academic activities.

As a special gift, I am grateful to have met Dr. Christoph Wecht who emerged as both a friend and business partner. We conducted various activities together and I would like to thank him for his support and his constructive, critical comments that truly helped to improve my endeavors.

As a point of honor, I also dedicate my gratitude and respect to my parents for their love and support, and the striving for education, leadership and discipline. In this same respect, I also thank my parents-in-law.

Finally, as a by-achievement of this thesis, my long-term dream to set-up an intellectual property related advisory group has become real by merging with two very suitable business partners to form a university spin-off. Most satisfyingly, I am grateful for the liaison with my former fiancée that evolved to a bond of matrimony and has blossomed into two new sparkles in our world. They have become my backbone for the spirit and purpose of life and it is to whom I dedicate this work.

St. Gallen and Rorschach am Bodensee   Martin A. Bader
June 2006

Table of Contents

1 Introduction

1.1 Increasing Competitiveness

At the beginning of the 21st century, the business world is dynamic and complex and competition is globalized. Success rates in innovation in such a context are low. Only 0.6% of innovative ideas are eventually successful. In the pharmaceutical industry, the success rate falls to 1 in 10,000. The requirements for handling innovations have increased in numerous ways: globalization of competition, explosion of technological knowledge, technological fusion, decentralization of knowledge, escalation of research and development costs, reduction of innovation cycles, and acceleration of innovation diffusion.

Globalization of competition: The intensity of competition has increased due to the opening of national borders and the expansion of multinational firms. The takeover of *IBM's* PC operations by the Chinese firm *Lenovo* in 2004 would have been inconceivable only a few years ago. Hence, in many industries it is no longer sufficient to merely sell and protect products locally. The power of economies of scale of production, along with a dramatic reduction in transportation and information costs has forced many players to go global.

Explosion of technological knowledge: The amount of knowledge doubles every seven years. The number of scientific journals has grown substantially over the last few centuries. The figure was estimated at only about 100 in the 19th century, increasing to around 1,000 in 1850, jumping to 10,000 in 1900, and coming close to 100,000 in 2000. At the same time, approximately 80% of technical knowledge in the form of patent applications is published. Over 90% of the information in patent documents is not protected, due to expiration, rejection, retraction or non-extension (Ehrat 1997). Not only is the greater part of technological knowledge openly accessible, but it can also be freely and openly used.

Technological fusion: Increasingly, there has been fusion of various technological knowledge areas. According to a 1998 report by the OECD, interdisciplinary research activities have great potential in the next 20 years.

Electronics has merged with optics (optronics), with mechanics on a mi-cro-technical level (mechatronics), and also with biology (biotronics). The important breakthroughs in the development and identification of the hu-man genome are thanks to the close linkage between computer science and genetic engineering.

Decentralization of knowledge: The increased globalization of research and development (R&D) in transnational enterprises has led to the decen-tralization of competence centers. In a number of investigations, a clear trend could be ascertained towards integrated network structures and the establishment of a definition of R&D competence centers. The complexity of innovation processes has clearly increased because of decentralization. The application of modern information and communication technologies becomes indispensable and opens up new forms of innovation; for exam-ple internet-based innovation networks (Gassmann 2001).

Escalation of R&D costs: Given the increased technology dynamics and more stringent requirements, R&D costs have risen dramatically. Yet, the 1990s were marked by a reduction in central funding for research. During the 1980s, the corporate research center in a company such as *ABB* was re-sponsible for 20% of the financing, with the remaining amount being in the form of company reallocations. Today, 80% of research funds must come from the various divisions or third parties. A larger portion of the R&D budget is allocated to patent rights. In technology-intensive industries, more than 5% of the R&D budget is reserved for the generation and pres-ervation of commercial protection rights, plus the costs for the infringe-ment and defending of own positions.

Reduction of innovation cycles: Despite rising R&D costs, companies are under increasing pressure to produce more products within a shorter time frame. The main reason for this is the fact that regardless of rising costs in R&D, innovation and technology leadership has become a substantial competitive factor (von Braun 1994). For example, the innovation life cy-cle for a mechanical typewriter remains at around 25 years, while a type-writer that is based on microprocessor technology only has one of five years. If one were to look at newer substitute products such as laptops and palm pilots, the cycle time has been reduced to a few months. The risk of late market entry has increased notably.

Acceleration of innovation diffusion: As a result of the globalization of knowledge, shortening of the innovation cycle and the aggravation of the price situation, the diffusion of innovation has accelerated. In the *electron-ics industry*, it is only a matter of months after a product innovation before there is an imitation product on the market, in the *toy industry* this time frame shrinks to weeks. The protection of innovation has become even more important for companies in technology-intensive industries. Legal and actual patent right strategies complement one another, in order to amortize the investment in product development. In the *automobile industry* 4–5% of turnover is invested in R&D, while in the *pharmaceutical industry* that number jumps to 18–20%.

The main challenges in the management of innovation in companies can be summarized by complexity, dynamics, and costs. Future-oriented organizations endeavor to achieve those projections on how to better handle innovation that were made in the years after restructuring. In order to handle high competition costs, companies are looking to achieve differentiation with customers. New products in the electronics, telecommunications, and software industries are usually associated with simultaneously increased input and reduced costs. Innovation is not limited to the development of new products, but also includes the development of new services and business practices. Hence, an essential component of innovation management is to establish differentiation advantages with the customer, and find ways in which to make these advantages sustainable and renewable.

1.2 Managing R&D Collaborations

1.2.1 Exceeding the Company Boundaries

In order to cope with these challenges, the ability to innovate therefore has become the key driver for an enterprise's success. Only those companies that can bring innovative ideas effectively and efficiently to the market are successful. Consequently, an increasing proportion of innovation no longer takes place solely within the boundaries of a company. In this context, R.Z. Gussin, Corporate Vice President Science and Technology of *Johnson & Johnson*, New Brunswick, NJ reasoned that "technology has become so sophisticated, broad and expensive that even the largest companies cannot afford to do it all themselves."

Over the past years, this phenomenon has been described in research and literature as *open innovation* (Chesbrough 2003a). Gassmann, Sandmeier and Wecht (2004) propose a holistic approach, based on a strategy, a process, a structure, a network and a cultural level, for integrating external sources of innovation. This concept aims to help companies cope with short innovation cycles and increasingly complex technologies.

Jones (2000) discovered that compared to internal R&D expenditure, the proportion of external R&D expenditure increased from 5% to 16% between 1989 and 1995 (in the pharmaceuticals industry in Great Britain). Whittaker and Bower (1994) observed the trend towards collaborative R&D among pharmaceutical companies in the US and Europe. Outsourcing of R&D activities has led to partnerships within and outside of the areas of core competence. The companies *ABB* and *Hilti*, e.g., implement mechatronic knowledge from expert firms that were spun-off from *ETH Zurich*. This confirms that the significance of technical services has increased sharply during the last few years (Gassmann and Hipp 2001).

Also the integration of customers into the innovation process can increase a company's potential for innovation (Urban and von Hippel 1988). A well-known method is von Hippel's lead user approach (von Hippel 1986) in which leading customers are identified and integrated. Other methods to integrate customers are the empathic design method that examines customers' use of existing products and analyzes their behavior (Leonard and Rayport 1997), and the virtual customer integration that applies purpose-designed toolkits and online communities (Dahan and Hauser 2002).

As a main consequence of larger innovative activities taking place beyond company borders, management's focus has to shift from intra-firm coordination to the coordination of complex innovation (Tidd 1997). Powell, Koput and Smith-Doerr (1996) determined that all phases of the innovation process (discovery to marketing) are increasingly executed through some type of network. According to Jones, Conway and Steward (2000), the motivation for networking is based on increasing pressure to share risks, to acquire market access, to achieve complementary assets and high speed to market. Tidd (1997) concludes that firms have to *collaborate* to further manage the innovation process effectively. Collaboration management based on outside innovation activities will thus have to become a core competence (Tapon and Thong 1999).

A benchmarking study by the Institute for Technology Management of the University of St.Gallen affirmed the general interest of companies in involving external parties in their innovation processes. This includes the management of collaborations with third parties, e.g. customers, suppliers or even competitors. The study further revealed that about two-thirds of the companies surveyed are already involving external partners in their idea generation process (ITEM 2004a).

1.2.2 Collaborative R&D

R&D collaborations are therefore of greater importance for companies today, due to the increased complexity of scientific and technological development, shortened innovation cycles and the higher risks and costs of generating innovation. Thanks to strategic technology alliances over several decades, the number of R&D partnerships has steadily increased (OECD 2002a; Hagedoorn 2002). The growth in technology alliances has been driven mainly by the high-technology industry (biotechnology), information and communication technology, and aerospace. Important criteria for characterizing collaborations include motivation, structure and performance (Kale, Singh and Perlmutter 2000).

Between 1980 and 1998 the number of strategic technology alliances has more than doubled, from 209 in 1980 to 564 in 1998 (Fig. 1). Their proportions of joint patents increased during the years 1980 to 1998 from almost 50% to over 70% (OECD 2002a).

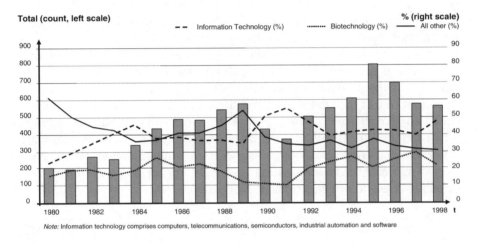

Note: Information technology comprises computers, telecommunications, semiconductors, industrial automation and software

Source: OEDC (2002a); National Science Foundation (2000)

Fig. 1. Amount of R&D partnerships from 1980 to 1998

Aspects of motivation. A collaboration between competitors is only meaningful when a win-win situation is created and the customer perceives the added value (Dixi and Nalebuff 1990). Major reasons for forming such collaborations include intense competition, opening of new markets, insufficient internal resources, lack of know-how and inability to generate opportunities alone (Müller-Stewens and Lechner 2003; Gassmann and Fuchs 2001). From a strategic point of view, collaborations further strengthen a company's competitive position on a long-term basis (Kogut 1988). However, transaction costs need to be kept low in order to achieve optimized benefits (Williamson 1985; Hennart 1988).

Aspects of structure. Collaborations can be classified in different categories based upon marketing strategy (Sydow 1992): Purchase contracts and barter deals are the most market driven forms of collaboration. On the other hand, profit center organizations are mostly driven by hierarchy. Inter-organizational networks can be formed through long-term supplier contracts, licensing and franchising contracts or joint ventures. Collaborations, especially on R&D, can be differentiated into three categories (Schögel 1999): Collaboration as partnerships among independent business units, suppliers and competitors. Typical inter-firm collaboration partners are completion partners, suppliers, customers or competitors.

With respect to investigating intellectual property management in R&D collaborations, a suitable criteria is the general level of competitiveness between the collaborating partners (Fig. 2). Typical inter-firm collaboration partners are completion partners, suppliers, customers and competitors. Completion partners offer products and services with added value for the customer. The level of competitiveness between the suppliers and their customers might vary, depending upon demand in the market and the exclusivity of the products and services offered, whereas customers play an important role in idea generation and the conceptionalization of production (Leonard-Barton 1995). Other types of collaboration partners can be formed at an intra-firm level, i.e. between independent business units that often aim for cross development or cross selling (Schögel 1999). Non-inter-firm R&D collaborations are also regularly formed with universities or public research organizations (OECD 2003a).[1]

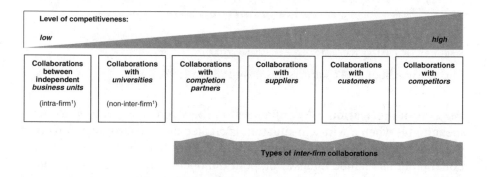

Fig. 2. Level of competitiveness with respect to collaboration types

---

[1]   This thesis excludes intra-firm and non-inter-firm R&D collaborations due to the collaboration partners' different situations and motivations compared to inter-firm R&D collaborations.

Aspects of performance. The overall performance and value creation that are achieved through collaboration are usually greater than what can be achieved by individual partner efforts. Belderbos, Carree and Lokshine (2004) analyzed the impact of R&D collaboration on firm performance, differentiating four R&D partner types: competitors, suppliers, customers and universities. Whereas competitor and supplier collaborations focus on incremental innovation, customer and university collaborations are considered as important sources of knowledge for firms seeking radical innovations. Ideally, the process of collaboration should challenge each of the partners (Beamish 1987; Harrigan 1985; Merchant 1997). Gaining consensus regarding the partners' individual views is a prerequisite for a successful collaboration (Kelly, Schaan and Joncas 2002). Therefore, considerable effort must be made by all partners to reach consensus during the early stages of collaboration.

1.2.3 Set-up and Early Stage

Various studies have shown that 50–60% of R&D collaborations fail (Spekman et al. 1996; Dacin, Hitt and Levitas 1997; Duysters, Kok and Vaandrager 1999; Kelly, Schaan and Joncas 2002). Most failures happen during the collaboration's set-up phase (Bleeke and Ernst 1993). A collaboration's set-up phase and early stages are known to be the important period for establishing a quality working relationship (Anderson and Weitz 1989; Sherman 1992; Doz and Hamel 1998) and thus crucial for its success.

There are several models to describe the formation process of collaborations (Much 1997; Meckl 1995; Fontanari 1995). With respect to Fontanari's model, one can describe the formation process as having four phases, of which the first three phases describe the set-up and early stages of the collaboration. There are four clearly identifiable phases in the collaboration formation process (Fig. 3):

- *Phase 1* consists of assessing the strategic goals and the business environment. This leads to goal setting and the definition of product and service portfolios. For example, companies would assess whether their respective strategic objectives can be achieved through such collaboration, or whether their internal resources are sufficient for the purpose.
- *Phase 2* consists of the search for and selection of suitable partners for the collaboration.
- During *phase 3* negotiations are carried out to formalize the individual contributions expected from each of the potential collaboration partners.

During this phase, common goals and motives need to be explicit and agreed on (Kanter 1994). In this phase it is also crucial to agree upon the existing and future intellectual property that is necessary for or that needs to be created through the collaboration. However, interestingly, the clarity of intellectual property definition at the set-up phase depends upon the experience that the partners have gained with intellectual property in earlier collaborations (Hagedoorn, van Kranenburg and Osborn 2003).

- During *phase 4* the details of all performance measures are worked out, including a possible exit criteria.

Trust between the collaborators decreases the risks based on transaction costs, enables conflict resolution and helps to adapt to change (Ring and van de Ven 1992; Parkhe 1998b).

Another important aspect of the set-up phase is the assessment of the potential partners' cultural compatibility, an element often underestimated (George and Farris 1999). The selection of the right people as part of the collaboration is crucial (Yoshino and Rangan 1995). Learning in the early stages is very important (Doz and Hamel 1998) and a communication culture has to be developed early so that it suits the needs of the collaboration (More and McGrath 1996).

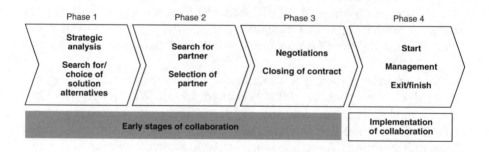

Source: According to Fontanari (1995)

Fig. 3. Formation process of collaborations

1.3 Managing Intellectual Property

1.3.1 Protecting Temporary Monopoly Profits

To justify high investment costs in R&D, companies have to gain competitive advantages. Only through realizing these temporary monopoly profits can such companies then continue to invest in research and development on a long-term basis. Therefore, these companies search for suitable protection strategies for their own innovations. Situationally adjusted protection strategies for internal innovations are essential. Traditional, factual protection strategies for the reduction of imitation risks are ever increasingly being supported by legal protection strategies to ensure freedom of action and block competitors (Fig. 4, p. 11). *Intellectual property* (IP) has therefore become a suitable instrument for influencing sustainability and returns-on-investments.

The demand to use and apply intellectual property rights increased dramatically at the end of the last decade. Worldwide, the overall demand for patent rights rose between 1998 and 2002 from more than 6.2 million to an all-time high of almost 14.8 million (Trilateral Statistical Report 2004). The trend shows an annual average increase of about 24%. This is a lot more than the global estimated economic growth as per the International Monetary Fund (IMF 2005: 4.4%).

Today many technology-intensive companies not only want to protect their products from being copied, but are now also looking to maintain and defend their *freedom of action* status by enforcing the rules of their intellectual property rights. This means that they intend to block competitors through specifically shaped intellectual property rights, e.g. by dependent patents.

Companies have created licensing departments, some of which are even structured and budgeted as profit centers. Furthermore, various external licensing and litigation companies have been established to support these business models. The approaches to and methods of enforcing intellectual property in pretrial or litigation cases are being increasingly applied in Europe to achieve economic goals. In Germany, Switzerland and Austria, universities and public research centers have even started to apply intellectual property rights to protect themselves from exploitation. These institutes patent and market their projects and research results on the basis of intellectual property.

Financial pressure is another reason why companies increasingly exercise their intellectual property, and do so by taking cost and benefit ratios into account. This means that they must minimize the cost issues while optimizing the effectiveness of the intellectual property, which can be done by shaping these with respect to internal and external market activities. Options for action include optimizing the portfolio of designated countries per invention with respect to own and third parties' products and the individual relevance of the invention. Relevant information that might include the characteristics of an invention, but does not have the potential for a valuable patent might not be further processed as a patent application. However, companies might choose to publish the related inventions in order to avoid patenting from other parties. It is still common in Europe to apply opposition procedures. If a company does not want its competitor to know which patents are the truly significant ones, it might be more useful not to run an opposition, but to rather collect valuable state-of-the-art and request an internal or external opinion. If there is an infringement, this opinion can then be used to bilaterally negotiate an advantageous licensing agreement without clearing a patent that might still have some value with respect to further parties.

During the last few decades, the characteristics of patentees have also changed. Public patent holders like universities and research centers play an increasingly important role. For example, a law change in Germany allowed universities to create their own patent and licensing departments in order to gain returns on their research investments. Previously, patents were generally held by large organizations. Nowadays, the percentage of patentees with only a single patent has grown to 63% in the *United States Patent and Trademark Office (USPTO)*, and 69% in the *European Patent Office (EPO)* (Trilateral Statistical Report 2004). The ratio of patent holders with more than 50 patents or patent applications is only 1% of those before the *USPTO* and *EPO*.

1.3.2 Generating Intellectual Property

When generating intellectual property, many companies do not sufficiently grasp that patents do not automatically provide a right of allowance. This is a common misunderstanding that still leads to unwise investments. In fact, patents are prohibition rights that allow the patent owner to stop third parties from copying and using the claimed invention. Products, systems, processes, methods, (subject to certain national restrictions), and even software and business methods are all patentable. It is obvious that national legislation is of major importance when dealing with intellectual property. However, in practical terms, intellectual property management also depends on the sensitivities of internal and external stakeholders concerning intellectual property issues.

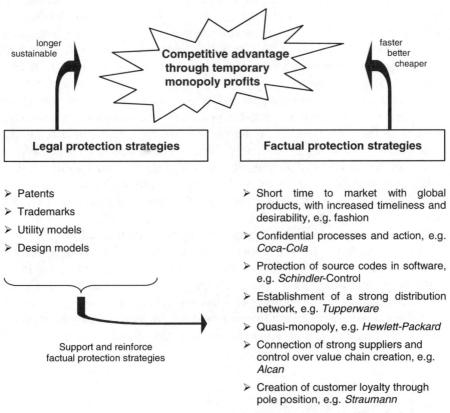

Source: Gassmann and Bader (2006a)

Fig. 4. Legal and factual protection strategies

The average life cycle of a patent today ranges from 10 years in Europe (*EPO*), to 12 years in the US (*USPTO*) and 18 years before the *Japan Patent Office (JPO)*. The average success rate of a patent-granting procedure ranges from 69% (*EPO*) to 63% (*USPTO* and *JPO*). Twenty-five percent of patent-granting procedures still take more than 72 months (Trilateral Statistical Report 2004).

The demand for patents is continually overshadowed by the high costs associated with procedures needed to grant a patent, including attorney and translation fees. Furthermore, maintenance fees have to be paid regularly after the issuance of a patent. Lately there has been strong criticism of the high transaction costs of patents when compared to their quality (Kahin 2002). It is commonly known that the costs of generating and maintaining a patent in Europe with a larger country selection for a period of 10 years amount to about 25,000 euro (Fig. 5).

Based on this background, the management of intellectual property has become a delicate issue. This specifically applies to inventions from the so-called high technology areas such as computer and automated business equipment, microorganisms, along with genetic engineering, aviation, communication technology, semi-conductors and lasers.

Patent statistics also reveal international differences concerning application behaviors: The actual demand to protect the aforementioned types of

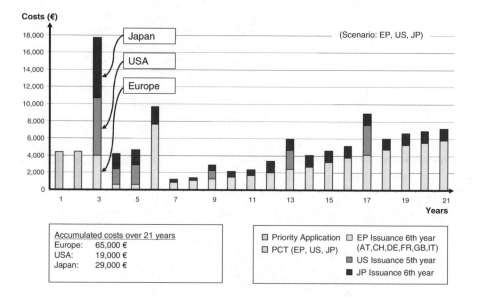

Fig. 5. Development of costs of an international patent application

high-end innovations varies from 23% before the *EPO* to 33% before the *USPTO*, as a proportion of applications in high technology areas being filed before patent offices (Trilateral Statistical Report 2004). Furthermore, while 57% of the patent applications and patents before the *USPTO* come from US patent holders, only 40% of the patent applications and patents before the *EPO* go back to patent holders from *EPO* member states.

The pressure in organizations to optimize cost and utilization considerations, takes on a role of great importance in the area of intellectual property. It is therefore essential to organize and optimize the patent management process. Our studies at the Institute of Technology Management at the University of St.Gallen found that three out of four organizations track legal protection strategies and have a documented patent strategy (ITEM 2004a). This strategy is balanced with business activities, implemented countrywide, and regularly checked and updated. The research and development departments are strongly integrated into the strategy process.

1.3.3 Enforcing Intellectual Property

Internal investigations often reveal that intellectual property strategies are not only restricted to mere defense mechanisms and protection from product imitation. Increasingly, intellectual property management is also becoming an area of competence and is generating licensing revenues by marketing existing intellectual property. A well-known leader in this area is *IBM*, whose overall licensing revenues are almost 1.5% of its total turnover. Now, every other company markets its intellectual property externally (ITEM 2004a). However, these types of activities need to be monitored carefully as areas such as overall core competencies and relative competitive advantage could be affected.

Achieving revenues from intellectual property such as patents is becoming increasingly important. In the US, earnings based on marketed patent licenses grew from 15 billion US dollars in 1990 to more than 110 billion US dollars in 1999. This is equivalent to an average annual growth rate of 25% (Rivette and Kline 2000b). Worldwide, the commercialization volume of intellectual property is estimated to have reached 100 billion US dollars and is increasing (Athreye and Cantwell 2005).

Most notably in R&D-intensive industries such as chemicals, pharmaceuticals, computers and electronics, medical and scientific instruments and software, it is becoming more commonplace to report information about royalty earnings in annual reports. A study on patent licensing revealed that between 1990 and 1998, on average, 14% of the overall earn-

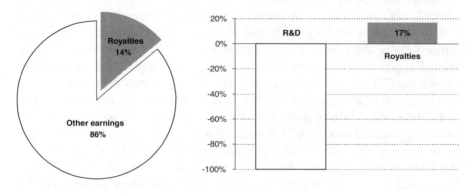

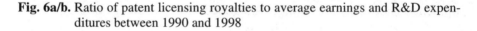

Source: Gu et al. (2000)

Fig. 6a/b. Ratio of patent licensing royalties to average earnings and R&D expenditures between 1990 and 1998

ings were provided by royalties (Fig. 6a). Royalty incomes comprised almost 17% of the R&D expenditures (Fig. 6b).

However, the environment of intellectual property rights enforcement has become both heated and frosty at the same time. Whereas 20 years ago courts had often still been chosen on a geographical basis, today it is possible to make a selection based on subject matter and time frame expectations. Previous (US) case law that was potentially advantageous to the rights of infringers has changed so that it now enhances the rights of patent holders (Rivette and Kline 2000a). The average cost of a US litigation case has grown from 400,000 US dollars in 1999 to 499,000 US dollars in 2001 per single case; a jump of 25% (AIPLA 2001). Persons or enterprises that seek litigation, or get involved in a case need a big war chest. The urge towards quick and often unfair settlements is therefore growing due to insufficient available financial resources.

1.4 Managing Intellectual Property in R&D Collaborations

Creating and sharing intellectual property externally. More and more companies use external intellectual property and do not further rely only on their own intellectual property (Chesbrough 2003a, b). During the 1990s outsourcing became a trend in R&D management. In addition, the number of acquisitions and mergers rose to a maximum. Today, pre-competitive technology alliances, open product architectures and collaborative product development and product marketing are integrated into many business strategies. Furthermore, an increasing number of companies are willing to share their intellectual property with external, third parties (Kline 2003). Intellectual property also plays a continuously growing role in international research collaborations (European Commission 2002).

While intellectual property can be acquired through internal processes, it can also be acquired externally, through collaborations, acquisitions or in-licensing. Intellectual property can be utilized both internally by multiplying its value through collaborating with other partners, and externally as a means of keeping other parties from selling or out-licensing.

Management of intellectual property has therefore become an increasingly important success factor for collaborations. However, before entering a collaboration, companies frequently try to secure as much intellectual property on their side as possible (Markwith 2003). In practical terms agreeing upon how to manage the intellectual property that comes from and arises during a collaboration, is a great challenge (Dillahunty 2002). It is recommended that the business plans and legal issues for the anticipated exploitation of the fruits of the collaboration, including the intellectual property should be agreed upon. However, collaborations' failure rates still vary between 30% and 90% (Fontanari 1996).

Intellectual property management in R&D collaborations therefore plays a decisive role in the early stages of collaborative processes as well. Early and explicit agreement on how the intellectual property ownership and benefits are generally to be allocated among collaboration partners is important. Finding solutions to the handling of intellectual property that evolves from R&D collaborations thus poses a big challenge to the collaboration partners and their strategists. However, the willingness to solve intellectual property issues and the success rate in R&D collaborations depend upon the collaboration partners' previous experiences with the joint patenting process (Hagedoorn, van Kranenburg and Osborn 2003).

Joint patenting amongst companies. Statistics on joint patent ownership can help to explain the general growth of inter-firm collaborations. There is empirical evidence that the number of jointly owned patents has been growing during the last few years. An exploratory study (Hagedoorn 2003) affirms that more patents are co-owned by two or more patent applicant companies today. While there were about 200 co-owned patents in the USA in 1989, this number tripled to almost 650 co-owned patents in 1998. The average annual growth rate of 14% is only slightly more than half the patent applications' general annual growth worldwide.

An empirical investigation reveals that even the share of co-patent-applications in triad patent families has been increasing from almost 7% in 1980 to more than 10% in 1995 (Fig. 7).

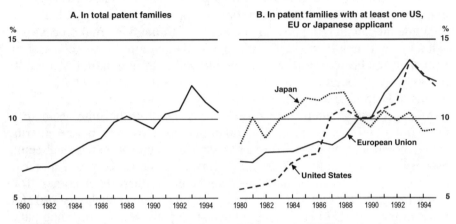

Note: A triad patent family is a patent applied for at the EPO and the JPO and granted by the USPTO for inventions that share one or more priority dates. Applications are sorted by priority date (date of first filing worldwide) for granted patents only (granting date up to 2000). Co-applications in patent families with at least one US, EU or Japanese applicant, as presented in the figure on the right, are not mutually exclusive.

Source: OECD (2002a)

Fig. 7. The share of jointly owned patent families is continually growing

The low ratio and relatively slow growth of jointly owned patents can be explained by the general tendencies of companies to avoid jointly owned patents, because they cause increased administrative efforts before and after the collaboration, and also pose greater risks of the exploitation of the intellectual property.

An empirical study conducted by the Institute of Technology Management of the University of St.Gallen also supports the understanding that managing intellectual property in collaborations already plays an important role in the collaboration processes' early stages (ITEM 2004a). More than 80% of the investigated companies agreed on this statement. It seems that the early and explicit agreement between collaboration partners to share the ownership and exploitation rights of the resulting intellectual property is important.

2 Literature Review

Based on the introduction in chapter one, the literature review for this research work covers the following literature streams:

- Managing R&D collaborations;
- Managing intellectual property;
- Managing intellectual property in R&D collaborations.

In this chapter, an overview of the current thinking as published in the above literature streams is concluded with a *white spot* analysis of where this research will go in detail.

2.1 Managing R&D Collaborations

The literature in this section is mainly focused on formal inter-firm R&D collaborations with respect to discovered success factors and their drivers as based on previous experience and relational trust. The early stages of collaborations and the early phases of collaborative innovation processes are also discussed (Fig. 8 and Table 1, p. 22).

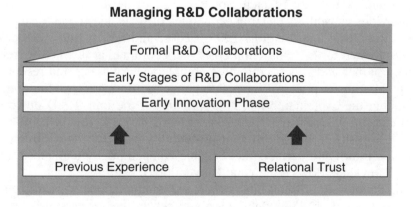

Fig. 8. Structure of literature streams in managing R&D collaborations

2.1.1 Formal R&D Collaborations

A broad spectrum of literature examines the increase in formal and informal R&D collaborations among companies (von Hippel 1988; Osborn and Baughn 1990; Hagedoorn 1993; Hagedoorn and Narula 1996; Granstrand 1998; Edler, Meyer-Krahmer and Reger 2002), mainly due to the growing complexity, and the risks and costs of innovation (Nooteboom 1999; Hagedoorn 2002). Miotti and Sachwald (2003) have examined R&D collaborations and observed that the need for knowledge access is the main reason for collaborating, while the complementarity of the partners serves as the main selection criterion.

Furthermore, formal inter-firm collaborations are based on joint R&D as one of the most significant reasons for forming alliances, especially in high-tech industries and the emerging technical industry sectors (Mowery 1988; Mytelka 1991; Hagedoorn 1993; Arora and Gambardella 1994; Colombo 1995). But even in other industries, e.g. the manufacturing industry, R&D collaborations may have a positive effect if there is sufficient absorptive capacity (Veugelers 1997). With respect to the information and communication technology industry: the more similar the technological portfolios of the collaboration partners, the easier it is to mutually absorb each other's capabilities (Santangelo 2000).

Joint R&D is sought by collaboration partners to complement internal resources in the innovation process, to support innovation input and output with regard to the company's R&D intensity and an enhanced probability of developing new products (Becker and Dietz 2004). The likelihood of an R&D collaboration increases with the company size and with R&D intensity, but not with the market share involved (Negassi 2004).

Collaboration activities furthermore involve opportunities and risks: Opportunities are joint financing of R&D, reducing uncertainty, realizing cost-savings as well as realizing economies of scale and scope (Campagni 1993; Robertson and Langlois 1995; Becker and Peters 1998). Risks are mainly related to the transaction costs, i.e. coordinating distinct organizational routines and styles, compiling complementary assets and resources, fixing the transfer prices of intangible goods as information on know-how, regulating the exploitation and appropriation of the joint R&D outcomes (Williamson 1989; Pisano 1990; Gassmann and von Zedtwitz 1999). The risks also result from the different profitability expectations regarding innovation return and partners that become competitors by unplanned, one-sided knowledge flows (Helm and Kloyer 2004).

The literature on formal inter-firm R&D collaborations is usually structured and based on the collaboration's effect on the partnership's overall success (Geringer 1991; Glaister and Buckley 1999). In general, this still depends on the type of collaboration partners and the innovations' techno-logical level (Tether 2002), whereas Belderbos, Carree and Lokshine (2004) have substantiated that collaborating firms are generally engaged in a higher level of innovative activities. The effect on the companies in-volved in the joint activities is described by Balakrishnan and Koza (1993), and also by Hagedoorn and Schakenraad (1994). A further litera-ture area has concluded that most collaborations may be embedded in a larger set of relationships and have a specific purpose, i.e. R&D (Levinthal and Fichman 1988; Heide and Miner 1992; Gulati 1995a, 1995b; Saxton 1997). Becker and Dietz (2004) confirmed that there is an increasing prob-ability of realizing product innovations as the number of collaboration partners involved increases.

2.1.2 Early Stages of R&D Collaborations

The early stages of an R&D collaboration are known to be the crucial pe-riod during which the quality of working relationships is established (Anderson and Weitz 1989; Sherman 1992; Doz and Hamel 1998). Trust reduces the risks based on transaction costs, enables conflict resolution and may help in adaptation to changes (Ring and van de Ven 1992; Parkhe 1998b).

Kelly, Schaan and Joncas's (2002) research is based on data from the Canadian high technology industry and looks at the barriers to successful alliances that develop during the early stages of alliances with four key themes: *People and relationship* issues, involving problems related to communication, culture and roles; *operation* issues, involving problems re-lated to the technical details of implementation, e.g. technology transfer and scheduling; *strategic agenda* issues or problems that are concerned with the venture's goals and objectives; and *results*, or problems, related to the venture's performance. They concluded their investigations by estab-lishing that relationship issues are the main challenge for partners during the early collaboration stage.

Collaboration with partners brings along risks that vary depending on the collaboration stage. Enkel, Kausch and Gassmann (2005) investigated the inherent risks of customer integration in respect of the collaboration stages, i.e. loss of know-how, dependency on customers, being limited to mere incremental innovations and niche markets, and misunderstanding. These risks can be reduced by comprehensive risk management methods. One major risk is the loss of know-how and the possible conflict regarding idea ownership, which can be reduced, e.g., by non-disclosure agreements, know-how contribution lists and agreements concerning the innovation process outcomes. The agreements should be adapted to the stage of the collaboration, for example, a non-disclosure agreement is best signed during an early collaboration stage and before sensitive information is disclosed.

2.1.3 Early Innovation Phase

In general, the innovation process can be divided into three main areas (Gerpott 1999):

- The early innovation phase, which operates in the front end of innovation – in the literature this phase is often described as the *fuzzy front end*. In this phase, people and innovation management are most dominant;
- The new product development phase. In this phase, project management under time and cost issues are most dominant;
- The commercialization phase. In this phase, marketing and sales issues are most dominant.

The early innovation phase presents the best opportunities for improving the overall innovation process. In order to conduct the new product development phase, it is very important to generate enough suitable high-profit ideas from the early innovation phase (for radical innovations significantly more often than for incremental innovations). The early innovation phase may be characterized by:

- A low structural level, although this is in an experimental phase and often involves individuals instead of multifunctional teams;
- Revenue expectations that are often uncertain, and predicting precise commercialization dates is often impossible;
- Funding that is usually erratic;
- Results that often end up in a concept, and do not achieve a planned milestone.

Kim and Wilemon (2002a) define the early innovation phase as the period between the point of a first consideration of an opportunity until an idea is judged ready for development. The outcomes are categorized into product definition, time, and people dimensions. Several strategies are available to manage the fuzzy front end by, e.g., assigning a fuzzy front end manager or a team, providing organizational support, understanding the sources of ambiguity, building an information system and/or developing relationships with supporters, partners and alliances. A product is more likely to be developed successfully and marketed when the *upfront* or *fuzzy front end* activities are understood and managed carefully. The key issue identified is the *collaboration* with external organizations during the early innovation phase.

Dahan and Hauser (2001, 2002) describe the product development process as an *end-to-end* process, differentiating the three process parts: fuzzy front end, designing and engineering of concepts and products, and the prototyping and testing of these concepts and products. However, Koen et al. (2001, 2002) attest that the division between the fuzzy front end phase and the following new product development phase is often fuzzy itself since technology development may be necessary to bridge the intersection.

Kim and Wilemon (2002b) confirm that the fuzzy front end of the product development process is the most important and difficult challenge for innovation managers. They define its outcomes as product definition, time and people dimensions and develop a framework to illuminate performance factors. Especially difficult seems to be the initiation of radical innovation projects (Rice et al. 2001; Walls 2002).

There is also research work that describes effective methods, tools and techniques for managing the fuzzy front end and how to apply it for new product development (Koen et al. 2001, 2002). The introduced model consists of three parts. First, five front end elements, (i.e. opportunity identification, opportunity analysis, idea generation and enrichment, idea selection, and concept definition), among which ideas are expected to flow, circulate, and iterate. Second, leadership, culture and business strategy and third, influencing factors, i.e. the environment. They evaluated their model at 19 companies. Highly innovative companies were found to be more proficient in the early innovation phase.

Khurana and Rosenthal (1997) studied front end activities and observed key best practices: Integration of a product strategy, product portfolio planning, a facilitating organizational structure with clearly identified customer needs, a well-defined product concept and a project plan.

2.1.4 Previous Experience and Relational Trust

The ability of companies to succeed in inter-firm collaborations significantly depends on their experience with collaboration processes as such (Kogout 1989; Barkema et al. 1997; Kale and Singh 1999; Anand and Khanna 2000). The wider the experience, the better the ability to extend existing collaboration relationships (Park and Ungson 1997) and to enter further future collaborations, i.e. knowledge about how to select a suitable partner, the right moment to enter and how to administer a collaboration (Oster 1992; Gulati 1995a; Powell, Koput and Smith-Doerr 1997; Dyer

Table 1. Literature streams in managing R&D collaborations

Research Focus	Authors
Formal R&D Collaborations	Mowery 1988; von Hippel 1988; Mytelka 1991; Osborn and Baughn 1990; Hagedoorn 1993, 2002; Hagedoorn and Narula 1996; Veugelers 1997; Granstrand 1998; Nooteboom 1999; Hicks and Narin 2000; Santangelo 2000; Edler, Meyer-Krahmer and Reger 2002; Miotti and Sachwald 2003; Becker and Dietz 2004; Negassi 2004.
Risks and opportunities	Williamson 1989; Pisano 1990; Becker and Peters 1998; Camagni 1993; Robertson and Langlois 1995; Gassmann and von Zedtwitz 1999; Helm and Kloyer 2004.
Overall success	Geringer 1991; Glaister and Buckley 1999; Tether 2002; Belderbos, Carree and Lokshin 2004.
One or more sponsors	Balakrishnan and Koza 1993; Hagedoorn and Schakenraad 1994.
Embeddedness in a larger set of relationships	Levinthal and Fichman 1988; Heide and Miner 1992; Gulati 1995a, 1995b; Saxton 1997.
Early Stages of R&D Collaborations	Anderson and Weitz 1989; Ring and van de Ven 1992; Sherman 1992; Doz and Hamel 1998; Parkhe 1998b; Kelly, Schaan and Joncas 2002; Enkel, Kausch and Gassmann 2005.
Early Innovation Phase	Khurana and Rosenthal 1997; Dahan and Hauser 2001, 2002; Koen et al. 2001; Rice et al. 2001; Kim and Wilemon 2002a, 2002b; Koen et al. 2002; Walls 2002.
Previous Experience	Kogut 1989; Oster 1992; Gulati 1995a; Powell, Koput and Smith-Doerr 1997; Barkema et al. 1997; Park and Ungson 1997; Dyer and Singh 1998; Kale and Singh 1999; Anand and Khanna 2000; Hagedoorn, Carayannis and Alexander 2001.
Relational Trust	Ring and van de Ven 1992; Gulati 1995b; Nooteboom, Berger and Noorderhaven 1997; Saxton 1997; Parkhe 1998a; Zaheer, McEvily and Perrone 1998; Kelly, Schaan and Joncas 2002; Segrestin 2005.

and Singh 1998; Hagedoorn, Carayannis and Alexander 2001). Due to increasing internal skills, companies can improve their reputation and attract better partners (Powell, Koput and Smith-Doerr 1997).

Another important issue in formal inter-firm R&D collaborations is a priori the level of trust between collaboration partners (Parkhe 1998a; Kelly, Schaan and Joncas 2002). This relational trust depends on the experience that the collaboration partners have had with each other in the past (Ring and van de Ven 1992). Multiple interactions, and especially prior relationships between the collaboration partners, positively influence relational trust (Gulati 1995b; Nooteboom, Berger and Noorderhaven 1997; Saxton 1997). The level of trust can also become institutionalized with a positive effect on the content exchanged between the collaboration partners (Zaheer, McEvily and Perrone 1998).

Segrestin (2005) argues that the building of a new collective identity requires specific managerial models to design simultaneously common purposes and collective identity.

2.2 Managing Intellectual Property

There are numerous literature sources relating to managing intellectual property. In order to be relevant to the research topic, literature dealing with strategy is assessed in this section. Some of the literature deals with the maintenance and management of intellectual property portfolios and the acquisition and exploitation of knowledge and intellectual property. It seems that several factors consistently influence the mechanisms between intellectual property management, intellectual property portfolio and entrepreneurial success. A suitable visualization of these literature segments is provided in Fig. 9 and is summarized in Table 2, p. 28.

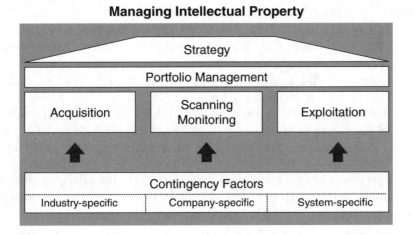

Fig. 9. Structure of literature streams in managing intellectual property

There is increasing awareness of the empirical relevance of intellectual property (Kortum and Lerner 1999). However, despite its increasing importance, there is also criticism as to whether technological and economic progress can really be stimulated by patent protection (Mazzoleni and Nelson 1998). This is especially acute in the software and information technology industry sectors, with respect to US legal changes (Coriat and Orsi 2002). The macroeconomic impacts of patenting software are currently being investigated in a considerable number of studies. Some studies deal with certain types of innovation, such as sequential innovations or complex systems (Bessen and Maskin 1999; Somaya and Teece 2001), while others deal with areas such as semiconductors, genetics or computing rules (Grindley and Teece 1997; Hall and Ziedonis 2001; Fraunhofer ISI 2001).

2.2.1 Strategy and Portfolio Management

Research has shown that there is a positive correlation between a company's success and the strength of its patent portfolio (Lerner 1994; Ernst 2001; Shane 2001; Ernst 2002c; Ernst and Omland 2003). An intellectual property strategy should therefore aim to develop a qualitative patent portfolio. Ernst and Omland (2003) have shown that young, technology-intensive companies, especially biotechnology enterprises, can boost profit and growth through patents that protect their products. Yet, secrecy remains an alternative approach to patenting (Arundel 2001). Trademarks also play an important role, especially in cases of service innovations (Miles et al. 2000; Klinger 2003; Jennewein 2005).

According to Ernst (1995, 1996, 2001), in the mechanical engineering sector, those companies that have an active and systematic patent strategy are significantly more successful than companies that remain inactive and non-strategic in this area. Patent applications usually lead to revenue growth within two to three years. Shane (2001) analyzed the patent portfolio of the Massachusetts Institute of Technology and came to the conclusion that patents of high value, i.e. with broad technical claims and a high citation index, increase the probability of commercialization either by licensing contracts or through spin-offs. In the field of venture-capital-financed biotechnology enterprises Lerner (1994) also provided evidence that patents with broad technical claims increase the financial rating of companies. Austin (1993) has shown that in the biotechnology sector, patent grants have a positive influence on the market value of companies.

Intellectual property has reached a level of greater importance in many successful companies (Grindley and Teece 1997; Sullivan 1998). Patents are specifically recognized as powerful instruments through which innovation and technology management can overcome discontinuities, although their use needs to be adjusted or combined with other instruments and tools (Harmann 2003). A variety of strategic management literature sources points out that an intellectual property strategy needs to be aligned with a company's corporate strategy (Lynn, Morone and Paulson 1996; Faix 1998; Brockhoff 1999; Hargadon and Sutton 2000; Ernst 2002a, 2002b; Smith and Hansen 2002).

An intellectual property strategy generally aims to improve the economic outcomes of investments made through innovations. The strategy should therefore address various key decisions such as: make or buy decisions, organizational association or isolation, innovation or adaptation of new technology, protection or exploitation of knowledge; public or private research funding, safeguarding or sharing of intellectual property, and pioneering advantages or disadvantages (Borg 2001; Harhoff and Reitzig 2001).

Above all, the main purpose of creating intellectual property is to protect earlier innovation investments, for example, to avoid copying by third parties. Thus a solid patent portfolio can also function as an important strategic weapon against competitors, as evidenced by Brockhoff, Ernst and Hundhausen (1999) in the field of cardiac rhythm management.

2.2.2 Acquisition and Exploitation

Intellectual property can be generated internally and externally (Ernst 2002a). Even when patent information is technically available, it appears to be rarely used for strategic R&D planning. However, by evaluating patent information technically, legally and strategically, it is possible to support competitor and technology analyses and consequently shape one's patent portfolio (Ernst 1998b; Brockhoff 1999; Ernst and Soll 2002).

The relationship between corporate spending on research and the number of patents has been examined by Ernst (1998a), who based his findings on data from 25 European and Japanese electronics companies. An increase in R&D expenditure can lead to an increase in the number of patent applications (Kondo 1999). However, investment in R&D should be supplemented by internal capabilities (Teece 1988).

Inward technology licensing has become a suitable alternative to in-house R&D, in the areas of product and process development (Lowe and Taylor 1998). In this context, intellectual property plays an important role for in-licensing and continuous learning; with the finding that Japanese companies are more open and dynamic than British companies (Pitkethly 2001).

An intellectual property portfolio can also be marketed externally, which is yet another motivation for having an intellectual property strategy. Arora (1997) demonstrated that in the chemical industry, producers use licensing as an important instrument for generating revenues from process innovations. An important and practical approach to exploiting the value of a patent portfolio is to use it for in-licensing valuable intellectual property from other parties, e.g. by bilaterally cross-licensing patent portfolios. This is quite common in the semiconductor industry (Grindley and Teece 1997). In the biopharmaceutical industry, licensing is applied as a commercialization strategy for new technology-based firms, especially for strategic reasons and for financially unattractive projects (Kollmer and Dowling 2004).

Numerous literature citations are available on the procedure for licensing intellectual property, which specifically focuses on marketing, negotiation and pricing (Ehrbar 1993; Fox 1999; Mobley 1999; Torres 1999; Aitken, Baskaran, Lamarre et al. 2000; Boss 2000; Bramson 2000; Fradkin 2000; Gu and Lev 2000; Gruetzmacher, Khoury and Willey 2000; Iwasaki 2001; Sudia 2001; Elton, Shah and Voyzey 2002; Linder, Jarvenpaa and Davenport 2003; Razgaitis 2003a, b).

The enforcement of intellectual property can, however, be time-consuming and costly. The value of a patent license depends on whether the patent has been proven valid and infringed. Settlement outcomes in patent litigation depend on the patented technologies' strategic value (Somaya 2003). Only 45% of patent litigation plaintiffs win their cases at trial court level (Sherry and Teece 2004).

2.2.3 Scanning and Monitoring

Extensive research has been conducted in this field, for instance the usage of patent information for knowledge management or for supporting the technology strategy formulation process (Behrmann 1998; Ehrat 1997; Reger 2001).

Ernst (1997) assesses the general suitability of patent data for forecasting technological developments, based on experiences in the CNC-technology industry sector. Geschka (1995) and Watts, Porter and Newmann (1998) also conducted similar research. A recent study based on Indian and US patent data confirmed this general suitability for understanding trends in technology development and innovation levels (Abraham and Moitra 2001). However, more sophisticated and reliable "forecasting" analyses are often only realistic in retrospect (Mogee and Kolar 1994; Mogee 1997).

Patent literature always includes a discussion of the state-of-the-art. In general, this is done by referring to earlier patent literature, as close to 90% of all technical information is disclosed in patent literature (Behrmann 1998). It has been proved over a period of time that patents that are cited by other patents have a positive influence on products and technologies' market values (Deng, Lev and Narin 1999; Hall, Jaffe and Traijtenberg 1999; Harhoff, Scherer and Vopel 2003; Reitzig 2003). Patents have therefore also been used as economic indicators (Griliches 1990, 1998).

Various studies have used patent data to understand and explain macroeconomic phenomenon (Pavitt 1982, 1985, 1988; Pavitt and Patel 1988). Cohen et al. (2002) compared intra-industry R&D knowledge flows in Japan and USA, while Stolpe (2002) investigated the knowledge flows for liquid crystal display technology. Other studies have looked at the dependence on technology, the internationalization of technology and the growth of embedded software-related patents (Guellec and van Pottelsberghe de la Potterie 2001; Tijssen 2002; McQueen and Olsson 2003).

Patent data can also be used for comparing the competitive strengths and efficiency of international R&D (Penner-Hahn and Myles Shaver 2005). Ernst (1998) distinguishes two types of patent portfolio. At company level, the quality of the overall technological positions can be compared with those of relevant competitors. On a technological level, patent portfolios can be effectively used to manage the allocation of R&D resources. In contrast, Erickson (1996) claims that there are certain limitations to using patent data for technological benchmarking, mainly due to the differences in national and individual firm situations with respect to technologies.

The technological strength of R&D-intensive companies can be analyzed by patent analysis techniques, e.g. for merger and acquisition transactions (Breitzman, Thomas and Cheney 2002). Information on key inventors might also play an important role in this context (Ernst, Leptien and Vitt 1999, 2000). Based on *USPTO* semiconductor DRAM-related patents, Yoon, Yoon and Park (2002) have established a visual portfolio analysis method with patent maps.

Table 2. Literature streams in managing intellectual property

Research Focus	Authors
Strategy and Portfolio Management	Austin 1993; Lerner 1994; Ernst 1995, 1996, 2001, 2002a, 2002b, 2002c; Hamel 1996; Lynn, Morone and Paulson 1996; Grindley and Teece 1997; Faix 1998; Brockhoff 1999; Brockhoff, Ernst and Hundhausen 1999; Hargadon and Sutton 2000; Miles et al. 2000; Arundel 2001; Borg 2001; Harhoff and Reitzig 2001; Shane 2001; Sullivan 2001; Smith and Hansen 2002; Ernst and Omland 2003; Harmann 2003; Klinger 2003; Jennewein 2005.
Acquisition	Teece 1988; Ernst 1998a, 1998b; Griliches 1998; Lowe and Taylor 1998; Brockhoff 1999; Ernst, Leptien and Vitt 1999; Kondo 1999; Pitkethly 2001; Ernst and Soll 2002.
Exploitation	Ehrbar 1993; Arora 1997; Grindley and Teece 1997; Fox 1999; Mobley 1999; Torres 1999; Aitken, Baskaran, Lamarre et al 2000; Boss 2000; Bramson 2000; Fradkin 2000; Gu and Lev 2000; Gruetzmacher, Khoury and Willey 2000; Iwasaki 2001; Sudia 2001; Elton, Shah and Voyzey 2002b; Linder, Jarvenpaa and Davenport 2003; Razgaitis 2003a, 2003b; Somaya 2003; Sherry and Teece 2004; Kollmer and Dowling 2004.
Scanning and Monitoring	Pavitt 1982, 1985, 1988; Pavitt and Patel 1988; Griliches 1990, 1998; Mogee and Kolar 1994; Geschka 1995; Erickson 1996; Mogee 1997; Ehrat 1997; Ernst 1997, 1998; Behrmann 1998; Watts, Porter and Newmann 1998; Deng, Lev and Narin 1999; Hall, Jaffe and Traijtenberg 1999; Ernst, Leptien and Vitt 1999, 2000; Schlake and Siebe 2000; Abraham and Moitra 2001; Reger 2001; Guellec and van Pottelsberghe de la Potterie 2001; Tijssen 2002; Breitzman, Thomas and Cheney 2002; Stolpe 2002; Cohen et al. 2002; Yoon, Yoon and Park 2002; Harhoff, Scherer and Vopel 2003; McQueen and Olsson 1993, Reitzig 2003; Penner-Hahn and Myles Shaver 2005.

2.2.4 Contingency Factors

The relationship between patent management, patent portfolio and entre-preneurial success is strongly influenced by several contingency factors that therefore play a major role in managing intellectual property. Ernst and Omland (2003) distinguish *industry-*, *company-* and *system*-specific contingency factors. In addition, there are also differences in the propensity to patent product innovations (36%), and in process innovations (25%) (Arundel and Kabla 1998). Even the frequency of patent opposition cases is higher in areas with strong patenting activity and with high technical or market uncertainty (Harhoff and Reitzig 2004).

Industry-specific contingency factors influence the effectiveness and impact of patent protection in certain industry sectors (Ernst 1996; Mansfield 1986). In the pharmaceutical and biotechnology industries, intellectual property is an important instrument for maintaining competitive advantage through temporary monopolies (Levin et al. 1987; Thumm 2001). Whereas in the semiconductor or telecommunications industries, strong mutual interdependencies force competitors to use open licensing policies, to cross license intellectual property and sacrifice their portfolios to standardization pools (Grindley and Teece 1997; Bekkers, Duysters and Verspagen 2002). In the service industry sector, patents have in general played a fairly minor role so far and are subject to deeper investigation in this research (Wehling 2002; FhG 2003). Table 3 provides a detailed summary of further findings in the literature with regard to the various industry sectors.

Company-specific contingency factors crop up due to differences between large and small companies, as the latter may apply more stringent criteria for inventions selected for patent applications (Table 4a; Täger 1989; Ernst 1996). Furthermore, small companies also tend to place more importance on their patents, possess patents with a higher utilization ratio and have less formalized patent management processes. On the other hand, small companies are less likely to find patents of greater value than maintaining secrecy in respect of product innovation (Arundel 2001). In the global data-processing industry, companies that carry out more basic research are more successful in passing on the *EPO's* requirements (van Dijk and Duysters 1998).

System-specific contingency factors relate to socio-legal aspects, i.e. national aspects of intellectual property legislation and also cultural and country-specific differences (Table 4b; Wyatt, Bertin and Pavitt 1985; Gerstenberger 1992; Leptien 1996; Kortum and Lerner 1999; Berkowitz 2000; Granstrand 2000; Jaffe 2000; Cohen et al. 2002; Coriat and Orsi 2002; Faber and Hesen 2004; Hagedoorn, Cloodt and van Kranenburg 2005).

Table 3. Industry-specific limited findings on managing intellectual property

Authors	Scope of Analysis	Subject and Measures	Main Results
Mechanical and Manufacturing Industry Sector			
Ernst 1998b	21 German, European and Japanese mechanical engineering companies.	Patent information about competitors' R&D strategies is rarely used in strategic R&D planning, although this information is viewed to be of significant importance.	• Patent portfolio on a company level differentiates patent strategy in terms of patent activity and patent quality; • Identification of core competences through technological patent portfolio; • Patent portfolios as a valuable tool for strategic decision makers; • Improvement of intelligence about competitors' R&D strategies through continuous and strategic analysis of patent information.
Lowe and Taylor 1998	128 manufacturing companies; United Kingdom investigation.	The role of inward technology licensing and in-house R&D as alternative and complementary strategies in new product and process develop ment.	• Licensing and in-house R&D are complementary strategies rather than alternatives; • A significant driver of technology strategy was found in product-market positioning; • Firms that pursue product differentiation are most likely to license.
Ernst 2001	50 German machine tool manufacturers; Germany; 1984–1992.	Relationship between patent applications and subsequent changes of company performance; cross-section data of sales and patent data.	• Higher impact of EU patent application on sales than national applications; • Increases in sales after a time-lag of three years; • Length of time-lag depends on the quality of technological invention; • Strategic patent analysis draws competitive future changes, especially foreign patent applications should be considered.
Cohen, Goto, Nagata, Nelson and Walsh 2002	826 R&D units belonging to R&D performing US manufacturing firms, 593 R&D performing Japanese manufacturing firms with capitalization over one billion yen, with the restriction of annual sales of US$ 50 million or more for all firms; 1994.	Comparison of the ability of the US and Japanese firms to appropriate the returns to their innovations, how these firms protect their innovations and the magnitude and channels of intraindustry R&D information flows in the two nations.	• Intraindustry R&D knowledge flows and spillovers are greater in Japan than in the US; • In Japan, patents play a central role in diffusing information across rivals; • Patents appear to be key reason for greater intraindustry R&D spillovers; • Patent policy can importantly affect information flows; • Strategic usage of patents, particular for negotiations, are more common in Japan; • Differences in the patent systems partly account for the differences in intraindustry R&D information flows.

Authors	Scope of Analysis	Subject and Measures	Main Results
Electronics and Semiconductor Industry Sector			
Grindley and Teece 1997	Case study on basis of four US companies in the semiconductor and electronic sector.	Licensing and cross-licensing practices and impact for innovation management.	• Licensing and cross-licensing has become a relevant issue in the semiconductor and electronic industry sector; • Using intellectual property to support core business; • Importance of developing a valuable patent portfolio; • Concentrate R&D where the firm is strongest.
Ernst 1998a	25 European and Japanese electronics companies; 1990–1994.	The relationship between corporate spending on research and patenting output. Differentiation of patent applications according to their quality in order to assess the technological and commercial impact of R&D activities.	• Higher R&D expenditures on research results in patents of relatively higher quality; • Japanese companies spend significantly more of their total R&D budget on research and receive patents of much higher quality; • Research serves as a base for inventions of higher technological and commercial importance.
Stolpe 2002	Field of liquid crystal display (LCD).	Knowledge spillover from R&D in the field of liquid crystal display technology.	• Patent citations in LCD technology indicate knowledge spillover; • Usage of patent information to explore the changing nature of the diffusion of knowledge and ideas in innovating economies exists.
Yoon, Yoon and Park 2002	193 dynamic random access memory (DRAM)-related patents from US Patent no. 5,079,613 to 5,681,773; 1992–1997.	Conventional patent maps are limited as the size of patent databases increases and the relationship among attributes becomes more complex. Sophisticated data-mining tools are required to use the full potential of information from patent databases.	• A self-organizing, feature-map-based patent map visualizes the complexity of relationships among patents and the dynamic pattern of technological advancement; • Reduction of the amount of data by simultaneously clustering and visualizing the reduced data on a lower dimensional display; • Patent maps serve for monitoring technological change, developing new products and managing intellectual property.
Information and Communication Technology Industry Sector			
Van Dijk and Duysters 1998	44 companies of the global data-processing industry; 1986–1990.	The investigation of how firms have coped with the patentability requirements in Europe.	• Basic research explores novel and unknown technical paths, while development aims more at modifying and redesigning existing products; • Results from basic-oriented research are expected to fulfill the patentability requirements relatively more often than the results from development.

Authors	Scope of Analysis	Subject and Measures	Main Results
Bekkers, Duysters and Verspagen 2002	11 largest suppliers of GSM mobile terminals, mobile telecommuni-cations; 1996.	The role of IPRs in shaping the GSM (global system for mobile communications) industry.	• Emergence of strong network positions is in line with the findings on essential IPRs; • Three out of four dominant network players' positions are based on the ownership of essential IPRs; the relationship between market power, essential IPRs and network centrality is found to be a positive one.
McQueen and Olsson 2003	Software-related patent applications across 118 IPC patent classes for 1988, 1993 and 1998.	The identification of IPC patent classes that comprise software-related patent applications and their rate of expansion.	• A majority of embedded software applications occurs in only two patent classes (electric communication technique and computing, calculating, counting); • The statistics relate to the technical problems solved by the invention in contrast to economic statistics on the distribution of embedded software over the branches of an industry, which characterizes the application of problem solutions.
Somaya 2003	Patent litigation data from the US federal district courts, computer and research medicine industry, suits filed from 1983–1993.	Reasons for non-settlements that can explain why firms are willing to continue fighting patent suits despite the costs.	Two main drivers of non-settlement in patent suits: • A strong strategic stake in litigated patent; • Combined multiple inventions in the systems-product industry due to the mutual blocking of patent rights.

Biotechnology, Pharmaceuticals and Chemical Industry Sector

Authors	Scope of Analysis	Subject and Measures	Main Results
Arora 1997	The relevance of patents and technology licensing in the chemical industry.	Chemical firms' patent and licensing behavior of during the 19th century to the post-World War II era.	• Today, patents are no longer used to form cartels; • Organic chemicals and petrochemicals, and chemical producers use licensing as an important means of generating revenue from process innovations.
Kondo 1999	R&D expenditure and patent applications in different industry sectors; Japanese industry; 1970 to mid-1980.	Quantitative analysis of the dynamic mechanism of an R&D patent function.	• R&D investment created patent applications with a time-lag of about a year and a half, directly and through accumulated technology stock; • In the chemicals industry (incl. pharmaceuticals), the cost to create a patent application is high and requires much time; • R&D expenditure to create a patent application appears to have decreased over time during the analysis.

Authors	Scope of Analysis	Subject and Measures	Main Results
Thumm 2001	103 European biotechnology firms supplementary telephone interviews with 22 participants.	How European biotechnology firms manage their inventions and make use of patent protection.	• Absolute number of priority applications in Europe is about one-tenth of that in the United States and Japan, except for UK files; • Patents are an important incentive for R&D in Europe's biotechnology industry.
Breitzman, Thomas and Cheney 2002	Merger between Glaxo-Wellcome and SmithKline Beecham (pharmaceutical industry).	Examination of patent analysis techniques for evaluating the technological strength of merger candidates and the technological quality of the merged company; The use of patent analysis methods for examining the market value of companies and determining whether a merger target is over- or under-priced.	• Patent analysis to measure companies' capacity to innovate, e.g. for a merger; • Techniques for R&D-intensive industries to assess other mergers in order to provide insight into the technological fit between the companies involved; • Patent analysis in order to value the companies in regard to the quality of their patented technology.
Harhoff and Reitzig 2004	Biotechnology and pharmaceuticals industry sector; 1978–1996.	The analysis of determinants of opposition to biotechnology and pharmaceutical patents granted by the European Patent Office.	• Likelihood of opposition increases with patent value; • Opposition is particularly frequent in areas with strong patenting activity and with high technical or market uncertainty.
IGE 2003; Thumm 2004	Survey of the Swiss biotechnology industry; 2003.	Analysis of the relevance of patents and their strategic uses in the biotechnology industry.	• Patents for biotechnology inventions are important as an incentive for investment in R&D; • Patents are an effective tool for protecting biotechnology inventions.
Service Industry Sector			
Wehling 2002	Insurance sector in Germany and Great Britain.	Analysis of legal protection intruments for insurance products.	• There is a wide variety of legal tools to protect insurance innovations; • Patents have so far played a minor role in protection against imitation, but might be applicable to technically based inventions.
FhG 2003	65 companies from the European service sector from 10 different member states.	Survey concerning the value of patents within the service sector; empirical case study research on basis of literature research, patent database analysis of service companies and selected in-depth case analyses.	Protection of services through patents can cause two kinds of problems: • Scope: not all service-related inventions can be protected by patents; • Implementation: one group of companies has no ambition to generate patents since they doubt the effectiveness of patent protection for their business; the other group complains about the limited scope of patents; the latter group is in general more experienced in handling patents and comes from manufacturing or hardware-related services.

Authors	Scope of Analysis	Subject and Measures	Main Results
Klinger 2003	Case study based survey within the service industry.	Analysis of protection mechanisms against imitation of service innovations.	Notional house of protection with various factual and legal protection tools, e.g. patents and trademarks, for service innovations.
Research and Public Sector			
Wessel 1993	Patent applications and patents issued, seven most productive government organizations; 1981–1990.	The evaluation of the NASA IP program to review the patent process at nine field installations and the headquarter offices, with particular interest in the three R&D centers.	Due to a reduction of disclosures of the R&D centers, two fundamental changes will be required: • First, goals regarding disclosures received, patent applications filed and patents issued could be established for each field installation on the basis of its R&D funding level; • Second, cost effectiveness could be measured more realistically by showing annual royalties received per million dollars of R&D budget.
Luukkonen 1998	5-year-evaluation of EU framework programs, early 1980s.	The evaluation and the effects of EU framework programs.	• Too little attention has been paid to the interaction between firms' R&D strategies and their EU collaboration activities in EU research programs; • The intangible, infrastructural effects, such as learning new skills and seeking new network relations are the impact most often mentioned by all partners concerned.
Guellec and van Pottels- berghe de la Potterie 2001	Database of patents of the EPO; 1985–1987 and 1993–1995.	The analysis of factors that affect the degree and pattern of the internationalization of technology.	• Patent-based indicators of the internationalization of technology reflect international cooperation in research and the location of multinational firms' research facilities; • The higher degree of technological internationalization in small countries and in countries with low technological intensity; • Collaboration factors: geographical proximity, technological specialization and common language.
Tijssen 2002	Nationwide mail survey amongst inventors in corporate and public research sector in the Netherlands.	A novel methodology to increase the understanding of the contribution of research efforts to successful technical inventions.	• 20% of private sector innovations are based on public sector research; • Citations in patents referring to basic research literature are invalid indicators of a technology's science dependence.

Authors	Scope of Analysis	Subject and Measures	Main Results
Cross Industry Sector			
Mansfield 1986	100 US manufacturing firms, twelve different industries; 1981–1983.	The influence of patent protection on the rate of development and commercialization of inventions and the extent to which firms make use of the patent system with regard to industries and time.	• Patent protection is not essential for the introduction of inventions during that period; • Effects of the patent system are very substantial, except for the chemicals and pharmaceuticals industries; • Patentable inventions are patented and patent protection is clearly preferred to trade secret protection.
Levin, Klevorick, Nelson and Winter 1987	650 high-level R&D executives of more than 100 manufacturing industries.	Identify those industries and technologies in which patents are effective in preventing the competitive imitation of a new product.	• Patents for products are more effective than those for processes; • Secrecy considered less effective in protecting products and processes; • Patents are a strong means of protection in chemicals and drugs industries; • Patents raise imitation costs by 40% for drugs, by 30% for chemical products and by 7–15% for major electronic products.
Arundel and Kabla 1998	604 European industrial companies, 19 industries; 1993.	Propensity for product and process innovations.	• Patent propensity increases with firm size and is higher among firms that find patents to be an important method of preventing competitors from copying both product and process innovations; • Patent protection is less likely to be used at firms that find trade secrecy an important protection method; • The R&D intensity of the firm has no effect on patent propensity rates for both product and process innovations; • The sector activity has a strong influence on product patent propensities, but very little effect on process patent propensities.
Ernst and Vitt 2000	43 acquisitions of German companies in the mechanical engineering, electrical engineering or chemical industry where both types of companies perform R&D; 1980–1989.	Impact of acquisition on the key inventors' behavior during the first three years after the acquisition of their company.	• Key inventors frequently leave their company or change their position; • Remaining key inventors reduce patenting performance; • Main drivers for this behavior: size of the acquired company, cultural differences between both companies' R&D departments and the complementarity of technological positions; • Creation of an incentive system and the integration of the inventor during the early stages of the acquisition process may reduce this behavior.

Authors	Scope of Analysis	Subject and Measures	Main Results
Arundel 2001	2849 R&D performing firms, data from the European Community Innovation Survey; 1993.	The analysis of the relative importance of secrecy vs. patents at R&D performing firms.	• A higher percentage of firms in all size classes rate secrecy as more valuable than patents; • However, the probability that a firm rates secrecy as more valuable than patents declines with an increase in firm size for product innovations, while there is no relationship for process innovations; • There is only weak evidence that participation in collaborative R&D increases the value of patents more than secrecy for product innovations.

Table 4a/b. Company- and system-specific limited findings on managing intellectual property

Research Focus	Authors
Company-specific contingency factors	Täger 1989; Ernst 1996; Arundel 2001; van Dijk and Duysters 1998.
System-specific contingency factors	Wyatt, Bertin and Pavitt 1985; Gerstenberger 1992; Leptien 1996; Kortum and Lerner 1999; Berkowitz 2000; Granstrand 2000; Jaffe 2000; Cohen et al. 2002; Coriat and Orsi 2002; Faber and Hesen 2004; Hagedoorn, Cloodt and van Kranenburg 2005.

2.3 Managing Intellectual Property in R&D Collaborations

In this section the effects of collaborations on intellectual property as an outcome are discussed, based on the literature streams concerning joint intellectual property and the role of intellectual property in collaborative standardization procedures (Fig. 10 and Table 5, p. 39).

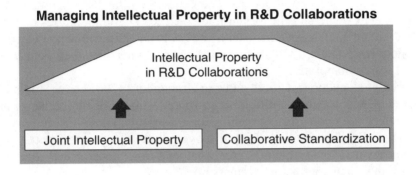

Fig. 10. Structure of literature streams in managing intellectual property in R&D collaborations

2.3.1 Joint Intellectual Property

A company's propensity to patent is significantly higher among R&D collaborators (Brouwer and Kleinknecht 1999). The exceptions still seem to be small and medium sized enterprises that rarely collaborate in obtaining patents, even though collaboration has proved to be a good way to solve problems concerning patents (Masurel 2002).

Hicks and Narin (2000) concluded that there is an increase in jointly owned patents due to a growth in collaborative R&D.[2] In fact, there is an increasing number and relative share of jointly owned intellectual property rights, especially in the form of joint patents: An empirical investigation reveals that even the share of co-patent applications in triad patent families has increased from almost 7% in 1980 to more than 10% in 1995 (OECD 2002a). However, jointly owned patents are still seen as sub-optimal due to

---

[2]   Joint intellectual property is characterized by two or more assignees from different companies or legal bodies that share the ownership rights of the individual intellectual property right.

necessary contractual and administrative regulations, which remain incomplete and reveal various legal and economic risks. Hagedoorn (2003) compared different industries with regard to their joint patenting behavior, which depends greatly on the sectoral patent intensity, partnering intensity and strength of intellectual property.

Hagedoorn, van Kranenburg and Osborn (2003) observed that formal inter-firm R&D collaborations could generate valuable results for the partners. Yet, "surprisingly" the collaboration partners did not recognize joint patents as a collaboration benefit. The general willingness of companies to share patent ownership in formal inter-firm R&D collaborations depends, however, on their experience with the joint patenting process. Once the partners have learned to process joint patent ownership, they continue to do so with collaboration partners.

Finally, Hagedoorn, Cloodt and van Kranenburg (2005) have studied the degree to which country differences in intellectual property rights protection affect the choice of companies for a particular mode of international inter-firm R&D partnering. They discovered that the country-specific protection level is a significant factor whether firms choose R&D joint ventures rather than contractual partnerships.

2.3.2 Collaborative Standardization

Standardization can either be based on a *de iure* or a *de facto* standardization procedure: Whereas the former procedure is stimulated by legislative bodies, the de facto procedure is based on competing technologies, each being sponsored by one or more companies. A company has then to decide if it wants or does not want to collaborate with other parties to promote the selection of a standard (Jorde and Teece 1990; Axelrod et al. 1995; Doz and Hamel 1998; Weiss and Sirbu 1990).

Companies that collaborate generally do so due to a lack of resources or competencies that are necessary to form an autonomous standard. Chiesa, Manzini and Toletti (2002) derived from their research that the motivation for a standardization procedure in the form of a developing collaboration is to reduce the risks and costs of standardization, to increase and complement the available skills and competencies and to increase the market power favoring the introduction of the technology to the market. Relevant for the choice of partners is the level of the complementarity of the shared resources, the level of trust between the partners and the market power of the coalition.

The role of intellectual property within standardization procedures has become significant, especially in the telecommunications industry and especially if the standardization players own *essential intellectual property* that is needed to implement the anticipated technology standard. The positions of the standardization coalition partners and their market power may depend heavily on the strength of their individual intellectual property portfolios influencing their negotiation power (Bekkers, Duysters and Verspagen 2002). However, actual investigations have confirmed that the higher the patent intensities of companies, the lower their tendency to join standardization processes, as they do not need the support of standards to market their products successfully (Blind and Thumm 2004).

Table 5. Literature streams in managing intellectual property in R&D collaborations

Research Focus	Authors
Joint Intellectual Property	Brouwer and Kleinknecht 1999; Hicks and Narin 2000; Masurel 2002; OECD 2002a; Hagedoorn 2003; Hagedoorn, van Kranenburg and Osborn 2003; Kline 2003; Hagedoorn, Cloodt and van Kranenburg 2005.
Collaborative Standardization	Jorde and Teece 1990; Weiss and Sirbu 1990; Axelrod et al. 1995; Doz and Hamel 1998; Bekkers, Duysters and Verspagen 2002; Chiesa, Manzini and Toletti 2002; Blind and Thumm 2004.

2.4 Research Gap

Managing intellectual property. As demonstrated above, a broad range of academic literature is available. Within the literature stream relating to *intellectual property management*, one can get a clear picture of how individual companies are managing their intellectual property, i.e. through strategy, acquisition, scanning, monitoring and maintenance of intellectual property, and portfolio management, including the influence of approved contingency factors. Information is also available on transactional levels where firms are competing on the basis of their intellectual property, i.e. valuation and licensing of intellectual property. However, there is very little information on managing intellectual property when two or more firms are interacting as collaboration partners.

Another limitation obviously seems to be the industry sector on which current research has focused so far. A relatively large number of intellectual property management studies are confined to the *mechanical* and *manufacturing* industry sector. Other ones are the *electronics* and *semi-*

conductor, the *biotechnology, pharmaceuticals* and *chemical* industry sector and, for some aspects, the *information and communication technology* industry sector (Table 3, pp. 30).

One can conclude that the current scope of research in the field of intellectual property management is additionally limited to current industry activities; but omits the impact on the next value chain generation, which is expected to become the future service industry sector (as further described in chapter four).

Managing intellectual property in R&D collaborations. In the literature stream of inter-firm *R&D collaboration management*, only a few studies have been conducted on the impact of intellectual property on collaboration partners. One substream has tried to understand and interpret the implications of joint patenting (Hagedoorn 2003; Hagedoorn, van Kranenburg and Osborn 2003). However, these studies focus only on certain aspects of the outcomes of such collaborations and place less emphasis on the formation phase and the entire collaboration process itself.

Furthermore, joint patenting between collaboration partners is only a very rough indicator (OECD 2002a). This is due to the following reasons:

- The total number of joint patent applications underestimates the total number of patented joint inventions. Because most companies, even when they collaborate and make joint inventions, prefer not to share patent ownership. In some cases this is due to political reasons and in other cases it is due to the high degree of administrative complexity and cost.
- Instead of taking the route of joint patent applications, collaborating companies might set up a common subsidiary as the owner of the intellectual property. Another widespread practice is for one of the collaboration partners to take the patent ownership and manage the formal patent application process. The owner then sets up cross-licenses on a royalty-free basis with the collaboration partners.
- There is a tendency to over-estimate joint patenting figures, especially in respect of those multinational firms that have several national and foreign subsidiaries, some of which may even operate using different company names. In such cases, parent companies and their subsidiaries might apply as joint patent owners together.

Thus it can be concluded that to date there have been no academic investigations into the role of intellectual property management in collaborations, specifically with respect to the following focus areas:

Research and development (R&D) collaborations: As intellectual property is still looked upon as the key outcome of technology-based innovation,

R&D collaborations are given the highest priority. Similarly, intellectual property has the highest impact on these kinds of collaborations.

Formal collaborations: Formal R&D collaborations are based on basically fixed contracts as a result of an early negotiation phase antedating the core collaboration phase. There is therefore a realistic probability that the partners will negotiate the issue of intellectual property and find solutions for it.

Inter-firm collaborations: Collaborations amongst companies need the highest level of professionalism in dealing with collaborations in general and intellectual property in particular. Even though universities and public research organizations have recently begun to treat intellectual property as an important asset, they generally do not have the same level of formal approach and experienced professionals as companies in the private sector do. To a certain extent, however, the theories on inter-firm collaborations could also be applicable to non-inter-firm collaborations.

Early stages of collaborations: During the early stages, it is important to take the various risks and opportunities into account before the actual collaboration phase begins. On the other hand, this is the most difficult phase because the partners are not yet fully aware of the true impact that anticipated intellectual property will have on the partners and their markets.

Early innovation phase of innovation process: Collaborations that take place during the early innovation phase are tricky, as at this stage the outcome of the innovation process is still quite unclear and is therefore characterized by a high level of uncertainty and risk.

The literature discussed so far deals with how to manage intellectual property as well as collaborations. However, there is very little information on managing intellectual property where two or more firms interact as collaboration partners.

The service industry sector is of particular interest for further research. Hardly any of the research carried out to date can be applied to the service industry because of its specific industry characteristics and limitations.

In conclusion, from intellectual property management's perspective, there is a gap with respect to the role intellectual property plays in and the impact it has on the early stages of formal inter-firm R&D collaborations. This research work therefore focuses on how companies manage intellectual property in the early stages of formal inter-firm R&D collaborations within the early innovation phase, especially with regard to the service industry sector.

3 Research Design

3.1 Research Question

Since managing intellectual property has emerged as an important issue within R&D collaborations (chapter one) and has not been sufficiently addressed by the research to date (chapter two), this work aims to contribute by bridging that gap. This research provides a guideline for R&D managers as well as for intellectual property, legal and innovation management experts and provides an answer to the following research question:

> *How can companies manage intellectual property in the early stages of formal inter-firm R&D collaborations, within the early innovation phase?*

This research question raises two more questions that are directly linked:

> *What modes are there for managing intellectual property in these collaborations today?*
>
> *What are important criteria for managing intellectual property efficiently and effectively in these collaborations?*

This research work aims to provide a typology of current intellectual property management models in the early stages of formal inter-firm R&D collaborations. It also intends to provide meaningful insights into current and potentially novel methods for managing intellectual property in collaborations. This research furthermore derives explanatory patterns and develops managerial implications and guiding principles.

3.2 Research Concept

As managing intellectual property in the early stages of formal inter-firm R&D collaborations has emerged as a very young empirical phenomenon, an exploratory method has been chosen for this research, focused on the qualitative approach of Eisenhardt (1989), Yin (1994) and Gassmann (1999).

This work applies the principles of generic research methodology by Ulrich and Krieg (1974), Ulrich (1981) and Bleicher (1991). Based on relevant practical situations, Ulrich's process defines fundamental and formal sciences to identify relevant theories and methods. At first, interesting situations, correlations and contexts from a practical point of view are observed and are then conceptualized (Ulrich 1981). The concepts can be repeatedly tested in practice and be refined. The iterative learning process will not only raise relevant questions, but will also generate theoretical and practical solutions to those questions (Kromrey 2002).

According to Kubicek (1977), Tomczak (1992) and Gassmann (1999), this approach could also be regarded as a highly iterative learning process that also considers empiricism as theory (Fig. 11). Empirical data collection includes real-life problems and results of focused case studies that explain certain occurrences or successful practices in qualitative terms. In parallel, a theoretical understanding is based on a first literature overview that provides a better understanding of the identified problems. In addition, scientific theories and hypotheses enable the researcher to answer the research questions in a thorough and unique manner. A quantitative confir-

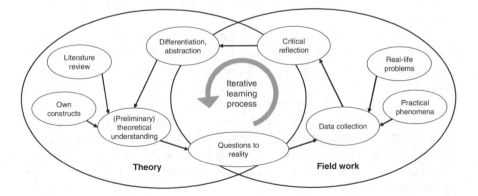

Source: following Kubicek (1977), Tomczak (1992), Gassmann (1999)

Fig. 11. Iterative learning process between theory and empiricism

mation of developed models or hypotheses may conclude the whole process, but does not lie within the scope of this research work.

3.3 Research Methodology

This research follows a multiple-case design with the formal inter-firm R&D collaboration, i.e. the joint project, as the single unit of analysis, described from one of the collaboration partners' point of view (Yin 1994). Additionally, small case studies will be used to illustrate theoretical concepts and approaches for coping with different R&D challenges. These mini-cases or narratives will be used throughout the work.

The main criteria in qualitative empirical research are validity and reliability of results. Usually, three types of validity can be differentiated: (a) *construct validity*, (b) *internal validity*, and (c) *external validity*. According to Yin (1994), construct validity can be increased by using multiple sources of evidence, establishing a chain of evidence between the question asked, data collected and conclusion drawn, and by getting the key informants to review the draft case study report and agree upon the outcomes. Internal validity of causal relationships requires a reliable process of analyzing data and comparing emerging concepts and theories with previous literature for generalization and theory building from cases. It can be enhanced by pattern matching, explanation building and time-series analyses. In addition, the concept of triangulation is key to internal validity (Lamnek 1995; Yin 1994). External validity confirms that the findings can be generalized. Lastly, reliability ensures that another researcher could successfully conduct the same research using the same procedure at later date (Eisenhardt 1989).

Validity and reliability are ensured during this research by combining the semi-structured data with the results of thoroughly conducted desk research, internal documentation and presentations by expert and management personnel. The interpretations are then confirmed with each of the participating companies through follow-up interviews.

Even though there is an increasing awareness of the relevance of intellectual property management, only few studies have been conducted about it from a management perspective. Therefore, the Institute of Technology Management of the University of St.Gallen, Switzerland conducted various research activities between the autumn of 2002 and the autumn of 2005, and these partly form the basis of this research:

- Various intellectual property-related bilateral projects have been conducted together with larger and medium sized companies from different industries, e.g., software, telecommunications, electronics, chemicals, pharmaceuticals and furniture component supply industries.

- Two specific intellectual property benchmarking projects were conducted. The first one was focused on intellectual-property-related processes and was conducted on a selected group of three medium sized companies from the machine tool, automotive supply and furniture component supply industries in early 2003. The second international benchmarking project was conducted over eight months from June 2003 to January 2004 and focused on strategic technology management. One of the four key focus areas was intellectual property management. The consortium benchmarking started with a review of 61 technology-intensive companies worldwide. Case studies were prepared from 13 of these companies' case studies, and the five leading companies were visited in Europe and USA for in-depth investigations (ITEM 2004a, Table 6).
- A series of workshops on intellectual property management was conducted from July 2003 to March 2004 with a group of nine multinational core participant companies and six guest speaker companies (Table 6). The objective was to assess how competitive advantage can be leveraged upon and sustained through contingently adapted intellectual property strategies. One of the six selected key issues on intellectual property management was its role and impact within R&D collaborations. (ITEM 2004b).
- A nine-month bilateral project was conducted within the service innovation sector together with a qualitative benchmarking research project covering the software, information technology, telecommunications and finance/insurance industries (ITEM 2005a, b).
- Various personal interviews were also conducted during the projects mentioned above, resulting from participation in conferences and expert groups as a speaker and/or participant. In total, about 450 interviews and discussions with managers and experts from R&D, innovation, legal and intellectual property have taken place, providing insights from companies in various industries, from legal and consulting firms as well as from academia in West and East Europe, the USA, Japan and Taiwan.

As already mentioned in chapter two, there are only a few academic findings on managing intellectual property within the service industry sector that has a high rate of collaborative activities. The sample of case studies for in-depth analysis has therefore been selected within the service industry sector. A triple iterative research process was applied to the selected

Table 6. Sample of analyzed companies

Company	Industry Sector	Region	Turnover [bill. euro]	R&D Expenditure [mio. euro]	Number of Patents[a]
Alcatel	Telecommunications	Germany	16.5	2.2	n.s.
Aventis	Pharmaceuticals	Germany	17.6	3,140	n.s.
Basell	Chemicals	Germany	5.9	n.s.	1,000[b]
BASF	Chemicals	Germany	32.2	1,135	89,000
Bayer	Chemicals	Germany	11.0	320	3,200[b]
British Telecom / BT Exact	Telecommunications	United Kingdom	28.1	571	14,000
Bühler	Engineering	Switzerland	0.95	39	300[b]
DaimlerChrysler	Automotive	Germany	149.6	6,156	23,300
E.I. du Pont de Nemours	Chemicals	United States of America	22.1	1103	400[b]
Eastman Kodak	Chemistry, Software	United States of America	10.7	665	9,100
Henkel	Consumer Goods	Germany	9.6	211	900[b]
IBM	Information Technology	Switzerland	81.2	5,600	37,000
Infineon Technologies	Semiconductors	Germany	5.2	1,100	9,000[b]
Leica Geosystems	Geomatics	Switzerland	0.7	81	150[b]
Novartis	Pharmaceuticals	Switzerland	13.9	2,840	n.s.
Philips	Electronics	The Netherlands	31.8	3,312	95,000
Roche Instrument Center	Medical Instrumentation	Switzerland	4.8	n.s.	n.s.
SAP	Software	Germany	7.4	875	350[c]
Schering	Pharmaceuticals	Germany	5.0	950	n.s.
Schindler	Engineering	Switzerland	8.0	139	800
Siemens	Electronics	Germany	84.0	5,600	43,600
Swiss Re	Insurance	Switzerland	28.4	n.s.	45[b]
Swisscom	Telecommunications	Switzerland	9.6	29	240[d]
Unaxis	Engineering	Liechtenstein	0.9	104	400[b]

Source: Own research (2002)

[a] Number of patents and patent applications in total
[b] Number by patent families
[c] Number of patent applications in year 2002
[d] Swisscom Innovations and Swisscom Mobile

four in-depth case study companies presented in chapter four, namely *IBM*, *SAP*, *Swisscom* and *Swiss Re*.[3] After each research cycle, the revealed outcomes were used to refine the research focus and to sharpen the questions used for interviews (Eisenhardt 1989):

- The four case study companies were subject to in-depth interviews with various internal company experts and managers. The focus of these interviews was to understand how the companies manage of intellectual property in inter-firm R&D collaborations during the period 2003–2005.
- Three of the four case study companies were furthermore subject to participation in the series of workshops on intellectual property management. One company participated during the entire eight-months period, two other companies participated as best practice example cases (ITEM 2004b).
- One company participated in the nine-month bilateral project (ITEM 2005a).
- The four companies finally participated in the benchmarking research project with a focus on intellectual property management in the service industry sector (ITEM 2005b).

In total, each case study company has therefore been subject to at least three iterative research cycles (Table 7):

Table 7. Iterative research activities concerning the in-depth case studies

Research Method	IBM	SAP	Swisscom	Swiss Re
Expert and management interviews	x	x	x	x
Participation in workshop series / bilateral project	x	x	x	x
IP benchmarking in the service industry sector	x	x	x	x

---

[3]   For the reason of simplicity, legal structures of companies are not specified in detail.

3.4 Research Structure

Fig. 12. Structure of research work

4 Case Studies in the Service Industry Sector

As discussed in the literature review in chapter two, only very little research has to date focused on managing intellectual property in that industry sector. This research work therefore aims to select case examples from within the service industry sector and therefore provides an introduction to the service industry sector in this chapter and selects the cases on the basis of a recognized service delivery typology. Descriptive analyses of the selected cases, namely *IBM*, *SAP*, *Swisscom* and *Swiss Re* are also presented.

4.1 Introduction to the Service Industry Sector and Case Selection

Trend towards software- and service-based innovations. As an overall trend, the value-creating activities of an organization lie increasingly in the software and service industries (Hipp 2000). More and more traditionally hardware-based products need software and service complements. Services in particular increasingly play an economic and strategic role in industrialized countries (Simon 1993). An example is the Swiss manufacturer of geomatics precision surveying equipment, *Leica Geosystems*, whose hardware-based products traditionally contain optomechanical components. The company, however, invests close to 50% of its R&D budget in software. The reason for this stems from image and data processing's ever-growing importance in providing a wide range of evaluation services around the equipment.

The trend towards services is enhanced by the fact that intensive competition at product level has resulted in a homogeneous market with reduced revenues (Belz et al. 1997; Homburg, Günther and Fassnacht 2002). Service products help regain profit margins as they function as an additional source for generating sustainable competitive advantage (Engelhardt and Reckenfelderbäumer 1999; Frambach, Wels-Lips and Gündlach 1997). In order to reduce the risk of decreasing margins, even manufacturing-oriented companies are increasingly interested in expanding into the service business in order to generate additional revenues and profits – and introduce a step-wise transition from products to services (Gebauer, Fleisch and Friedli 2005).

Companies are furthermore focusing on core competencies and are more likely to outsource non-core activities to increase flexibility. Therefore, new opportunities arise for service providers to take care of these activities (Oliva and Kallenberg 2003). Another reason for the extension of the service industry sector is because product life cycles tend to decrease, which forces companies to recoup their outlay quicker in order to develop and manufacture goods. This acceleration process can be enabled by services. The current understanding is that value creation and related revenues that can be realized through services are much higher than value creation through products alone (Potts 1988; Knecht, Leszinski and Weber 1993; Gadiesh and Gilbert 1998; Wise and Baumgartner 1999). Besides higher revenues in the service industry sector, further advantages of service innovations are the positive marketing effect and the strategic potential of services (Mathieu 2001).

Businesses that led to the field of industrial services being established, led to academic research activities in the field of service innovations (Casagranda 1994; Fassnacht and Homburg 2001). Industrial services should be understood as services between two enterprises (Homburg and Garbe 1996). Excellent services establish strategic advantage by hampering imitation and by increasing market barriers (Simon 1993; Heskett, Sasser and Schlesinger 1997); furthermore, they can help to sell more products (Mathe and Shapiro 1993). One of the characteristics of services is intangibility, which means that services as such cannot be stored or transported, and this leads to the following success factors for the service sector (Meffert and Bruhn 2003): materialization of immaterial services; intensive coordination of production and demand; requirement for flexible capacity planning; management of short-term demand management.

Greater market differentiation and increased economic success can be attained by combining products with services and by offering problem-oriented service solution packages (Anderson and Narus 1995; Boyt and Harvey 1997). By doing this, further competitive advantage can be created that are difficult to imitate and therefore strengthen the firm's uniqueness (Simon 1993). The service component might only be small, might complement products, or might even be the core product itself. Complementary services help to strategically stabilize volatile product business by adding an extra value component (Quinn 1992).

Overall, there are four relevant factors behind the continuing increase in and extension of services (Gebauer 2004): Increase in the differentiation and uniqueness of companies by applying services; increasing customer needs; toughening competition; and better business opportunities in the service sector.

An example is the American information and technology specialist *IBM*, which acquired the consultant firm *PwC Consulting* in 2002 and formed *IBM Global Services* with more than 75,000 employees. *IBM Global Services* was already considered strong in systems integration and IT outsourcing. By insourcing *PwC Consulting*, *IBM* extended the strengths of its former *Business Innovation Services* unit with respect to vertical industry expertise, especially in the four industries: pharmaceuticals; oil and gas; aerospace and defense; and automotive. *PwC Consulting* is considered to be a dominant player, particularly in respect of pharmaceuticals. As an endorsement, *IBM* spun off its hardware-based, mass-market, personal computer business to the leading Chinese PC maker *Lenovo* in 2004. *IBM* has therefore taken significant steps to back out of the mere hardware product business and to be prepared for the industry trend toward more comprehensive and integrated software and consulting services.

Service innovations change business models and value chains. The trend toward services is driven by information and communication technology facilitated by computer science technology (Schmid 2000a). Based on that, process, product and service designs have evolved and will do so further in the near future. Customers may now procure bundles of services that could only have been obtained via various sources and which the customer himself still had to integrate (Österle 2000). The critical success factors have moved from production chain control to managing competencies in information and communication, therefore from production management toward information and communication management; especially when designing new products or services and when communicating customer benefits (Schmid 2000b). Production and communication of information are the foundation of service solutions. While former business models collapse, relating service models have to be reinvented. However, the underlying technology and its industries change the structure of the economy that is based on the division of labor, i.e. the value chain system – making it faster and more sustainable. Due to the high speed of innovation and the assimilation of modern communication and information technologies, technical infrastructure has become a very important success factor for service innovations (Olemotz 1995; Müller 1998). The new productivity therefore requires and forms new business models by radically changing traditional value chains.

Information and communication technology influences the specialization process within a labor-divided society. Further productivity increases are achieved through the increasing accumulation of knowledge by specialized groups. Knowledge and information have become key factors for productivity, both for products and pre-deliverables, and for process knowledge (Schmid 2000b). Furthermore, services help to bridge the gap between the producer of goods and the procurer of these goods – a distance that is growing due to the increase in specialization in core competencies. A large number of public and professional service platforms have appeared in the last decade, e.g. internet-based trade, market and auction places, and search platforms, e.g. *yet2.com*, *ebay* and *Google*. They follow the business model that bridges information gaps between suppliers of goods and services, and potential customers.

The *Swiss Reinsurance Company (Swiss Re)*, one of the largest reinsurance enterprises worldwide, is an example. The company has over 70 offices in 30 countries worldwide. *Swiss Re* has been involved in reinsurance since its inception in Zurich in 1863. With its three divisions: Property & Casualty, Life & Health, and Financial Services, *Swiss Re* can offer a wide variety of products and services to help manage capital and risk. However, during the last decade e-business based reinsurance products were introduced on the market. These new solutions started to use internet- and browser-based information technology solutions to optimize reinsurance transactions. The introduction of these kinds of innovations changed the competition in the financial services sector.

Modern information technology is based on formalizing logic and on rationalizing work flow processes. Through formalizing, work flow processes can be described, mechanized, automated and transferred to and applied by computer technology. By formalizing information and data processing, collaborative systems and internal process flows can be planned and shaped (Schmid 1999).

Communication between computer technologies changes these systems into a productivity factor that is available globally without any time delay. Through this, almost everybody can have access to very strong production means with very low entry barriers. Information and communication technology therefore necessitates the reconfiguration of value chains. On the one hand, new values might then be offered at new low cost prices, on the other hand, traditional values and production of goods are reshaped and might be substituted. If a value chain is only changed on a local basis, the changes can be described as *evolutionary*, if large parts of the entire value chain are substituted, a *revolutionary* transformation takes place (Schmid 2000b).

An example is the German software company *SAP* that develops software that helps companies to improve customer relations, to enhance partner collaboration, to create efficiencies across their supply chains and business operations, and to support databases, applications, operating systems and hardware from common vendors. Powered by the *SAP Net-Weaver*® platform to drive innovation and enable business change, *my-SAP*™ *Business Suite* solutions are helping enterprises around the world improve customer relationships, enhance partner collaboration and create efficiencies across their supply chains and business operations. Today, *SAP* has international operations and has grown into the world's largest business-to-business software company and the third largest independent software supplier worldwide. The current software is an open integration and application platform that reduces complexity and total cost of ownership, and provides outsourcing and support services, while empowering business change and innovation.

As another important factor in the service industry sector, the speed at which different changes take place is accelerated by information and communication technology. The automation and availability of formalized and integrated information have changed the production of goods and services and have dramatically decreased production cycles from product idea via realization to market entry. Often, the value of a product is reduced to its transfer costs in being distributed, e.g. in *electronic mailing* or in the *music industry* which is eroded by internet-based exchange platforms. In these cases, the transfer costs are more or less induced by the bare costs of information communication (Schmid 2000b).

An example is the Swiss telecommunications provider *Swisscom* that is considered Switzerland's leading telecommunications service provider. *Swisscom* offers a comprehensive range of telecommunications products and services, and is the market leader in mobile and fixed voice and data communication as well as internet-based services. Without the divested German *debitel* group, *Swisscom* currently has more than 15,600 employees and expects to close the current financial year with a consolidated revenue of around 10.1 billion Swiss francs and a net income of 1.6 billion Swiss francs (2004). As a company that previously primarily focused on its home market, *Swisscom* aims to keep its focus on its core businesses of fixed network and mobile communication in future. The company wants to invest in related growth businesses and strengthen its position further by targeted investments in Europe. An example of this is *Swisscom Eurospot*, a subsidiary founded in early 2003, which sets up and operates *Wireless Local Area Networks* (WLAN) at busy public locations across Europe such as hotels, airports and conference centers.

Service innovations typologies. From the point of view of a service provider, information and communication technologies allow the substitution of human production steps with technologies for the generation of service innovations. There is, moreover, a high potential for reducing process flows to increase productivity through the standardization of service components, and technologies can help both to improve the quality of services and to reduce service costs. Services also help to collect and structure information on customers and competitors and help to leverage this information with respect to the customer and market focus (Hesket, Sasser and Schlesinger 1997). Information and communication technologies enable the development and marketing of differentiating services to attract and keep customers, and may even bring about a positive effect with which to motivate employees. From the point of view of a service procurer, information and communication technologies improve the availability and accessibility of service innovations. Customers do, of course, implicitly benefit from the higher quality and productivity as well as from improved service innovations' lower costs.

Table 8. Benefits of modern information and communication technologies for service innovations

Potential benefits for service *providers*	Potential benefits for service *procurers*
▪ Cost improvements and standardization ▪ Better quality of services ▪ Attraction of customers ▪ Improvement of innovation, differentiation and image ▪ Higher motivation of employees	▪ Higher availability and accessibility of services and information ▪ Better quality of services ▪ Cost improvement and higher productivity

Source: According to Sanche (2002)

Service innovations have a wide variety of characteristics. In order to manage service-based companies, however, it is important to know what influence these characteristics have on the management process. One category of characteristics is the service process's level integration (Engelhardt, Kleinaltenkamp and Reckenfelderbäumer 1992). The level of integration has two relevant dimensions (Wohlgemuth 1989; Corsten 1990): The *level of interaction* indicates how much interaction is necessary between the service provider and service recipient to provide the service. The *level of individualism* indicates how much the services can be standardized and still satisfy customer requirements. The two dimensions support the identification and deduction of clear and useful activities for managing the contribution of services (Meffert and Bruhn 2003). On the one hand, it is possible to describe the necessity for integrating the customer's external values into the service being provided, e.g. social context, goods, virtual goods, information and other background knowledge. The level of interaction therefore indicates how much interaction with the customer is necessary to create the service. On the other hand, it is possible to describe the focus and direction of the service provided with respect to customers' specific environment. The level of individualism therefore indicates how much a service product has to be adjusted to customer-specific needs for it to be successful.

A more common typology for service innovations has, however, been introduced by Schmenner (1986), who proposes a two-by-two service process matrix that is based on three characteristics of service delivery systems: Labor intensity, customer contact, and service customization. As a first dimension of the service process matrix, *labor intensity* is defined as the ratio of the labor costs with regard to the value of the equipment involved. High labor intensity involves a relatively high investment of worker time, efforts, and costs in comparison with the necessary equipment. Low labor intensity involves high equipment costs or financial assets in comparison to the labor costs and effort. The second dimension of the service process matrix combines *customer contact* and *service customization*. High customer contact enables the customer to actively get involved and intervene in the service process. High service customization focuses on individual needs and preferences. As a second dimension, the combination of both measures is high when a high level of contact as well as a high level of customization for the customer is necessary to offer a service. The service process matrix has been empirically tested and refined by Verma (2000) with regard to category-specific management challenge relationships.

On the basis of the aforementioned two dimensions, the service process matrix identifies four different types of services for analyzing service operations: the service factory, the service shop, the mass service and the professional service. With regard to service providers based on information and communication technology, the categorization would be as follows:

- *Service Factory:* Low degree of labor intensity combined with low customer contact and low customization. Services that are based on high investments in infrastructure, but only need relatively low customer contact and customization, are to be found in the telecommunications service industry that, on the one hand, uses expensive telecommunication equipment such as base stations, servers and routers, but, on the other hand, is based on strongly standardized processes and tools. A representative firm in this field is, e.g., *Swisscom*.

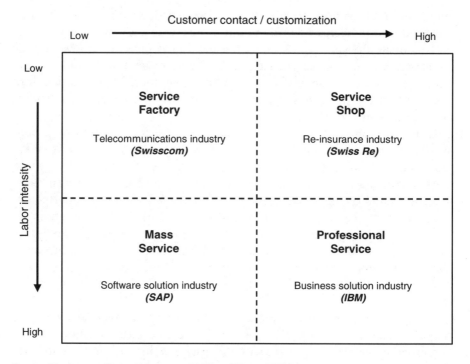

Source: Matrix according to Schmenner (1986) and Verma (2000)

Fig. 13. Typology of service delivery systems and selected cases

- *Service Shop:* Low degree of labor intensity but high customer contact and high customization. The expenses for equipment and financial assets still count more than labor costs. However, various customized services are provided to customers. This kind of service type is to be found in the insurance business, especially in the re-insurance business. While considerable financial securities are necessary, the services have to be individually customized to develop the right insurance package. A representative firm in this field is, e.g., *Swiss Re.*
- *Mass Service:* High degree of labor intensity combined with a low customer contact and low customization. The labor costs exceed the costs of equipment as in the case in brainwork-based software development, which in general is developed independently of individual customer preferences. Even a business-to-business software service business is based on the development of largely standardized software modules. A representative firm in this field is, e.g., *SAP.*

- *Professional Service:* High degree of labor intensity combined with high customer contact and high customization. The labor costs exceed the costs for equipment, and service development needs the customer's direct involvement. A representative firm in this field is, e.g., the firm that introduced a new trend in business solution delivery in the information and communication industry with the program *Innovation on Demand*, which is *IBM*.

Based on the service process matrix (Fig. 13), the relationships between the introduced service categories and specific legal intellectual property protection strategies will be further investigated on the basis of the four introduced service innovations companies, namely *IBM*, *SAP*, *Swisscom* and *Swiss Re*.

4.2 IBM

IBM is well known as the leading information technology company worldwide. *IBM* – also known as *Big Blue* – has survived in a very dynamic and competitive environment that required major internal transformations. However, decreasing margins in the hardware and software industry still provide *IBM* with challenges, and induce the company to extend its range of activities to services, so that technology increasingly only serves as an enabler. *IBM* recently invested in the *On Demand Innovation Services* (ODIS) with which it should gain a better understanding of customers' business problems and be able re-incorporate the resulting knowledge into its research. At the same time, *IBM* divested its hardware-based PC business division. Like many companies, *IBM* seeks to strategically *in-source* external components in order to provide customers' solution concepts.

IBM's traditional core business is the development and manufacturing of computer systems, software and network systems, storage and micro-electronics. Its main business segments are *Global Services*, *Hardware*, *Software*, *Global Financing* and *Enterprise Investments*. In 2004, *IBM* achieved a turnover of 96.5 billion US dollars and a net income of 8.4 billion US dollars with its total of 319,000 employees.

IBM operates worldwide, although its headquarters is in Armonk, New York. The company focuses on the integration of technology, products and services. The core business is increasingly moving towards services in information technology: Almost 60% of the turnover is generated by services and 40% by *IBM* products.

4.2.1 Research and Innovation

At *IBM*, research and development are two separate entities, each with its own central company activities. The *Research Group* interacts with the entire organization: divisions, companies, wholly-owned subsidiaries, partnerships, joint ventures, and others. Its role is to transfer innovation projects from idea to prototype and further to the market launch.

The Research Group therefore has a technical vision that covers all of the *IBM* businesses, and continually adapts to the realities of the marketplace. Headquartered at the *Watson Research Center* in Yorktown (NY), *IBM Research* employs more than 3,440 people in eight main research sites worldwide:

- T.J. Watson Research Center, Westchester County, NY, USA;
- Almaden Research Laboratory, CA, USA;
- Zurich Research Laboratory, Switzerland;
- Austin Research Laboratory, Texas, USA (launched in 1995);
- Tokyo Research Laboratory, Yamato, Japan;
- Haifa Research Group, Israel;
- China Research Laboratory, Beijing, China (launched in 1995);
- Solutions Research Centre, Delhi, India (launched in 1998).

IBM Research used to be substantially inwardly focused; the developers tended to *mind the science* and they assumed that this would lead to best results. At the same time, it was recognized that moving an idea or a proto-type from *research* to development was not a simple process. *Joint projects* were therefore established. These are programs which are funded by a product group and which are largely staffed by a workforce that consists of researchers working on research sites. Other researchers, funded from a base budget, and developers at their own sites form additional staff for these kinds of programs. With these joint projects, *IBM Research* has been able to smooth the transfer of ideas into development by creating early links in a program, and by starting with a shared vision and a shared agenda.

In the mean time, *IBM Research* expanded with the goal of developing joint program activities with customers. Multiple disciplines are leveraged in the research labs to help customers achieve a competitive advantage.

Research programs. Vital to *IBM's* future success is the achievement of *IBM Research's* goal of developing ideas towards successful market launches. This goal has now been pursued for over ten years and it will determine how *IBM* will be viewed in terms of its science and technology. *IBM* recognizes the role that the *Research Group* should play within the organization, which has led it to become deeply involved with other parts of the company, usually with excellent results.

IBM Research therefore follows seven strategic streams: *Technology, Systems, Storage Systems, Personal Systems, Software, Services,* and *Exploratory* (Table 9).

Table 9. Research programs of IBM

Research Thrust	Vision	Focus Topics
Technology	Enable high-speed inter-connectivity	High-speed interconnect
Systems	Enable high productivity computing systems (HPCS)	Reliable computing systems (PERCS)
		Programmer productivity, ease-of-use, cost of ownership, reliability, effective performance
Storage Systems	Enable vast reliable, size-, cost- and power-reduced storage systems	Collective intelligent bricks (CIB)
Personal Systems	Enabling digital TV market	Digital set-top-box (STB)
Software	Enable software development environments for e-business on-demand enquiries	Build and deploy business applications over the web, application servers, messaging software, business integration tools, portal creation tools
Services	Enable e-utility services	Continual optimization
		Reduce infrastructure costs
Exploratory	Identify new materials and processes to increase computer performance at lower cost	Novel insulators
		Organic semiconductors
		Nanoscale magnetic materials

4.2.2 Managing R&D Collaborations

At the *IBM Zurich Research Laboratory*, the main part of the research work is nowadays done in collaboration with partners, other internal *IBM* entities, and external third parties.

Historically, the research organization used to work mainly with colleagues in the world of science and technology. It later diversified by working with other *IBM* units and today it works with customers, often entering into new collaborations with leading customers. There are various ways in which *IBM* works with its customers: Joint Programs, Service Collaborations, i.e. *On Demand Innovation Services* (ODIS), and *First of a Kind* (FOAK) deals.[4]

---

[4]   See also http://www.gartner.com/reprints/ibm/102530.html.

Due to changes in research areas, e.g. nanotechnology, and changes to business requirements, e.g. increased focus on services and stronger industry focus, *IBM* expects a further increase in the importance of collaborations.

Joint programs. Joint programs are research projects that run in a coordinated program with an *IBM* product organization. These types of projects are 50% funded by the *IBM* product organization, and centrally coordinated by a joint program manager across the labs. This is particularly true of research in the fields of software, server and semiconductor technology.

IBM Research used to be more or less centrally funded. Currently, two-thirds of the people at *IBM Research* are centrally funded, while one-third are funded by the business lines as a joint program headcount.

On Demand Innovation Services (ODIS). *IBM's* innovations have made the transition from hardware to software and are now heading toward services. A new approach has been set up to offer these innovation services through the services organizations. The development of a new research field is first of all based on the existing competencies in science and technologies. Second, the engagement of the research competence focuses on the development and the generation of innovations for *IBM* customers. Finally, there is close collaboration between *IBM Research* and the *IBM Business Consulting Services Group* (BCS) in the marketing and developing of solutions for customers. *BCS's* "innovative thinking", which is considered to be a key element of the *BCS* value proposition, is strengthened through this systematic linkage with *IBM Research*.

Through the *IBM Business Consulting Services Group, IBM* customers can gain access to *IBM Research*'s innovation services. Competitive differentiation is gained by obtaining access to cutting-edge ODIS capabilities, and by providing a proven methodology for innovation processes. Pilots and proof of concepts take place with fast time to market and reduced risk, which form the main benefits for customers.

The *Zurich Research Lab* works together with the *Haifa Research Lab* to provide business consulting services covering Europe, the Middle East and Africa (Fig. 14).

To leverage research and business consulting capabilities in order to enhance value to clients, the ODIS team has to act as a *gearbox* between *BCS* and *IBM Research*. Therefore, the ODIS team in the *IBM Zurich Research Laboratory* consists of researchers and *BCS* on-site consultants. This means combining and leveraging both groups' capabilities, facilitating and marketing leading-edge research consulting, providing *BCS* with a competitive advantage, and serving as a catalyst in winning large deals to

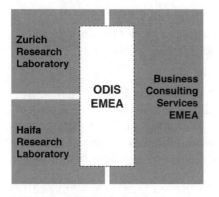

➤ Combine and leverage *IBM Research* and BCS capabilities;

➤ Facilitate and market leading edge research consulting;

➤ Provide BCS with a competitive advantage;

➤ Serve as a catalyst in winning large deals;

➤ Strengthen *IBM* brand.

Source: IBM Research (2005)

Fig. 14. On Demand Innovation Services (ODIS) in EMEA

strengthen the *IBM* brand. ODIS started in 2003 and has grown to a team of about 15 researchers in Zurich. The team has no direct contact with customers, as customer relationships are still owned by client managers. *BCS* is supported by ODIS at several points during demand generation, opportunity management and project engagement. In the following focus areas, ODIS has in Zurich gathered the following micro-practices:

- Security & Privacy, i.e. assess, design and implement enhanced security processes and tools;
- Mobile Enablement, i.e. automate and enhance business processes with mobile technologies;
- Business Optimization & Analysis, i.e. optimization, planning, modelling, and analysis to transform businesses to on-demand, e.g. pricing, workforce and product innovation.

First of a Kind (FOAK). As soon as a technology has reached a level where a practical benefit can be achieved, *IBM Research* partners with a leading-edge client that is prepared to test the technology in a real-life situation. The FOAK Program is a collaborative effort between *Sales and Distribution* (S&D), *IBM Research* and *IBM*'s customers. The goal of the program is to accelerate the delivery of leading-edge research technologies to the market by applying them to real customer problems and creating reusable assets for *IBM*.

Prototype solutions in key areas are yielded through the FOAK program. The research technologists partner with industry experts to collaborate with clients in their environment. S&D drives the client/partner and strategic solution selections, while *IBM Research* provides technology leadership and direction in defining the specific solutions and deliverables. The FOAK program creates valuable intellectual capital for *IBM's* portfolio and provides a steady stream of advanced prototype exhibits for the *IBM Research's Industry Solutions Labs* (ISL), which host major clients, key industry events and CEO conferences.

First-hand experience with emerging technologies and new business models are the main motivation factors for customers to participate in these projects. Benefits include early adopter market advantage; access to world-renowned researchers; and early access to game-changing technologies. Furthermore, customers can benefit from *IBM* skills and knowledge transfer and may provide direct input for the *IBM* requirements process. The investment funding model minimizes investments from customers.

IBM's benefits include acceleration of the delivery of new technologies to the market and of the sales of solutions. The projects establish a link from strategic research initiatives to real customer problems and provide insight into emerging market opportunities, while providing an opportunity to share knowledge and gain valuable experience.

A very successful *First of a Kind* project was *IBM's* teaming up with *New York's Memorial Sloan-Kettering Cancer Center* and *Massachusetts General Hospital* in Boston. The project resulted in the creation of *MedSpeak*, a specialized speech recognition application for radiologists, whose distinctive technical vocabulary made recognition easier. *IBM* expanded into legal dictation as soon as the technology improved. Subsequently, *IBM* moved into general products, e.g. the *ViaVoice* line that turned into a leading product in the speech recognition business.

To validate a prototype, FOAK projects have to include a collaborative customer or partner. However, the customer has to participate in the funding of the project. In general, the project takes twelve months. The standard FOAK agreement contains some of the following key terms:

- *IBM* maintains ownership of all intellectual property created during the FOAK project;
- No exclusive rights shall be granted to any customer;
- *IBM* has freedom of action to utilize ideas, concepts, know-how obtained from the FOAK engagement related to *IBM*'s business activities;
- *IBM* should not be precluded from assigning its employees in any way it may choose or from providing similar products and services to others;
- The work product is provided, "as-is", without any warranties that the work product will be made commercially available;
- There is no maintenance or support beyond the scope of the FOAK project;

- A non-disclosure agreement needs to be in place to ensure that *IBM*'s confidential information is protected.[5]

4.2.3 Managing Intellectual Property

IBM has a long history in which intellectual property and its protection played a major role. In the past, industrialists such as John Patterson, CEO of *National Cash Register* (NCR), who had a lot of influence on the management of *IBM*, consistently used patents to eliminate or block competitors and aggressively sued *infringing companies*. Also Tom Watson, Sr. actively defended *IBM's* monopoly by exclusively licensing products instead of selling them, e.g., in the market for punch cards. Like many other software companies at that time, *IBM* hid its source codes, which enabled the company to keep control over its own products. *IBM's* market dominance was further strengthened by other practices, such as a functional pricing policy and the applied *tie-in* system. These protectionist actions created resentment and dissatisfaction among *IBM*'s competitors, customers and the public. As a reaction, the then US President F.D. Roosevelt launched an antitrust lawsuit against *IBM* (Mühlbauer 2001). Without an appropriate protection of punch card technology through patents, however, aggressive competition could not have been avoided, which would have ended up in a fierce price war. Thanks to its history in intellectual property and its protection strategies, *IBM* managed to become a very innovative player at the forefront of IT development. Without it, *IBM* probably would not have grown to one of the world's most recognized brands.

During the eighties, the potential of intellectual property's commercialization practices was recognized by *IBM*. The company started developing strategies for licensing intellectual property and thereby generating returns on R&D investments. This change of direction in the company's philosophy turned out to be highly successful. Income increased by about 5,000% to 1.7 billion US dollars within a decade (Chesbrough 2001). Over the past ten years, approximately 10 billion US dollars were generated in intellectual property royalties.[6] In 2004, *IBM* received 3,248 patents from the *United States Patent and Trademark Office*, to add to a portfolio of more than 10,000 patent families with almost 40,000 active patents worldwide including more than 23,000 US patents (Fig. 15).

---

[5]   An example for a model agreement for the exchange of confidential information is provided in the appendices, pp. 229.
[6]   See also http://www.ibm.com/news/us/2003/01/131.html.

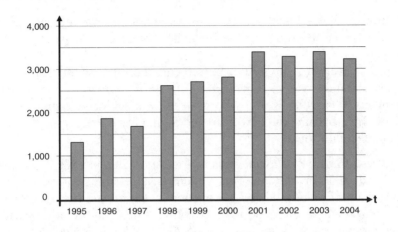

Source: IBM Research (2005)

Fig. 15. Yearly issued US patents by IBM

Strategy. Creating an environment that stimulates innovation and investing in R&D is *IBM's* philosophy. This is contrary to the *old* world in which patents were seen as creatures of the labs. A paradigm shift was, however, achieved with the development of the internet division, and the areas of creative algorithms, solutions and integrations, as well as network computing innovations.

With the growing importance of *IBM's* strategy, it is essential that employees understand the meaning of innovation. Clear and visible internal processes for patent disclosure, patent application and publication are established. Easy information gathering while working with these processes is facilitated by intranet sites owned and maintained by the intellectual property department. A patent learning tool is an excellent example of how *IBM's* philosophy is supported.

Organization. *IBM* has internal patent departments located worldwide that conduct the various in-house activities concerning generation, management, maintenance and enforcement of intellectual property. The *IP Law* group is a corporate organization which employs more than 100 patent attorneys, located worldwide including in locations like the USA, Germany, France, the United Kingdom, China, Japan, Korea, Switzerland, Taiwan and Canada. The *IP Law* office in Switzerland employs three patent attorneys and two administrative support employees. Their task is to conduct patent protection mainly for lab inventions, to solve *IBM* corporation trademark matters in Switzerland and to support the lab staff in intellectual-property-related matters. A consistent and long-term intellectual property strategy is ensured by a designated team of central patent portfolio managers.

Yet, to ensure a stronger business focus, the internal intellectual property organization was re-organized as the *IP & Standards* department by December 2004. John Kelly, who used to be a senior vice president of a business line, became the new head and Senior Vice President Technology and Intellectual Property.

Processes. *IBM's Worldwide Patent Tracking System* (WPTS) centrally collects all *IBM* inventions. This system is accessible worldwide and, is based on a *Lotus Notes* database. For each invention and file, it contains an event and deadline database (Fig. 16). Inventions can already be entered during the conception state and can successively be optimized. The system enables the traceable decision and status paths of each invention as well as its prosecution process.

Shared online evaluations for each invention, including actual business and strategic information, are facilitated by the WPTS. The evaluation itself, which is based on multiple-choice questions, is conducted and calculated by what is called an internal *Patent Value Tool* (PVT). The qualitative and quantitative analyses are done by an interdisciplinary team that

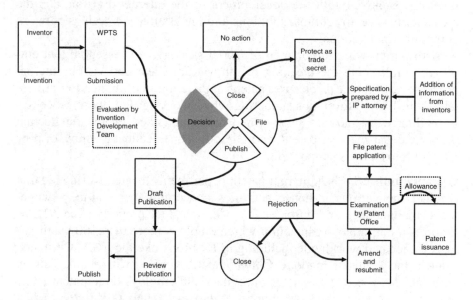

Source: IBM Research (2005)

Fig. 16. IBM invention disclosure handling process

consists of inventors, technical experts and patent professionals. The evaluation is carried out before a decision is made to file, publish or close an invention.

When the decision is made to *publish* an invention, an article is placed in the *IBM Technical Disclosure Bulletin* (TDB) or in another publication. The TDB was specifically established with the purpose of making innovations public. This formal publication helps to ensure that *IBM* is free to act in areas where *IBM* scientists, engineers, programmers and technicians have made innovations, and it prevents others from obtaining patents on innovations similar to those made earlier by *IBM*. When the decision is made to *close* an invention, this means no further patent action or formal publishing action is undertaken. This may occur, when there is insufficient development or experimental data to set up the operability of the invention. When there is additional operability proof, this decision might be reassessed.

Cultural aspects. *IBM* introduced awards to reward and acknowledge innovative individual and team activities. The researchers are encouraged to submit disclosures of high value to *IBM*, to assure *IBM's* freedom of action, to disclose their work-related ideas (which may be filed or published), and to provide ongoing support for filed patent applications up to and after a patent issuance. *IBM* remunerates a wide variety of significant contributions, such as key innovations, creativity, breakthrough thinking, technical leadership, outstanding teamwork, knowledge sharing and superior execution of key projects, creative problem solving and other achievements. The awards can be given to individuals or teams and can be transferred in the form of cash or non-cash recognition, such as verbal public recognition, personalized merchandise, a plaque or a certificate, participation in a special event or personal time off.

The potential licensing value of the patent and/or the patent portfolio forms the basis for the monetary-enriched awards. *IBM* introduced different types of invention achievement awards:

- Patent Application Awards;
- Plateau Awards;
- Patent Issue Awards;
- Patent Team Awards;
- Special Incentive Awards;
- Others.

Patent Application (Filing) Awards are granted for a petit patent or a regular patent: A *petit patent* is awarded for design or utility models, such as the shape of a car or the shape of a laptop. Innovative and creative ideas such as the invention of a car that runs on grass clippings, or a new chip design that improves laptop processor speed are awarded with a *regular patent*. A qualified inventor who makes his or her first petit patent application will receive a cash award, a framed certificate and one point, provided the criteria are met. *Plateau Awards* are acknowledgements of people who reach a certain level of inventive activity by accumulating patent points that were earned by awards like the *Patent Application Award* and/or the *Patent Issue Award*. The above-mentioned plateau is reached when a total of twelve points is accumulated, provided that at least six of the twelve points are patent points (not Technical Disclosure Bulletin points). Cash payments plus a framed certificate are then handed to the inventor.

Licensing. *IBM's* approach towards patent licensing for products in the information technology field is rather fair and unprotected. Generally, non-exclusive licenses under reasonable and non-discriminatory terms and conditions are granted to those who, in turn, respect *IBM's* intellectual property rights.

IBM has established an *Intellectual Property and Asset Commercialization Team* (IP&AC Team) to coordinate the process of commercializing the *Intellectual Property Service Components* (IPSC). The IPSCs are intellectual property assets that can be commercialized from multiple sources, for example, from work done inside *IBM,* or from client engagements in which *IBM* has retained ownership rights to the results.

The tasks of the IP&AC Team are various and range from assisting in the development of the customer value proposition; defining a pricing structure together with the *Intellectual Property and Legal Department* (IP&L); setting up a development organization; drafting a license agreement or intellectual-property-related T&Cs in the service contract, to setting up internal presentations on the intranet to raise awareness of the value-added of licensing intellectual property.

IBM has developed or acquired thousands of intellectual property assets over time. Most of these can be licensed to third parties and used in customer engagements, although only about 300 of them have been identified and described in the *Intellectual Property Asset Catalog*. This catalog has been set up to make integration into customer offerings easier. For each of these intellectual property assets, the catalog provides information such as detailed descriptions, customer benefits, one-page value propositions, pre-qualification checklists, pricing information or terms and conditions for licensing. In the Intellectual Property Asset Catalog, assets are categorized by industry, solution category and customer benefit.[7]

4.2.4 Managing Intellectual Property in R&D Collaborations

IBM differentiates between three different types of third party collaboration partners:

- Commercial partners;
- Non-commercial partners;
- Partners in government-funded projects, e.g. FP6, KTI.

Commercial partners. *IBM* may collaborate with commercial partners on the basis of joint development agreements, cross license agreements, evaluation agreements or field test licenses.

Handling intellectual property in joint development agreements: In these kind of agreements, an *Invention* can be any idea, design, concept, technique, invention, discovery or improvement, whether patentable or not, conceived or first reduced to practice solely by one or more employees of a single party (*Sole Invention*), or jointly by one or more employees of one party together with one or more employees of the other party (*Joint Invention*), in the performance of work under the agreement.

A *Sole Invention* is the property of the inventing party, including all patents issued on it. Any *Joint Invention* is jointly owned and each partner is entitled to all patents issued relating to it. All expenses, including those related to preparation, prosecution and maintenance are jointly shared. Furthermore, each party has the right to license third parties, without the need for consent from or accounting to the other party.

Handling intellectual property in cross license agreements: Companies do license their widespread patent portfolios on different technologies to enable a faster market entry of products. Under the terms of the cross-licensing agreement, each company will receive a license under all patents that relate to their specific field of interest. *IBM's* portfolio includes fundamental patents on a wide range of networking technologies, including server access, server load balancing, web caching, ATM, Ethernet and To-

---

[7] One pre-requisite is that such asset should have a valid Certificate of Originality: If an asset includes software or microcode material, the relevant *IBM* product or project manager should fill in a Certificate of Originality and Copyright Questionnaire for *IBM* Software Material. To obtain full product and service clearance, copyright registration, and the inclusion of the asset in the Intellectual Capital Management database, this document needs to be submitted to the Intellectual Property Law Department in a timely fashion.

ken Ring technologies as well as network interface cards and network management, policy-based networking and virtual private networks. By sharing patents under licensing agreements, companies can compete in new information technology market segments with newly developed products.

Handling intellectual property in evaluation agreements or field test licenses for IBM software: In this case, *IBM* provides software to customers at no charge for evaluation and feedback purposes. *IBM* owns all software rights and grants the licensee a non-transferable, nonexclusive and revocable license to use and execute the software only for the purposes of the Evaluation Agreement. The licensee assigns any copyright in written evaluation reports to *IBM*.

Collaborations with commercial partners provide opportunities to leverage existing know-how. A complementary long-term goal and a similar business understanding are essential in a successful collaboration. A difficulty might be the financial reliability of the partner. As collaboration is a process, the partners' individual objectives might change. It has often occurred that the ownership of intellectual property has been a serious source of disputes.[8]

Non-commercial partners. *IBM* may collaborate on the basis of joint research agreements, sponsored research projects, and evaluation agreements or field test licenses with non-commercial partners.

Collaborations with non-commercial partners offer the opportunity to benefit from collaborating with highly skilled partners, from the leveraging of existing know-how, from *IBM's* visibility in the research community, and from networking. Difficulties may include insufficient budget. Often, project management skills are lacking and there may be a differing culture, goals and views on timing. Again, ownership of intellectual property may be a serious source of disagreements and disputes.

Partners in government-funded projects. Currently, the *IBM Zurich Research Laboratory* participates in numerous FP6 projects that are funded by the European Union. *IBM* has established an internal infrastructure providing a central location for legal and intellectual property support for all research labs worldwide. To enhance and support the FP6 work, there is also an FP6 team in Belgium with installed contacts to the European Commission. In these FP6 projects, *IBM* handles intellectual property with respect to:

---

[8]   Examples for model technology license and patent license agreements are provided in the appendices, pp. 201 and pp. 220 respectively.

- *Background IP*: Intellectual property specially listed as pre-existing intellectual property and excluded from the beginning;
- *IP for execution of the project*: If needed for project work, granted royalty-free, non-exclusively, internally (but including access to affiliates), always within confidentiality limits;
- *IP for use after the project*: Non-exclusive, worldwide, internal license granted on RAND[9] terms;
- *Foreground IP*: Joint intellectual property – each joint owner has unlimited right to use, grant and assign licenses without the need for accounting or compensation to co-owners;
- *Co-owners*: Co-owners agree that they may jointly apply to obtain and/or maintain the relevant patent protection or any other intellectual property right to such joint invention;
- *Sole IP*: IP owned by the inventing party, others are granted access if needed royalty-free.

Government-funded projects offer the opportunity to collaborate with other technology leaders, to capitalize on *IBM's* visibility in the research community, including networking, and to smooth access to public funding. Difficulties may include long negotiations before the start of the collaboration, a high level of bureaucracy, different partners with different goals combined with limitations regarding partner selection. Sometimes it is difficult to properly assess coordinators' project management skills beforehand. It is therefore necessary to balance the projects' priority with facilitated obtaining of funds.

With regard to the anticipated benefits of the individual collaboration projects, *IBM* evaluates three critical issues when they collaborate with third parties (Fig. 17):

- Generation of tangible value;
- Freedom of action;
- Protection of competitive advantage.

Generation of tangible value. The most important costs of collaboration projects are the opportunity costs for the *IBM Research* organization. Therefore the Business Development Department makes an opportunity assessment in which they evaluate whether it is the right project with the right partner:

---

[9]   RAND = Reasonable And Non-Discriminatory.

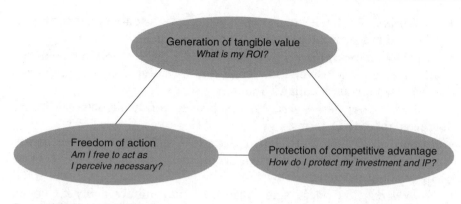

Source: IBM Research (2005)

Fig. 17. Critical issues in any 3rd party collaboration (IBM)

Is this the right project? Does the project conform to strategy? Does the project create the required leverage and return on investment (ROI); in US dollars, intellectual property, marketing value or other measures? What are the risks of the project and how can the risks be mitigated?

Is this the right partner? Do the partner's objectives match *IBM's*? Does the partner have the resources and skills to achieve the objectives? Are the business policies of the organizations compatible, e.g. open source for *Microsoft*? Do the partner's soft factors strengthen those of *IBM*?

Freedom of action. In order to protect freedom of action, *IBM* prefers not to obtain any confidential information from a third party. Yet, where this is unavoidable, confidentiality language has to be included, either bilaterally, one way in, or one way out. In this case, residual clauses and inherent disclosure clauses are the negotiation issues. However, most contract parties, especially in Europe, are unfamiliar with this confidentiality language, which can lead to extended negotiation processes.

Protection of competitive advantage. When collaborating with third parties, *IBM* generally tries to address the following issues contractually:

- Confidentiality;
- Intellectual property protection;
- Patents (sole and joint inventions), copyrights, trade secrets;
- Rights to prototypes and materials;
- Restrictions;
- Liability/warranty;
- Export language;

- Communication and marketing, e.g. the use of brand and references, and the publication of results;
- Defining pricing structure;
- Setting up development organization;
- Including intellectual property issues in service contracts;
- Raising awareness of value added of licensing intellectual property.

Summary IBM. *IBM* is increasingly involved in service innovations, especially if enabled by technology. Traditionally, the company follows a leadership strategy in the field of the generation and commercialization of intellectual property. *IBM* is also still involved in true research activities that are conducted by *IBM Research*, which is based in eight research sites worldwide.

IBM seeks research and development collaborations in order to cope with changes in research areas, such as nanotechnology; and to meet business requirements that have changed due to an increased focus on service innovations and a stronger industry focus. Within research and development collaborations, *IBM* applies its intellectual property as a basis for technology transfers and eventual licensing revenues. Key learnings from *IBM* are:

- Innovation is one of *IBM's* key interests;
- New ways to push innovation so that it responds to customers' needs are being developed constantly;
- Extensive investment in innovative culture and maintenance of appropriate processes to ensure the best leverage of created intellectual property;
- Collaboration (internal and external, commercial and non-commercial) and technology transfer are crucial to *IBM's* innovation culture.

4.3 SAP

SAP was founded in 1972 by five former *IBM* systems engineers. *SAP* is the world's leading provider of business software solutions. Today, more than 28,200 customers in over 120 countries run more than 96,400 installations of *SAP*® software – from distinct solutions addressing the needs of small and midsize enterprises to suite solutions for global organizations.

SAP's growth is based on the development of business software solutions that are designed to meet the demands of companies of all sizes – from small and mid-sized businesses to global enterprises. Their first product was *R/1* in 1972, followed by *R/2* and *R/3* introduced in 1979 and 1992 respectively. In 2003/2004, *SAP* brought the business solutions family *mySAP Business Suite* and *SAP NetWeaver*® to the market. *mySAP*^{TM} *Business Suite* is a complete package of open enterprise solutions which links up all people, information, and processes and thus increases the effectiveness of business relationships. It is based on the *SAP NetWeaver* technology platform and can be seamlessly integrated with practically every *SAP* and *non-SAP* solution. *SAP NetWeaver* is an open integration and application platform that reduces complexity and total cost of ownership, while empowering business change and innovation.

SAP industry solutions support the unique business processes of more than 25 industry segments, including high tech, retail, public sector and financial services.

Furthermore, *SAP* strives to strengthen its position as a technological think-tank. *SAP Ventures* invests in emerging companies that are developing and advancing exciting new technologies. The goal of *SAP Ventures* is to grow businesses that create shareholder value for everyone involved.

The main purpose of *SAP Labs* is to discover and understand new technology trends around the world. The focus is on short-term innovation projects that are closely aligned with current *SAP* products and customer requirements.

SAP's corporate research organization, *SAP Research*, prepares the groundwork for future growth by acting as *SAP's* information technology trend scout. The group focuses on identifying emerging information technology trends, researching and prototyping in strategically important *SAP* business areas, as well as leveraging entrepreneurial inventive talent.

Headquartered in Walldorf, Germany, *SAP* is listed on several stock exchanges, including the Frankfurt Stock Exchange and the New York Stock Exchange, under the symbol "SAP".

For the fiscal year ended December 2004, *SAP's* revenues totaled 7.5 billion euros with a net income of 1.3 billion euros. The company's revenues are derived from four distinct sources: software, maintenance, consulting and training.

4.3.1 Research and Innovation

SAP maintains a corporate research group, called *SAP Research. SAP Research* is headquartered in Walldorf, Germany. *SAP Research's* mission is to prepare the groundwork for future growth by acting as *SAP's* information technology trend scout. The group focuses on identifying emerging information technology trends, researching and prototyping in strategically important *SAP* business areas, as well as leveraging entrepreneurial inventive talent.

Its two key groups are *SAP Research Centers & Campus-based Engineering Centers* and *SAP Inspire;* each with a dedicated focus (Fig. 18). *SAP Inspire* is the corporate venturing unit with an innovation and project focus from six months to two years. *SAP Research* carries out applied research with an innovation and project focus of up to three or even five years. Each department is assisted by dedicated support functions, such as *Research Business Development* and *Research Operations*. Internally, these groups seek a research transfer engagement with the business units.

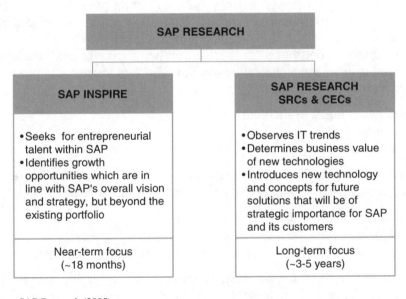

Source: SAP Research (2005)

Fig. 18. Structure of SAP Research

Externally, they aim for innovation collaboration as trusted innovators, with governmental organizations and in partner alliances as well as through customer engagement in the industry sectors. Communication, media and event activities round up the picture. *Research Operations* comprises the functions *Finance*, *Legal* and a *Project Management Office*.

The vision of *SAP Research* is to always be a world-class knowledge and thought leadership partner to *SAP*, and its customers and partners. *SAP Research* executes its research either on its own, or as is often the case, in collaborative research projects with academia, potential technology partners or potential customers. These kinds of research projects are often partly publicly-funded.

SAP Inspire. Throughout its history, *SAP* has renewed itself and successfully created innovative business in new areas. With the Inspire initiative *SAP* recognizes that a major part of its renewal process takes place within the minds of its employees. They require the right environment and support to successfully turn creative ideas into winning business.

The corporate research group of *SAP* includes the internal venturing group *SAP Inspire* which brings all this together – innovation, the entrepreneur's passion and *SAP*.

It is dedicated to seeking entrepreneurial talent within *SAP* and looking for growth opportunities. These opportunities must be in line with *SAP's* overall vision and strategy, but beyond the existing portfolio. The corporate venturing group manages the full innovation process from idea generation to commercialization and incorporation into businesses.

SAP Inspire contributes to *SAP's* long-term growth and leadership through business and technical innovation. The venture business process is based on four process steps:

- Idea gathering & evaluation;
- Prototype building;
- Transition.

Idea Gathering & Evaluation: Ideas that fit into the *SAP* vision are collected continuously from internal sources using tools such as:

- An intranet-based capturing solution for ideas;
- *SAP Inspire* think-tank sessions;
- Special initiatives such as idea contests (*NextGeneration@SAP*).

Furthermore, *SAP Inspire* systematically scans emerging trends. The knowledge gained from these two perspectives identifies potential new business ideas that might result in successful Inspire projects.

Once an idea has been submitted, the *SAP Inspire* team begins with the idea evaluation by gathering additional information, and collaborating with experts. The *SAP Inspire* reviewer tries to find answers for questions such as innovation substance, existence of similar solutions within the *SAP* product portfolio, potential technical feasibility, and strategic fit with *SAP* core business, high-level market potential, competitive situation and capacity for execution. Based on these questions, *SAP Inspire* decides to pursue the due diligence process by building a business case which aims to justify the investment.

Prototype Building: The business case describes problem and background, solution, innovation degree, strategic fit, project planning and estimation, benefits and go-to-market.

Only the most promising ideas are developed further in the *SAP Inspire* incubator, which offers necessary development resources to build prototypes as the basis for further product development.

Furthermore, *SAP Inspire* helps with access to *SAP's* support system, e.g. legal, communications, and human resources. This uniquely combines the best practices of internal corporate venturing and venture capital activity.

In comparison with other research projects, however, the Inspire projects have a much shorter project time scope for prototype building, i.e. only nine to twelve months duration. The business lines get actively involved and can expect results for their business and product development process.

Transition: The Inspire team provides proactive support to successfully reintegrate the idea prototypes into the organization and optional to pilot customers. This transition phase normally requires three to six months. As a basic outcome, *SAP* seeks to either merge the Inspire results into existing business units or creating new ones.

SAP Research Centers (SRCs) and SAP Research Campus-based Engineering Centers (CECs). The *SRCs and CECs* are corporate technology research locations that support *SAP's* long-term strategy of establishing *SAP* as a leader in the area of innovative and breakthrough information technology. They monitor current and upcoming information and technology trends. They determine the business value of new technologies for *SAP* and introduce new technology and concepts for future solutions that will be of strategic importance to *SAP* and its customers.

The *SAP Research* location strategy follows two approaches: either the research team is hosted by an *SAP* subsidiary (*SAP Research Center/*

Group) or *SAP Research* founds a *Campus-based Engineering Center* (CEC) in close vicinity to a university. Existing research locations are:

- Karlsruhe (CEC), Germany;
- Darmstadt (CEC), Germany;
- Dresden (CEC), Germany;
- Belfast (CEC), UK;
- Sophia Antipolis (SRC), France;
- Montréal (SRC), Canada;
- Palo Alto (SRC), USA;
- Pretoria (CEC), South Africa;
- Brisbane (CEC), Australia.

The research branch has identified long-term research programs with a focus on technologies, platforms and business solutions. They act – if necessary – on trend-driven information technology or market changes.

Research programs: SAP Research runs various research programs conducted by global teams across the various research locations (Table 10). The research programs establish a vision for how to address the challenges of an area of strategic interest for *SAP*. The program provides guidance for individual researchers on the one hand and for research projects or proposals for implementing the vision as part of the project charter and avoiding duplication of effort on the other. Furthermore they help to challenge individual research contributions such as invention disclosures, while also setting up doctoral theses and internships within the different projects to provide synergies between the stakeholders involved.

Table 10. Research programs of SAP

Research Programs	Vision	Focus Topics
Smart Items Research	Enabling the real-time enterprise by bridging the gap between the real and the digital world	AUTO-ID, sensor nets and embedded systems technologies Distributed hierarchical Auto-ID infrastructure
Security & Trust	Provision of user-centric security solutions for dynamic, collaborative and adaptive inter-enterprise business scenarios	Authorization and trust management Secure services and composition Security engineering
Knowledge People Interaction	Integrated knowledge-intensive collaborative working environments	E-learning and knowledge management technologies Knowledge integration and innovation Smart human computer interaction
Software Engineering & Architectures	Computer assisted engineering practices for *SAP's* standard development processes	Model-driven software development Software quality and non-functional aspects Software architecture for virtualization
Business Process Management & Semantic Interoperability	Highly configurable process-oriented applications and semantically enriched service-oriented composition of applications	Collaborative business processes between enterprises Model-driven architectures and engineering Semantic Web services; SoA Interoperability of applications and enterprises

4.3.2 Managing R&D Collaborations

The research process. *SAP Research* is closely following the technology market and academic trends in order to identify those of strategic relevance for *SAP* within the next three to five years to be prepared when the market is ready and the customers request it.

The applied research process of *SAP Research* is rather a classical stage gate process but a lively process with manifold interaction between the various research phases, the overall *SAP* product innovation lifecycle as well as with the necessary feedback loops within the engagement with the product groups. The main focus is on new technology concepts and their potential integration into the *SAP* software environment (Fig. 19):

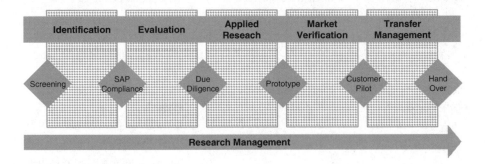

Source: SAP Research (2005)

Fig. 19. Research process at SAP Research

1. Identification: Screening of technology and research dialog with the research community will lead to the identification of opportunities that will be expanded by a research outline.

2. Evaluation: The research outlines are then validated with the state-of-the-art, technology providers and their prototypes and academia as well as initial investigations into the business relevance. A research proposal is written to enable the start of a collaborative research project, white papers or conference papers are being submitted for further dialog with the scientific and the real world.

3. Applied Research: This stage can mark the start of the collaborative research project and may include the preparation of an initial feasibility study, anticipated usage cases, business scenarios and technical concepts, for example technology evaluation studies, technology due diligence studies, research concepts, guides, recommendations, good practices and methodologies. Moving on with the project, demonstrators and prototypes will be built to show the technical feasibility, or e.g. the ease of use or the novelty of the concept.

4. Market Verification: The prototype will be taken out of the lab into real life environment; customer-specific requirements will be applied to the prototypes or demonstrators. A trial or research pilot will evaluate the business potential and may result in a customer requirement study.

5. Transfer Management: Throughout the research process transfer is driven by Research Business Development communicating and engaging with the *SAP* internal development or solution management teams. White-papers, technical concepts, forums or workshops facilitate the know-how transfer and/or technology decision processes. When the product decision has been made a dedicated transfer project, based on terms of engagement, is being carried out.

SAP Research executes its research either on its own, or, which is more often the case, within collaborative research projects with academia, potential technology partners or potential customers. These kinds of research projects are often partly publicly-funded.

Collaborative research activities. Partnering has traditionally played an important role for *SAP*. The company works together with numerous partners on various engagement levels.

To build further on this, the Research Business Development team moderates collaboration with partners from industry and academia as well as other research organizations. It also drives the generation of joint research roadmaps with partners of strategic interest to *SAP Research*. Typical characteristics of collaborative research projects are: duration of two to three years; competency augmentation through diverse consortia; risk sharing through cost sharing and joint applications for partly governmental funding.

A research partner network is important because it speeds up the value of the innovation process and monitors the competitiveness of *SAP's* research focus. Before a collaborative project starts, *SAP Research* assesses potential partners. Sometimes, competing partners come together and discuss these issues in a steering committee, striving to manage the co-opetive situation for the benefit of joint research.

The total number of partners has consistently doubled during the last few years, to reach about 200 collaboration partners in 2004 (Fig. 20).

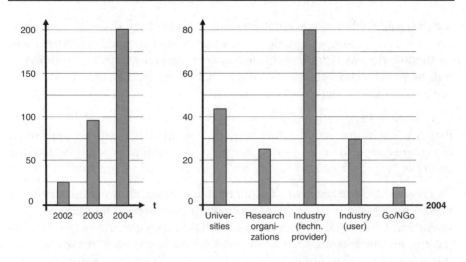

Source: SAP Research (2005)

Fig. 20. Evolution of the SAP research network (amount of research partners)

The main collaboration partners for *SAP Research* are:

- Academia;
- Technology partners;
- Customers.

Academia. Academic partners are mainly involved in joint innovation sourcing projects and provide the basic research within the collaborative projects. The goal is to make *SAP Research* a strong partner for collaborative research and to manage the development of the research partner network: public calls for proposals are introduced, opportunities are identified, the proposal process is facilitated and reviewers are provided.

SAP Research maintains research agreements with leading universities worldwide.

Technology partners. Strategic research alliance partners help to align research roadmaps and prepare future product synergies. *SAP Research* applies joint technology validation projects with strong use cases. Strategic research collaboration includes well known SAP Alliance partners but also technology providers that are new to the SAP community.

Customers. Existing and potential *SAP* customers act both as pilot project partners as well as a target for innovation marketing. Facilitated by Research Business Development *SAP Research* demonstrates thought leadership to the *SAP* community and invites them to join in future research to be prepared for upcoming technology potential and to by themselves be perceived as thought leaders.

4.3.3 Managing Intellectual Property

Twenty-five years came and went before the German software giant *SAP* established its own patent division in 1998. During its globalization process, *SAP* experienced stronger competitiveness, with patents playing an increasingly important role. This was mostly due to stronger activities in the US market, where the company became aware of its risk exposure resulting from conflicts with third party intellectual property. Furthermore, the patent situation in the United States also made it necessary for *SAP* to protect its own software (FAZ 2001).

Hence, *SAP* has recently undertaken the usual practice in US industry – to generate its own patents so that it has a trade currency if competitors sue for infringements of theirs. Today, *SAP* takes numerous measures to protect its intellectual property. These include written notification of copyright infringements, registration of patents, trademarks, and other marks. This also entails the conclusion of licensing and confidentiality agreements, and the installation of technical precautions against infringement.

> **IP risks in the US software market:** A small company called *Patriot Systems*, claimed to have written to 155 IT companies as part of its patent infringement fight against PC vendors. The firm sent letters warning of potential infringement of its US Patent number 5,809,336. *Patriot* did not provide company names in its announcement, but it is widely expected that nearly every large IT company received a letter. The small IT firm asserted it contacted the world's largest electronics firms in the semiconductor, communication equipment, computer hardware, electronic instruments, computer peripherals, scientific and technical instruments, computer storage, computer networks and office equipment business segments. *Patriot* said microprocessors operating at speeds above 110 to 120 MHz are in violation of portions of its patent portfolio. From the time its patents were issued, *Patriot* estimates that more than 150 billion US dollars worth of microprocessors have made use of its technology. It has given no indication as to what compensation it is seeking for a license.[10]

---

[10]   Source: SAP Info / Edittech International (05.05.2004).

Strategy. Today, *SAP* is confronted with the following situation:

- Offers for patent cross license agreements are received;
- Critical reflection of own patent portfolio;
- Decisions are made early enough with respect to time requirements.

SAP therefore follows the main strategy of growing a large and valuable patent portfolio. An important action that reduces the risk of patent conflicts is reaching patent cross license agreements with major competitors. As such, *SAP* has not to have significant conflicts with other parties' patents yet.

As a comparison, competitor *Microsoft* is estimated to file 2,000 to 3,000 patent applications each year. However, with the current application procedure before the *United States Patent and Trademark Office*, it takes about five years for software applications to be issued.

Patent protection, however, is not always considered to be the best solution, especially in cases of hidden functions inside *SAP* products. An infringement would be very difficult to pinpoint, let alone to prove. Hence, secrecy is sometimes considered to be the far better alternative. While coding or algorithms are generally not patented either, strategic issues are filed with a very broad protective range in different countries in order to secure a competitive advantage over several years. Due to its high impact leverage, it would therefore be desirable to file software-related patents therefore mostly for user-computer interfaces (interaction).

Patent cross licensing agreement SAP – Microsoft: In 2004 *SAP* and *Microsoft* entered into a patent cross-licensing agreement to provide a better environment for joint technical collaboration and solutions development.

During discussions with *Microsoft* regarding the joint development partnership for Web services, *SAP* confirmed that *Microsoft* had approached it in 2003 about a potential merger. The preliminary talks stalled, with no plans for their resumption. However, the two parties entered into a joint development partnership for Web services and a patent cross license agreement. The joint road map detailing both technology deliverables and business engagement is designed to deliver significant business value to customers, and enable the extension and connection of *SAP* deployments using *SAP NetWeaver* and *Microsoft.NET*.[11]

Portfolio management. *SAP* focuses its patent portfolio on main markets. All of the patent applications are filed in the US. One half are then selected to be filed in Europe, with about 10% in Australia, Canada, China, and Japan.

---

[11]   Source: SAP Press (07.06.2004, 12.05.2004).

SAP has been striving for a greater number of patent applications. In 2002, *SAP* filed 350 patent applications, followed by 750 in 2003. Due to the late start of its patent activities, *SAP* has issued 49 patents in the US so far (Fig. 21).

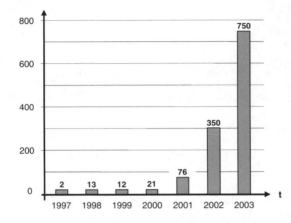

Source: SAP IP Group as available through public patent databases (2005)

Fig. 21. The birth of SAP patent portfolio (yearly filed patent applications)

The direct effect of the *SAP* patent portfolio on the software market is still unclear. For example, various small and medium software enterprises with no more than 50 employees regularly adapt to *SAP* software and re-program certain functions that have proven to be successful. By repro-gramming they avoid conflict with copyright laws.

The temporal distance between *SAP* original modules and repro-grammed versions currently ranges between two to three years. A patent protection with a maximum of 20 years, however, would severely disrupt the current equilibrium. But in general, most small and medium software enterprises still doubt that an investment in the protection of intellectual property would pay off, nor do they monitor the intellectual property of others. So the passive power of *SAP's* patent portfolio likely has a signifi-cant influence in this industry segment.

Organization. Intellectual property management has increased in impor-tance for *SAP* over the past ten years. While *SAP* started with only two patent attorneys, today the intellectual property office employs numerous people. The *Global Intellectual Property Department* is situated in the

Source: SAP Annual Report (2004)

Fig. 22. Global Intellectual Property Department as part of the CEO's Office[12]

United States, in Palo Alto, California. The United States department houses about six US patent attorneys supported by three paralegals, while the German headquarters in Walldorf has eleven patent professionals and six paralegals.

The *Global Intellectual Property Department* reports directly to the head of the board of directors of *SAP* and is legally separate from the legal department, yet there is strong cooperation between the two entities (Fig. 22).[12]

Each patent professional has dedicated internal customers, whether it is a certain lab site, unit or location. There is specialization in various fields, e.g. one patent officer in the US specializes in risk management in patent conflicts. Other fields of competence include:

- Administration;
- Contracts;
- European law;
- Remuneration;
- Searching;
- Standard committees.

Processes. The global intellectual property department manages the intellectual property budget and takes necessary decisions. The idea-to-invention process at *SAP* is kept on a simple level:

---

[12] In 2005, the *SAP* organization has been restructured with an organizational model following the value chain.

- Idea;
- Invention;
- Search procedure;
- Prosecution.

SAP uses a software and intranet-based portal to gather invention disclosures. The global patent department becomes involved, as soon an invention disclosure is internally published. The anticipated economic value of the invention is estimated by the inventor and is approved by the supervisor and the patent department.

The search for state-of-the-art is carried out by the patent department with the help of the inventors. A substantial portion of the reported inventions are filtered out in this process step, reflecting high standards.

Drafting, filing and prosecution of the patent applications is largely outsourced to private practice law firms. While in the US branch of the *Global Intellectual Property Department* all inventions are prosecuted externally, the German branch does some internally.

Cultural aspects. *SAP* actively lobbies its experts to divulge the number of inventions being disclosed. There is a first monetary award given for each invention disclosure being filed as a patent application and also a second monetary award given for the issuance of a patent. In countries such as Germany, where invention remuneration is required by law, these awards are accounted against the legally necessary payments.

The corporate research department, *SAP Research*, has even established an average invention deliverable value for its research teams. It demands a certain delivery target concerning invention disclosures per research group per year. In general, *SAP Research* delivers a number of inventions that is significantly above the overall *SAP* average per person.

4.3.4 Managing Intellectual Property in R&D Collaborations

Generally, *SAP* insists on its own standard agreements for collaborative projects. This is where it is decided whether intellectual property, in the specific context, refers to patents, trade secrets, copyrights, brands (seldom). Furthermore, they state that intellectual property belongs to the inventor, while joint intellectual property will be shared.

However, this may vary depending on the interests of the partners. Generally, *SAP* tries to gain the ownership rights to the whole intellectual property. This is often difficult to achieve, especially with large companies looking to make their own stipulations. Here, factors such as company size, relative power and the broader network surrounding the partner, will all have an influence on the collaborative agreement. In some cases, *SAP* has even paid for the intellectual property rights when a close analysis indicated good market potential.

Since *SAP* is an international company that often gets involved in cross-national development projects, additional questions regarding intellectual property typically come into play. For instance, the partners have to decide which laws should be applied. It is common to choose the legal system of the county where the larger or more committed partner is located. In any case, the system that is more beneficial for the parties is most often the one that is used. Jointly developed intellectual property is considered the main source of disagreements. Where previously joint patenting was sometimes used during transition phases or to access certain markets, today *SAP* generally avoids joint patent inventions with third parties.

Licensing agreements can take different forms. Occasionally, the partners decide on a 50%-rule, which means the product and maintenance revenues are shared. Licensing-in contracts only exist for software from third parties integrated in *SAP's* own products. Furthermore, patent protection is not always considered to be the best solution, such as in cases of hidden functions inside *SAP* products.

General rules for collaborating. A typical *SAP* collaboration project distinguishes temporally between created *knowledge* and the related intellectual property of each of the partners. There is the knowledge and intellectual property that is created *during* the collaboration phase, and *pre-existing knowledge* and related intellectual property that was owned by the parties *before* joining the collaboration. For *SAP*, it is important to keep its pre-existing intellectual property and knowledge exclusive, where it relates to their standard products, e.g. *SAP NetWeaver*. Collaboration partners or other parties are generally denied rights of access to these products and tools. On the other hand, *SAP* does provide the preexisting knowledge of the open interfaces, which are necessary to access their standard tools and products. These are oftentimes published via a special internet address (http://ifr.sap.com/).

CoBIs case. This project aims to improve smart items peer-to-peer communication for transport pallets, including a search for new business models. Project duration is two and a half years, stretching from August 2004 to February 2007.

R&D: The technical areas were easily divided between the partners. Only *HardwareCorp* is focusing more on software. The project outcomes will be very conceptual, meaning that it might take four to five years for commercialization. Success will be based on whether results can be used by project partners (Table 11).

Intellectual Property Management: Each partner keeps the intellectual property created by its team. Therefore, intellectual property created by *SAP* remains exclusively with *SAP*. In this situation, partners try to avoid joint inventions (case-by-case basis).

A general research agreement with the *University I*, states that inventions will be transferred to *SAP*.

Before starting with the project, the preexisting know-how is evaluated and distinguished between inclusion and exclusion items as part of the collaboration contract. *SAP's* philosophy is to exclude their standard products. As interfaces are made public, they can be included into and improved within the collaboration.

Table 11. Research partners of the EU funded project CoBIs

CoBIs Partners	Country	Function
*SAP**	Germany	Software
HardwareCorp	Austria	Technology (hardware)
NetCorp I	The Netherlands	Hardware/network/SME
TransportCorp	United Kingdom	End user/application
University I	Germany	Research network
University II	United Kingdom	Research network
University III	Netherlands	Research network

* Collaboration co-ordinator

Consensus case. This project focused on mobile web applications. It aimed to create application software that would be independent of the end device, and it would simplify the interface with the end device, e.g. mobile phones from various manufacturers. The EU-funded project started in April 2002 and ended in March 2004.

R&D: The project partners were chosen on the basis of trust, along with technical and market experience. (Table 12, p. 91):

- *MobileCorp* was chosen as a producer of mobile end devices to represent the device market. These partners possessed large market share, EU nationality, strong EU project experience, membership of the E3C standardization committee, and turned out to be very active and collaborative partners.
- *TechnologyCorp* was chosen as a partner for infrastructure and service area for providing and distributing information. This partner was also a member in the E3C standardization committee, was seen as close to development but not as a competitor. *TechnologyCorp* also provided

strong human resources, including good research management and the ability to play the role of an active collaboration partner.

- As project coordinator, *SAP Research* provided the environment for software development and worked on the business cases for the visualization of data on end-devices.
- Validation of pilot projects was provided by a system integrator. *TestCorp* was chosen to perform the independent testing on *SAP* software-based applications for various end devices.
- Usability experts needed to be independent, e.g. a research institute such as *ExpertCorp* in Austria to develop test cases with pilot users for mobile devices.
- Support for voice-based applications like *VoiceXML*, e.g. *CommCorp* in Belgium.

Competitors were not chosen; also no third German enterprise due to an otherwise uneven distribution of European countries.

The work packages were divided between the partners. Work packages were completed together, e.g. problem definition and analysis, first construction of solution and architectural design. The implementation and integration of the results in the work and product environments would be carried out separately by each of the partners.

Intellectual Property Management: Various inventions were filed as *SAP* patent applications. The specific results for each of the collaboration partners were:

- *SAP Research* is currently working on an internal transfer of the project results into the business lines.
- *TechnologyCorp* has placed the applications on its servers.
- *MobileCorp* has not pursued the issue since it wants to refocus on its customer base of end consumers.
- *TestCorp* has tried to use the results with its customers, which involves the open source modules but no intellectual property of *SAP*.

The project was considered to be a success. Overall solutions could be retrieved, standardization was brought forward, and the application development costs were reduced (two test applications). Also, the interface software component for the servers was published as open software modules in order to speed up distribution and provide accessibility for further evaluation. Furthermore, the results, including the problem description and solution areas, were presented to the W3C standardization committee.

Table 12. Research partners of the EU funded project Consensus

Consensus Partners	Country	Function
SAP*	Germany	Software
ExpertCorp	Austria	Usability expert
TestCorp	Finland	System integrator/ testing
TechnologyCorp	Germany	Technology
CommCorp	Belgium	Voice applications
MobileCorp	Scandinavia	End user/ applications

* Collaboration co-ordinator

Mosquito case. *Mosquito* is a follow-up project partly funded by the 6th EU framework program within the *SAP* research program *Security and Trust*, which is based on the results of the former 5th EU project *Witness*. *SAP Research* filed about four patent applications on the basis of the former project. For the new project *Mosquito*, the partner selection was based on criteria as follows:

- Former active collaboration partners were reselected;
- Formerly passive, inactive or unfit collaboration partners were not selected again;
- Each selected former partner brought in its own results from former projects, which form pre-existing knowledge that could be used by all partners;
- New partners replaced the updated work packages of the de-selected partners.

Table 13. Research partners of the EU funded project Mosquito

Mosquito Partners	Country	Function
SAP*	Germany	Software
ChipcardCorp I	Germany	Chip cards
ChipcardCorp II	France	Chip cards
SoftwareCorp	Germany	Software
ResearchCorp	France	Research
NetCorp II	Finland	Networks
TelecomCorp	The Netherlands	Telecommunication
ConsultCorp	Germany	Consulting

* Collaboration co-ordinator

MobileCorp case. In 2000, the first initiative for a bilateral collaboration between *SAP Research* and *MobileCorp* was undertaken. *MobileCorp* was contacted in the USA via an external *SAP Research* consultant based in Palo Alto, California. With this partnership, *SAP Research* wants to build an interface from *SAP* to *MobileCorp* devices by creating a development infrastructure for *Wireless Application Protocol* (WAP) enabled enterprise software solutions. The goal is to provide easy "data on the fly" deployment of handheld WAP enabled devices, with the *SAP* enterprise software *mySAP.com Mobile Workplace*. Customers and partners of *SAP* would benefit from being able to develop mini-applications (*MiniApps*) that can be deployed on mobile devices. Companies can tailor MiniApps for internet economy workers who rarely stay in their office and rely on mobile phones and handheld devices to accomplish their work.

SAP approached *MobileCorp* because the mobile company's WAP server is the most widely used WAP server technology. Interfacing this widely accepted server technology with *SAP's* enterprise solutions, enables users to access and update enterprise information online from a WAP enabled mobile device. Customers get flexible access to critical inter-enterprise data and applications, enabling them to conduct business activities from virtually any location. In addition, they can take advantage of internet-enabled mobile computing capabilities and wireless information management as quickly and productively as possible. Further reasons why *SAP* chose *MobileCorp*:

- *SAP* wants to grow with the help of partners, especially in the US market;
- *MobileCorp* is a large customer of *SAP*;
- *MobileCorp* would serve as a pilot to test the systems, which would be a significant advantage.

Advantages for *MobileCorp* from this partnership include:

- Opportunity for *MobileCorp* to sell more devices;
- *MobileCorp* can create its own distributable middleware;
- The interface between *SAP* and *MobileCorp*, i.e. *Application Program Interface* (API) might be certifiable but would stay non-exclusive and open to users, so customers could still create their own interface connections to personalize their systems.

In 2000, the field of mobile computing was very tangible, but moved quickly toward *Radio Frequency Identification Device Technology* (RFID). It took some time for both companies to individually develop competences in this field. Today, *SAP* has an RFID architecture with strong potential.

Intellectual Property Management: The parties do not grant any intellectual property rights to each other, e.g. know-how and patents.

Notably, the pre-existing knowledge of both parties' hardware, software solutions, and interfaces will remain exclusive. However, strictly for the purpose of the project, the partners provided each other with a limited, non-exclusive license to remotely access the hardware and software solutions of the other party.

As the existing knowledge is developed by the parties during the collaboration, a concept design is to be provided. It describes the functional specifications of the respective party's interface, which is necessary for the linkage between the two interfaces.

Both parties accepted that any unexpected knowledge, e.g. independently developed software that may not be based on confidential information, might end up competing with the hardware and software solutions of the other party.

Summary SAP. The inter-enterprise software giant *SAP* can look back on a long period of growth since its founding in the early 70s. During the late 90s, the patent situation in the US compelled *SAP* to start protecting its software with patents.

SAP conducts its research activities via the corporate group *SAP Research* that relies on various research and campus-based engineering centers around the globe to source first-class research resources and to keep their interdisciplinary research program going. Key learnings from *SAP* are:

- *SAP* maintains a large research partner network with about 200 collaboration partners;
- The collaborative research outcomes therefore emerge from the entire *SAP* ecosystem, and not from single players;
- Intellectual property management plays an important role in these R&D collaborations – *SAP* seeks single ownership and only rarely undertakes joint patenting.

4.4 Swisscom

Swisscom is the country's prime source and incumbent provider of tele-communications services in Switzerland. Although *Swisscom* and its predecessor, *Telecom PTT,* have had a monopoly for several decades, they have always showed willingness to and have been proved capable of providing one of the most modern telecommunications networks of the world.

Even the German-Swiss language has been influenced by *Swisscom*'s marketing strategists calling a mobile phone as *Natel*, an abbreviation of "Nationales Autotelefon", which means national car phone. This has not only become a commonly used expression for car phones, but for all kinds of mobile phones in Switzerland, regardless of whether the phone is operated by Swisscom or by a competitor.

In 2004, the *Swisscom* achieved a turnover of 10.1 billion Swiss francs and a net income of 1.6 billion Swiss francs, with about 15,500 FTE positions. The company offers all products and services for mobile, fixed and internet protocol-based voice and data communication, to date mainly in Switzerland but also increasingly across the border.

Swisscom's innovation power has always been one of the company's strengths. Even the entirely state-owned predecessor of *Swisscom, Telecom PTT*, always guaranteed its mobile customers the most advanced worldwide roaming network available at that time. Illustrative of *Swisscom's* innovation power is the recently presented mobile network solution for internet access. The patented *Mobile Unlimited* technology is designed to allow customers to experience uninterrupted broadband connectivity while on the move. Being the first of its kind, *Mobile Unlimited* automatically switches between networks in order to ensure the best possible connectivity in respect of time and place, while supporting GPRS, UMTS and WLAN.

When founded, the *Swisscom* was made up of a portfolio of connected entities of which the most important are *Swisscom Fixnet* and *Swisscom Mobile*. *Swisscom Fixnet*, a 100% affiliate of the *Swisscom*, operates the network infrastructure and sells communication and network services to both private and institutional clients. In 2004, *Swisscom Fixnet* generated a net revenue of 5.7 billion Swiss francs and therewith accounts for slightly more than half of the group's revenue. *Swisscom Mobile*'s ownership is divided between *Swisscom* (75%) and *Vodafone* (25%), and the company is the group's mobile services provider. *Swisscom Mobile* was the second largest group company in 2004, with a net revenue of 4.4 billion Swiss francs.

Traditionally, most of the company's revenues are generated in Switzerland, which is also its primary business focus. With the liberalization of the European telecommunications markets, *Swisscom* aims to gain a market share in different markets abroad. Market-entries in Austria and Germany were *Swisscom's* first initiatives, but due to political and business reasons they were abandoned. A fully owned WLAN provider called *Eurospot,* which has been set up in ten European countries, is the rather profitable initiative that followed.

4.4.1 Research and Innovation

Swisscom Innovations is *Swisscom's* entity that does research activities for the whole group. It is part of the headquarters and operates both autonomously as well as by mandate of one of the group companies. Individual group companies, like *Swisscom Mobile* and *Swisscom Fixnet*, are also engaged in innovation management.

Swisscom Innovations with its headquarter in Bern, employs about 170 people in three offices worldwide of whom 160 are found at the headquarters and the rest in Zurich and San Francisco. Most of the work is done at the innovation center in Bern. The satellite station in San Francisco was established to monitor technological progress in this progressive geographical area. In 2004, *Swisscom Innovations'* revenue represented 0.4% of the group revenues, and amounted to about 40 million Swiss francs in total.

At *Swisscom Innovations*, the criteria for innovative power and innovations are customer orientation and the usability of the resulting products. To ensure that this is achieved, the company's workforce is a mixture of various academic backgrounds. The recently established usability laboratory is also an example of the importance of usability.

The focus of the research activities at *Swisscom* is limited to applied research. *Swisscom* uses academic institutions' results and buys in technological solutions if necessary, but rarely enters into partnerships or outsources research activities regarding potential basic research.

The role of Swisscom Innovations has two focus areas (Table 14):

1. Looking for disruptions;
2. Permanent observation of the market.

1. Looking for disruptions: Disruptive technologies can appear in every field of business and have the potential to drive an otherwise competitive company out of business overnight. The history of the Swiss watchmaking industry is a good example. Worldwide, Swiss watches were distinguished for their high quality and perfect finishing, as the entire industry had been optimizing the technology in use for centuries. With the arrival of quartz watch technology, the profitability of the conventional industry was endangered almost overnight. As the example shows, disruptive technologies may lead to a complete redefinition of the business environment even in traditionally slow-paced industries – even more so in the short-cycled, highly technology-dominated telecommunications industry in which *Swisscom* operates.

Disruptive technologies therefore form a permanent threat for *Swisscoms'* operations. Consequently, one of *Swisscom Innovations'* primary tasks is the permanent observation of technological developments and the evaluation of new technologies with respect to their disruptive potential. This task is critical for the vitality of the whole corporation, as both the business cycles and investment requirements of the different businesses fields in which *Swisscom* operates largely differ. Generally, the longer the business cycle of a particular technology or product, the sooner top management needs to be convinced to invest in the early innovation phases. Therefore, one of *Swisscom Innovation's* challenges is the collaboration with the group's top management.

2. Permanent observation of the market: Swisscom Innovations also permanently observes the markets in which *Swisscom* operates and delivers detailed information about changes to the group companies.

Swisscom Innovation's mission is the scanning, exploration and evaluation of emerging technologies that enable *Swisscom Innovations* to build sound knowledge of available technologies, which can then be submitted to the group companies.

The three most common methods of knowledge transfer at *Swisscom Innovations* are depicted in Fig. 23. Example (a) illustrates a remote activity. The transferred knowledge is not of immediate importance, but future op-

Table 14. Activities and tasks of Swisscom Innovations

Activities	Tasks
Innovation projects (core activity)	Feasibility studies, pre-business cases, demonstrators
Technology strategy consulting (core activity)	Concepts and overviews based on technology and market watch
Engineering (support activity)	Architectural support, development, technical support
Innovation consulting (support activity)	Business models

portunities are monitored. Case (b) refers to potential synergies between the group companies, with the result that all possibly affected group companies are involved in the information flow. Illustration (c) shows the circumstance in which *Swisscom Innovations* reports on an activity beyond the company's current strategy and points to possible new businesses. In all cases, *Swisscom Innovations* pursues joint development and a *side-by-side* working approach with the group companies involved.

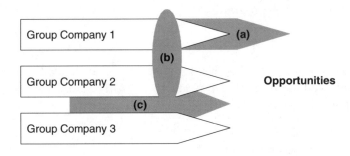

Source: Swisscom Innovations (2005)

Fig. 23. Knowledge transfer within the Swisscom Group

Innovations at *Swisscom* usually follow a process that consists of six steps:

- Idea generation;
- Definition phase;
- Concept phase;
- Prototype phase;
- Development phase;
- Rollout.

Swisscom Innovations is largely involved in all steps except for the rollout. Activities in the first four process steps are usually performed and led by *Swisscom Innovations*. After the fourth step, the prototype phase, innovations are handed over to the commissioning group company, which then leads the development phase in which it, together with *Swisscom Innovations*, further works out the innovation details. The rollout is then carried out by the relevant group company.

4.4.2 Managing R&D Collaborations

Swisscom Innovations' collaborative research activities amount to about 5% of its overall budget. The company has a wide external network of collaboration partners which includes:

- Academia;
- Industrial partners;
- Standards bodies;
- European Union research programs;
- Eurescom;
- US Outpost (Silicon Valley).

Swisscom Innovation's activities are organized through innovation programs. These innovation programs are made up of projects aimed at different group companies in order to:

- Exploit synergies between related projects;
- Ensure a comprehensive thematic approach;
- Achieve leadership in selected technological areas.

To ensure a broadbased approach, each innovation program team consists of members with different skill areas.

The design of the innovation programs varies to maximize the probability of covering all areas relevant to future business. Besides these innovation programs, there are two more initiative-types. To support the potential of unconventional ideas, the *out-of-the-box* projects have been set up. On the other side of the spectrum, *INO Ventures* have been created to make mature ideas visible and ready for commercial use.

Research partnerships. The main reasons for *Swisscom's* close contact with academic partners are, on the one hand, because the company is knowledge-driven. It is therefore interested in, e.g., the exploration of emerging technologies, the performance of usability studies and the set-up of pre-business cases. On the other hand, *Swisscom* has a recruiting interest in order to ensure a future workforce. The *University of St.Gallen*, the *University of Bern* and the *Hochschule für Technik Rapperswil* are frequent partners. The first two are recruiting targets; the latter is a partner in research. Further research partners are *CSEM* and other academic partners are, e.g. *ETHZ* and *EPFL*.

Industrial partnerships. These partnerships are focused on driving the market introduction of new technologies and are normally established on a project basis. *Swisscom*, for example, developed a *Service Level Agree-*

ment Management (SLAM) with *Whitestein Technologies*, a former project partner of *Swisscom Innovations*, The main goal of this collaboration was "to define and implement a tool-set for enabling dynamic *Quality of Service* (QoS)-based creation and deployment, allowing for consequent optimization of network resources and increased benefit to the end-user by means of an agent-based approach":[13]

- Iimplementation of a flexible recommendation system to establish adaptive SLAs;
- Creation of pro-active resources and SLA management, including proactive QoS monitoring;
- Dynamic and automated SLA re-configuration based on the current network state.

This project lasted only four months and is being internally further pursued by *Whitestein Technologies*. Another form of partnership was established with a supplier of *Swisscom*. To support the ideal use of applied software, a joint development program was set up with *Virage*, a US-based provider of media communication and content management software. Other industrial collaborations include companies such as *Dartfish*, a producer of home video sports training programs, and *PacketVideo*, an American mobile-media software provider.

Swisscom is not committed in standard bodies anymore, although the company actively follows standards. The need for standards in the telecommunications business is obvious: Communication between different parties can only occur if there is a common basis of understanding, both from a psychological as well as a technological perspective. From a business point of view, standards limit companies' differentiation potential, but in essence, they allow markets to develop, shape and grow. Moreover, standards are considered indispensable for different devices and protocols to work together. Standardizations mostly do not affect the competition space: in spite of the declared standardizations of certain properties, there are always possibilities and omissions in the policies that guarantee a worthwhile freedom to differentiate.

4.4.3 Managing Intellectual Property

In spite of being a rather new player in the intellectual property area, *Swisscom* has already become aware of the potential benefits of active in-

---

[13]   Source: *Whitestein Technologies*, see also: http://www.whitestein.com/pages/research/projects.html.

tellectual property management. Patents and other forms of intellectual property can, of course, be used in the traditional way as a legal instrument or as a marketing instrument. Yet, it could also serve other purposes, like generating revenues or the interchanging of rights with other companies and competitors.

For a long time, *Swisscom* had not needed to deal with intellectual property questions, due to its specific company and market history – being a formerly state-owned company with a monopoly – which is also true for *Swisscoms'* competitors in the neighboring countries. As markets were guaranteed by law and expansion, it was neither desired nor possible to protect intellectual property. Only in 1994, when the market conditions changed, there was a reduction in government protection and the entry barriers were lowered, did *Swisscom Mobile* start its patenting activities to prepare itself for the future. From that point onwards, the company has used intellectual property to defend itself against possible intruders and competitors. Defend oneself in the *shared battleground* is, however, only part of the game. Due to the ongoing integration of technological communication devices, companies with different technological backgrounds have to compete against one another while, simultaneously, the same companies' customers force them to establish common standards for the sake of technology usability.

In recent years, *Swisscom's* traditional commercial model has been continuously weakened. This was again due to the liberalization of the market and this has led to increasing value chain disintegration. The communication services value chain can be divided into three subcategories: services access, network access and device access. *Swisscom* used to have a monopoly in all three categories. These days, other companies such as *Nokia*, *Siemens* and *Ericsson* develop, manufacture and distribute communication devices. Network access is provided by a multiplicity of providers. Together with *Eurospot*, *Swisscom* forms only one party among many others in the market. *Swisscom's* leading domain is communication services, e.g. voice, e-mail and internet, but it faces serious competition here as well. It is therefore crucial to strengthen *Swisscom's* market position in the already diminished value chain. Intellectual property management and especially patents contribute to the legal protection of *Swisscom's* position in the market.

Strategy. *Swisscom's* intellectual property strategy can be partially derived from its market position. As the biggest player in the Swiss telecommunications market, further expansion within the country's borders is nearly impossible. Only emerging technologies could allow new market entries and this might broaden the scope of *Swisscom's* business portfolio. Understandably, *Swisscom* has a rather defensive posture as it tries to protect its traditional market in all types of voice communication. Legal protection of patents might help to avoid conflicts, and business relations with competitors can be smoothened with the help of patents.

Patents can also contribute to the company's overall financial performance, as they can form an additional source of income by generating revenues via royalties or sales.

The development of the patent portfolio of *Swisscom* is depicted in Fig. 24. *Swisscom* is looking for measurable criteria with which to objectively measure the performance of their innovative power. The patent portfolio, as one example, serves as a benchmark tool for innovation. More importantly, recognizable innovation steps, each represented by patents, may foster innovation in the company and nurture the will to enter external collaborations.

A challenge for *Swisscom* is the alignment of the overall company strategy and the intellectual property strategy. To date, *Swisscom* has created a correlation between the group companies' intellectual property strategy and their product and marketing strategies. This correlation was achieved through the group companies' responsible intellectual property managers' high degree of autonomy.

Organization, processes and cultural aspects. *Swisscoms' Chief Technology Officer* (CTO), who is the head of *Swisscom Innovations*, coordinates the intellectual property management activities between the group companies. However, every group company is responsible for its own intellectual property and for the tasks associated with it, such as patent screening.

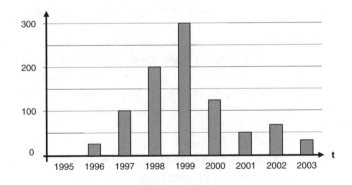

Source: Swisscom Innovations (2005)

Fig. 24. Development of the patent portfolio of Swisscom (applications per year)

Simultaneously, it is necessary to ensure that all the individual group companies are in line with *Swisscom's* strategy in respect of managing intellectual property. This decentralized organizational approach is therefore practiced as follows: Each group company nominates one person, situated in the specific group company's legal department, to be responsible for the intellectual property management. This person is responsible for the evaluation of newly acquired or developed intellectual property. Following its evaluation, intellectual property is graded into different categories, and handled in different ways. Depending on the evaluation of the matter at hand, the best way is chosen. Patent filing, which is used to secure legal protection, is one of the ways in which intellectual property can be handled. Other treatments may involve publication, classification as trade secret, or no action at all.

Within *Swisscom, Swisscom Innovations* is the main generator of intellectual property. The question is whether and how intellectual property is exploited in the organization. *Swisscom Innovations* files patents that are mostly the result of developments on behalf of one of the group companies. The resulting intellectual property is transferred from *Swisscom Innovations* to the group where it will have the best chance of being utilized. The ultimate responsibility for the allocation of patents to the group companies lies with the CTO, who also leads the biannual patent board meetings. This practice means that *Swisscom Innovations,* the main developer of intellectual property, has a portfolio of 50–60 patents at its disposal, while *Swisscom Mobile* now holds about 180 patents in its portfolio.

Swisscom also screens patents of third parties – a task that is partly executed by the group companies' intellectual property managers and, to some degree, outsourced to external patent attorneys. This approach allows the company to keep track of recent developments and to oppose potentially dangerous patent filings by other companies within the period of objection. *Swisscom Mobiles'* portfolio of monitored patent families has exceeded 1,000 and has led to an active opposition policy. So far, its experiences with objections against patent filings by competitors have been surprisingly good. The opposed parties mostly offer negotiations instead of reacting angrily. Some of these negotiations have even resulted in collaborative activities.

It is again emphasized that innovation is of central importance to *Swisscom* with the result that the generation of intellectual property is constantly gaining in importance over other targets. The company's culture therefore includes a proactive approach towards emerging technologies.

Licensing. There is no explicit licensing strategy at *Swisscom* yet, due to the intellectual property management's emerging level of maturity. Nevertheless, the company is actively searching for and interested in licensing relationships with other companies.

Although a first external licensing contract was recently signed with *id-Quantique*, intellectual property rights in general do not seem very promising to the company from a financial perspective. This is due to *Swisscom's* relatively small patent portfolio and the fact that intellectual property has only recently gained attention in this industry sector. Cross license agreements, a common instrument in many other industries, e.g. the software and semiconductors industries, are not yet common in the telecommunication services industry.

4.4.4 Managing Intellectual Property in R&D Collaborations

R&D collaborations are a fairly new experience for *Swisscom* in general and for *Swisscom Innovations* particularly. R&D collaborations are not very widespread in the telecommunications industry as yet, with the exception of multilateral EU R&D organizations such as *Eurescom*. *Swisscom's* primary focus is on market-oriented opportunities. *Swisscom* is therefore open to all kinds of collaborations and actively seeks potential partners with complementary knowledge. Most realized collaborations are based on an asymmetric spread of information between the partners, which, if combined, can lead to a new technology or application in a given product. *Swisscom's* experience illustrates that this can be achieved through a combination of knowledge from otherwise totally separate fields of technology.

At the moment, *Swisscom's* collaboration approach is not driven by intellectual property issues as these are still considered to be a side-product. Nevertheless, their role cannot be neglected. Based on past experiences and the will to yield results while keeping the danger of inefficient and ineffective collaborations as small as possible, *Swisscom Mobile* has developed an informal pattern of pre-entering checks. This procedure allows the company to quickly identify potentially fruitful fields of collaboration with respect to both partners' intellectual property.

Fig. 25 shows a four-step approach which describes the most important criteria for the choice of collaboration partners from the intellectual property manager's perspective.

- *Analyze potential partners' patent portfolios:* Scanning the partner's portfolio enables *Swisscom* to draw conclusions regarding the company's research traditions and technology portfolio. Knowledge of the

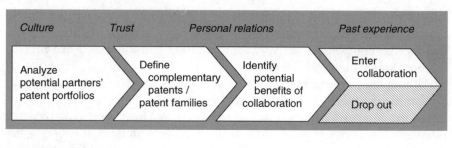

Source: Swisscom Mobile (2005)

Fig. 25. Selection procedure for collaboration partners at Swisscom Mobile

partner's patent portfolio is of essential importance for the successful generation of new intellectual property during collaboration.

- *Definition of complementary intellectual property:* One of the key motivational factors for *Swisscom's* collaborations is complementary knowhow. The combination of knowledge from otherwise different fields of technology can lead to new marketable solutions. The potential of this approach is best illustrated by the successful collaboration with *Atrua Technologies* during which the combination of two radically different businesses led to a new product.[14]
- *Identification of potential benefits:* The mere existence of complementary intellectual property cannot guarantee the success of any collaboration. Therefore, the identification of potential benefits needs to be explored during the assessment of the collaboration possibilities. Possible results need to be anticipated and checked against the background of market conditions and marketability. Critical issues concerning the legal distribution of resultant intellectual property have to be addressed and agreed on during the set-up phase.
- *Entering the collaboration or dropping out:* An overall assessment of the opportunities and threats leads to a conclusion as to whether to collaborate or not. The final decision will also take into account other aspects such as the diffusion of *Swisscom Mobile's* intellectual property to the partnering corporation, and any legal concerns that might occur.

But there are other issues that play a major role besides these core criteria. For *Swisscom Mobile*, these issues form a general background for any collaboration. The *cultures* of both companies need to be compatible to a certain degree in order to allow smooth team collaboration. *Trust* and reli-

---

[14] See *Atrua Technologies* case at the end of this section.

ability are of crucial importance in any collaboration, as the partners will gain highly sensitive knowledge about each other. *Personal relations* are not only an enabler during the initial phase of the collaboration, but will also allow increased efficiency during later stages. *Past experience* with the collaboration partner is not a prerequisite, although it could facilitate the work. Experiences from former collaborations will, in general, have a strong influence on the design of any future collaboration.

At *Swisscom*, the number of collaborations are neither limited by company rules, nor are there any restrictions on potential partners. From the strategic and the legal points of view, the only constraint regarding the choice of potential partners is the prevention of antitrust suits. As a former monopolist, *Swisscom* has to specifically take antitrust legislation into consideration and needs to apply the utmost caution in collaborations of all kinds with direct competitors in order to prevent suspicions of cartel forming. Long-term collaborations with competitors are therefore not considered, especially not with those acting in the same geographical market.

With the group's R&D affiliate *Swisscom Innovations, Swisscom* pursues an applied research policy as opposed to a basic research policy. R&D collaborations are relevant for the company's ongoing innovation aims, as *Swisscom's* developmental work focuses on the exploration and realization of innovations. In a collaboration project, the development of common intellectual property is a possibility, and the costs and profits are shared. *Swisscom Innovations* often takes the leading role in collaborations and consequently manages to take ownership of later patents. *Swisscom* accepts all the later patents' related costs and a non-exclusive right of use is granted to the partner. If the collaboration leads to the development of new products, each partner can be asked to defray costs, as each of them is responsible for any associated fees and costs.

In order to avoid future problems with partners, *Swisscom* is strongly interested in establishing clear regulations and guidelines in respect of intellectual property issues in collaborations. Some exemplary notable problems could be: a partner does not stick to the agreed processes and wants to register an idea prematurely, or a partner deliberately contravenes a condition of the contract.

Swisscom's search for collaboration partners is mainly based on the criterion of potential market development. The breadth of the potential partner's patent portfolio may help in the assessment of a collaboration partner. The need for this careful approach is twofold: *Swisscom* itself is not a technology group and its market is geographically limited.

Swisscom Mobile tries to avoid the risk of joint patenting that may lead to future entanglements. This is based on former experiences in respect of the joint patenting of intellectual property in a project that failed. *Swisscom* therefore has an interest in building up knowledge to be able to recognize any potential litigation in good time. The company has generally found it difficult to split costs and revenues in a way that leaves both parties satisfied with their input and revenue ratio. Also the proper split of employee activities between the employee's work within the collaboration, and the work carried out exclusively for *Swisscom* is a difficulty that regularly occurs in its collaborations. This issue needs thorough examination in the set-up phase and should be part of the intellectual property allocation agreement, because this could determine whether the resulting intellectual property is or is not part of the collaboration. *Swisscom Mobile* therefore tries to ensure that there is a clear understanding of those employees temporarily assigned to work on the collaboration project and those not involved. Furthermore, classification agreements are closed to prevent intellectual property that originates from collaborations from being diffused into the partner companies before the property rights have been defined.

Although *Swisscom Mobile* does not have an established research network like *Swisscom Innovations*, the company is active in several areas and engaged in different projects to develop marketable products. Mobile communication, being a relatively young industry, is mainly dominated by rivalry and the battle for market share. Collaborative research activities are therefore not very common yet. Additionally, the fast pace of development seems to focus the companies' attention on operational issues. Potential cost savings from, for example, shared development activities have not yet gained the attention of the responsible managers. Nevertheless, a project with the US enterprise *Atrua Technologies* (Askar 2005) is an example of *Swisscom Mobile*'s market-oriented innovation collaborations:

Atrua Technologies case. *Atrua Technologies* "provides intelligent touch controls, a new class of user input device for accessing and using advanced applications and services on today's mobile phones" (Atrua 2005). *Swisscom Mobile* and *Atrua Technologies* are major partners in the field of mobile network operators. Together, the two companies developed a biometric identification system that can be implemented in mobile phones, replacing the conventional *Personal Identification Number* (PIN) system. The biometric sensor scans the fingerprint of the user and the data collected is then transferred to the *Subscriber Identity Module* (SIM) card, where it is checked for identity with the reference information saved on the card. Access to the mobile phone and, thus, to the server applications is only granted if the test result is positive, i.e. the data on the SIM card and the fingerprint are identical. This newly developed technology improves the handling of mobile phones by the customers and releases *Swisscom Mobile* from the elaborate PIN renewal process: About 5% of all incoming calls to the *Swisscom Mobile* customer call center are due to the loss of a PIN, causing capacity absorption and costs within *Swisscom Mobile's* call centers.

Yet, the ability to communicate with the mobile phone's SIM card, and the resulting data stream, which is a specific implemented feature of the device, has been patented by *Swisscom Mobile*. The intellectual property in respect of the biometric sensor for the identification of the user's fingerprint belongs to *Atrua Technologies*.

Swisscom Mobile plans to license this technology by supporting suitable projects to generate a related market, thereby earning royalties on the jointly developed technology.

Summary Swisscom. The former telecommunication provider *Swisscom* has to cope with the liberalization of the Swiss telecommunication market and is currently planning expansion activities outside Switzerland. Consequently, *Swisscom* strives for innovations such as the patented internet access technology *Mobile Unlimited* that will allow it to enter new markets, or to broaden the company's business scope. The company's research activities are conducted by the central group *Swisscom Innovations* that relies on an external research collaboration network.

Since the opening of the national market, *Swisscom* has started to use patents as marketing instruments and has also exchanged intellectual property rights with competitors and other companies. Key learnings from *Swisscom* are:

- A comparatively young patent portfolio;
- Division-specific intellectual property strategies with a high level of autonomy;
- Developmental collaborations with different kinds of institutions, mostly project based;
- The developing licensing practices in the industry;
- Standardization as a means to shape markets while leaving space for competitive behavior.

4.5 Swiss Re

The *Swiss Reinsurance Company (Swiss Re)* is one of the leading re-insurance organizations, and the world's largest life reinsurer. *Swiss Re* was founded in 1863 in Zurich. Today, the company has more than 70 offices in 30 countries worldwide. *Swiss Re* has maintained the highest official security rating, "AAA", for decades. The reinsurance business is about insuring primary insurance companies, and therefore a business-to-business activity. The insurance business is based on managing the volatility of risks, i.e. to decrease probability of ruin, decrease tax burdens and cost of capital, and to secure returns to shareholders. Traditional reinsurance products therefore cover the entire spectrum of underwriting risk in the life and non-life areas. Examples of such products include accident, property, third party, car, and travel insurance. In addition, *Swiss Re* offers insurance-based solutions for enterprise financing and support services for risk management (Swiss Re 2004b).

To absorb risk volatility without endangering itself as a reinsurance company, *Swiss Re* has to be big, diversified and – most importantly – has to understand the insured risks. *Swiss Re* runs three divisions: *Property & Casualty*, *Life & Health*, and *Financial Services*, offering a wide variety of products and services to help manage capital and risk. The business group *Property & Casualty* offers "non-life" reinsurance products as they are termed, *Life & Health* has everything related to human life, and *Financial Services* is responsible for investments, credit and art. There is also a *Corporate Center* that hosts an IT group, a finance group and the *Group Intellectual Property Department*.

At its headquarters in Zurich, Switzerland, *Swiss Re* announced a fiscal profit of 2.5 billion Swiss francs for 2004. *Swiss Re* employs over 8,000 employees, 3,000 of whom are based in Switzerland. Notable competitors include *Munich Re*, *Hannover Re*, and *GeneralCologne Re*. *Swiss Re* ranks second to *Munich Re* in terms of premium volume, with 29.4 billion Swiss francs (2004).[15]

4.5.1   Research and Innovation

Within the (re–) insurance business, there are no typical research and development activities. Instead, there are numerous decentrally organized

---

[15]   In November 2005 *Swiss Re* announced it had agreed to acquire *GE Insurance Solutions*, the fifth largest reinsurer worldwide, from *General Electric Company*. *GE Insurance Solutions* had net premiums earned of USD 6.2 billion in 2004 advancing *Swiss Re* to the world largest reinsurance company.

and conducted technical projects. Their goal is to develop in-house information technology solutions, especially if there are no outside, off-the-shelf products on the market. These types of research and development activities are important for *Swiss Re* to defend itself against attacks by hackers, to simulate natural catastrophes and develop epidemic models, pricing models, tools and reserving methodologies. Further targets are e-business solutions and specific product developments. These project activities absorb significant human and financial resources. In the (re–) insurance business, the engineer's function is therefore replaced by the actuary's function.

(Re-) insurance products are, however, often characterized as possessing a relatively easy imitativeness. Competitive advantage can thus be achieved by emulation of existing products. This is often described as the *second-mover advantage*. Furthermore, first-mover activities, e.g. the introduction of a new product on the market, are considered to involve high-risk components and hence lack attractiveness.

Financial service providers and insurers are now devising new methods to protect their competitive advantage: business models and software solutions are more patentable, something that has become common practice in the United States and Japan. Typical areas of concern for insurance patents include risk transfer schemes, insurance products, e-business solutions, or pricing instruments.

4.5.2 Managing R&D Collaborations

Swiss Re gets involved in innovation collaborations in order to gain access to new resources, particularly technologies. The sought after technology plays a decisive role in partner selection. The basis for choosing a partner therefore boils down to the technologies and subsequent intellectual property that can be gained by collaborating.

Swiss Re's collaborations are designed and aligned to the company philosophy taking a long-term perspective. Often a long-term intensive partnership results in a win-win situation for both sides.

As an internationally active enterprise, *Swiss Re* has entered into collaborations with a wide array of partners worldwide. For a major part, collaborations are formed with research institutes and universities. There are also collaborations with competitors; but, those arrangements are dependent on the decision of the respective department within the company.

4.5.3 Managing Intellectual Property

In the financial services sector, banks and insurance companies are increasingly becoming aware of the opportunities created by patent innovations. In particular, they are examining patent business models that run on computer systems. However, the application of pure business models is rare, as even in the United States the patent-granting process for submitted inventions is both tangible and comprehensive. A large number of patents in this industry can be attributed to original patent holders and large companies that have many years of patent experience, characteristics not often associated with the (re–) insurance industry. This situation stems from the New Economy hype from a few years ago, when dot-com companies were vying for patents on software and business practices to make their financial situation more attractive to investors (Cuypers 2003).

Typical specifications for patents include, for example: systems and methods for user authorization, verification and audit systems, devices and process for calculating options, and internet-based insurance products. Following the US trailblazers, e.g. *Citigroup* and *Merril Lynch, Swiss Re* has caught on to the trend: establish dedicated patent departments and announce in-house patents. The company is one of the first (re–) insurance organizations to create its own patent department and carry out a consistent internal strategy.

Today, *Swiss Re* files about 30 patent applications per year. The company's intellectual property portfolio has increased significantly, thanks to

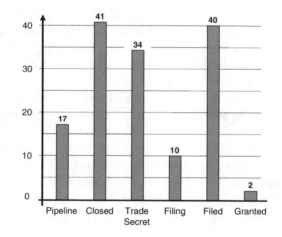

Source: Swiss Re Group IP (2005)

Fig. 26. Intellectual property activities of Swiss Re (number of activities)

approximately 100 inventions and more than 40 submitted patent applications (Fig. 26). Another ten were classified as trade secrets, while fifteen others were deemed not new and hence rejected. Two US patent rights stem from the acquisition of *Lincoln Re* in October 2003.

Beginning of the intellectual property era. The introduction and establishment of intellectual property within *Swiss Re* can be traced to the introduction of e-business-based reinsurance products. The goal of these e-business solutions is to achieve high efficiency in the processing of reinsurance transactions. In this framework, one can see how the internet- and browser-based IT solutions disrupted and altered competitors' specifications. This has been legitimized by the *State Street Decision*[16] in the United States, which followed a large and sudden growth in business model patent applications. *Swiss Re*, whose core competencies lie in the evaluation of risk and chances, is significant for two facts:

* At one time there was a risk of the infringement of patents from:

    a) Competitors;
    b) Other third parties not in direct competition with *Swiss Re*.

* *Swiss Re* faced more than just risk, as simultaneously there were other opportunities:

    a) Publishing of trade secrets that until recently had been protected by patents;
    b) Hedging of investments and income from research and development activities;
    c) Greater autonomy from key knowledge sources;
    d) Maintaining and taking stock of internal know-how.

This scenario led management to set up a task force in fall 2000, which was to investigate the potential of an in-house intellectual property department. The establishment of a central intellectual property department was finalized in August 2001, and it was placed under the Risk & Knowledge Division at the *Swiss Re* corporate headquarters in Zurich. This new department supports a division that already provides a number of services in the firm.

At the time of the new department's establishment, no patent infringement complaints or their like had been submitted. The intellectual property department's initial focus was on the generation and supervision of patents. The legal department already handled copyrights, and external law-

---

[16]   *State Street Bank and Trust Co. v. Signature Financial Group, Inc.*, 149 F.3d 1368 (Fed. Cir. 1998).

yers handled trademarks on a regional basis. The goal of the intellectual property department was and still is primarily to minimize risk.

This scenario led management to set up a task force in the fall of 2000 that had to investigate the potential of an in-house intellectual property department. The establishment of the central intellectual property department, called *Group Intellectual Property Department*, was finalized in August 2001, and it was placed under the Risk & Knowledge Division at the *Swiss Re* corporate headquarters in Zurich. This new department supports a division that already provides a number of services in the firm.

At the time of the new department's establishment, no patent infringement complaints or their like had been submitted. The Group Intellectual Property Department's initial focus was on the generation and supervision of patents. The legal department already handled copyrights, and external lawyers handled trademarks on a regional basis. The goal of the intellectual property department was and still is primarily to minimize risk.

Initiation of intellectual property activities. With the initiation of patent activities, the *Group Intellectual Property Department* launched an awareness program. Activities related to the program included: internal and external publication of articles relating to intellectual property, a company intranet site with information on intellectual property, active participation in international conferences; and internal and external interviews on intellectual property in order to establish a bilateral dialogue and team meetings. The Group Intellectual Property Department also specifically created a new pamphlet called *Welcome on Board* for incoming employees. The specific challenges facing *Swiss Re's* intellectual property department during the initial stages of establishing patent activities included:

- Sufficient sensitivity towards patents and intellectual property. The first challenge was to raise awareness within *Swiss Re* and help employees to understand the new issues surrounding a new patent department.
- To deal with supposedly "unimportant" ideas that the public could access and that could have an impact on patent protection. Even if internal experts knew about the Group Intellectual Property Department, their inventions were not always properly acknowledged and recognized. Inventors still lacked the specific ability to identify and evaluate their inventions.
- The acceptance and perceived value of intellectual property for (re–) insurers.
- The ability to point out improvements and changes that could be achieved through the internal Group Intellectual Property Department and its related patent activities.

Strategy. *Swiss Re* pursues an internal patent application and activity process so to protect its intellectual property, while building up a respectable and well-diversified patent portfolio to protect itself against potential conflicts. Where reinsurance products are concerned: the better the statistical findings on risk are, the easier that premiums can be calculated. Hence, a good model focuses squarely on profit.

As a rule, reinsurance products are relatively easy for competitors to copy. This is especially true when the development steps and related know-how are done by different parties. This means exposure to those handling or accepting the contracts distributed to customers. There is thus an incentive to protect this model with a patent. The advantages of such protection include:

- Product development or subtasks can be split into separate parts internally, ensuring that competition is not exposed to sensitive information. The development process can therefore be streamlined and costs lowered.
- R&D collaborations can be entered into in respect of patents; something that was not possible before without the additional protection of intellectual property.
- In addition, products can be passed on to customers without fear of being copied by third parties. This also frees up their use in other contexts and situations. Previously, projects (especially smaller ones) were not pursued vigorously if their application and project range were too small, since there was no incentive to develop and exhaust all the project's possibilities.

The intellectual property activities of *Swiss Re* are based on the three strategically aligned foundations:

- *Defense:* (Patent-) Infringement against *Swiss Re* should be anticipated, prevented and handled. The Group Intellectual Property Department maintains a strategic partnership with management.
- *Action: Swiss Re's* R&D activities should be identified, promoted, protected, and then used to the firm's advantage. The Group Intellectual Property Department maintains a strategic partnership with management.
- *Leadership: Swiss Re* wants to become an industry leader in handling intellectual property. The central Group Intellectual Property Department maintains a strategic partnership with management.

The above strategic points were developed by the central Group Intellectual Property Department with the insight and understanding of *Swiss Re*'s corporate leadership. These points are in agreement with

Swiss Re company policy. A strong and diversified patent portfolio is a necessary prerequisite for successful strategy implementation.

The following guidance rules were derived from the intellectual property strategy that is available to any *Swiss Re* employee. These fundamental points are of particular importance to key employees who have frequent contact with third parties.

- *Novelty:* Novelty is a fundamental criterion for having an invention patented. Inventions, before they are registered via patents, may not take on a publicly recognizable form to avoid the risk of losing patentability. Beyond this, there is the danger of a damaged reputation if the object to patent has already been revealed or inferred to by internal or external publications.
- *Identification and proof of patent infringement:* In some cases where it is difficult to prove patent infringement, it is better to classify the invention as a trade secret.
- *Usefulness for third parties:* If the patent application is too specified and for the benefit of *Swiss Re* only, the potential economic usefulness is questioned. Hence, the protected technology should be of use for other organizations as well.
- *Relevance to Swiss Re:* If an invention falls within the core competencies or other important areas of the firm's business, and if it can be avoided, competing firms should not be allowed to establish their own patents. In such a case, classifying an invention as a trade secret would be a dangerous option. The registration or publication of the patent is more advantageous than other strategies that could be detrimental to its novelty.

Swiss Re first registers inventions with strong distribution potential in Europe. As a rule, patent applications with reference to information technology are usually referenced with a higher level of technicality. *Swiss Re* systematically places patent applications in India and China, as patent applications procedures there are not too expensive and these countries with their many inhabitants are considered emerging markets. However, the emphasis on application activities generally still resides in the United States.

Organization. The central Group Intellectual Property Department, i.e. *Group IP* (GIP) at *Swiss Re* is staffed by three intellectual property managers and a part-time administrative officer. All *Swiss Re* patent activities at its headquarters and worldwide for are coordinated from Zurich. The GIP is responsible for patents, trade secrets and innovation. Lately, the

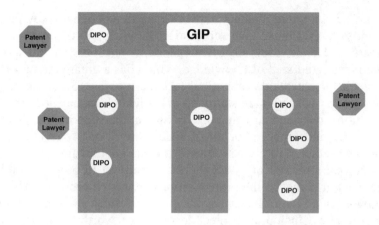

Source: Swiss Re Group IP (2005)

Fig. 27. Intellectual property infrastructure at Swiss Re

GIP has also taken over responsibility for trademarks, domain names and copyrights.

For decentralized support, *Divisional Intellectual Property Officers* (DIPOs) make themselves available to the patent departments in larger local offices (Fig. 27). They devote about 5% of their time to interests relating to intellectual property. There are three major task areas:

- *Identification of potential patent infringements:* The DIPOs compare the patent activities of third parties with the business activities of their own division.
- *Identification of inventions:* Firstly, the sensitization for intellectual property interests is increased through consultation with inventors. Secondly, the DIPOs develop a network with numerous inventors and oversee their R&D activities.
- *Identification of business opportunities:* On the one hand, the DIPOs must investigate possible patent infringements by *Swiss Re*. On the other hand, licensing opportunities with other parties should also be sought, as long as they fulfill a need or have a use for *Swiss Re* products.

The DIPOs are specifically responsible for adherence to the principles of defense and action within the *Swiss Re* intellectual property strategy. "DIPOs should be aware of any new development or invention at the earliest stage, preferably at conception", (Swiss Re 2004a). In order for DIPOs to be effective, they must be accepted throughout the organization. In addition, they must be well versed and connected within the various business areas, and have a strong contact network that includes many key partners. Importantly, DIPOs must have substantial knowledge in their area of market expertise. Hence, they are often placed in *hot spots*. A hot spot is a highly concentrated area of knowledge, which has a great potential for the development of patentable inventions. At the moment, *Swiss Re* employs 13 DIPOs, eight of whom are stationed in Zurich. Other locations that have key function areas and are in need of invention support are Germany, Great Britain, and France. For all of Asia there is only one DIPO, since there are no predicted future activities in this area at this time.

The internal structure of *Swiss Re* has turned out to be particularly favorable when it comes to the protection of intellectual property. The structure allows for an overall view of the projects, and can decide upon the proper resources, including project leaders, for worthy and appropriate projects. As a rule, DIPOs interact with project leaders on site – for the most part this occurs at the GIP. The goals and objectives of a project are discussed, and a general discussion is held to inform all sides and determine the possibilities of future actions; including patenting if necessary. The number of projects that concern the development of software is rather remarkable. Other internal target groups include actuaries and risk engineers whose job it is to simulate and analyze risk. All together, the internal *client team* is made up of close to 100 people.

The integration of the locations might optimize the central patent department even more: DIPOs' mandates can at present only be fulfilled to a certain extent. Thus, DIPOs undertake their tasks at various levels of commitment and engagement. There are power conflicts between the GIP and line management concerning the amount of work that DIPOs can allocate to intellectual property activities.

Processes. An important component of intellectual property management is the identification of inventions. *Swiss Re* sees itself first as a knowledge organization: the decision-making capabilities that are found within the minds of the employees (Swiss Re 2004b). In order for inventions to be properly identified and duly protected, *Swiss Re* has introduced a number of processes and instruments:

- *Integration of larger projects into the project management organization process:* The decision as to whether an invention is patentable depends on the project manager and the project review committee. If the project introduces novel components, the central GIP is notified and henceforth involved in the decision-making process.
- *Responsibilities of DIPOs in smaller projects and local development:* Since the DIPOs have a good network of business units at their disposal, potential inventions can be identified relatively quickly.

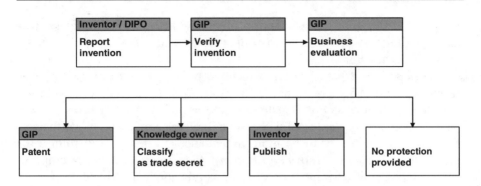

Source: Swiss Re Group IP (2005)

Fig. 28. Intellectual property workflow at Swiss Re

- *Informal network of the central patent department:* Through conversations with employees, intellectual property managers attempt to identity the current status of inventions at the company.

The most effective instrument in the identification of inventions has by a large margin been the GIP informal network: "I find out about most inventions during my coffee break" (Cuypers 2003).

A significant problem in the implementation of this strategy is that the patent department is often notified too late about patentable inventions. The reason for this often stems from premature disclosures of inventions, for instance at talks and conferences or during casual discussions with third parties.

The inventions are reported to the GIP either directly by the inventor or through the DIPO. The GIP verifies the invention and evaluates the related business opportunities on the basis of the aforementioned evaluation criteria, i.e. novelty; detection and proof of infringement; importance to third parties; importance to *Swiss Re*. The outcome is either to patent, to classify as trademark, to publish, or to provide no protection (Fig. 28).

During the invention verification process, the GIP looks for relevant prior art. At the moment, however, *Swiss Re* does not undertake complete patent analyses, due to a lack of resources. The GIP is still in its infancy, which is why there is still difficulty in discerning between tasks of equal and similar importance. In five to ten years, fully established patent analysis of (re–) insurance activities should be well underway. And with it, an ability to properly detect market trends and potential infringements. The need for and pursuit of potential collaboration partners will also be an indispensable attribute of this process. The first step of this process occurred in spring 2003, with the acquisition of multi-functional search classification instruments. With these instruments, refined analyses will now be possible in the future.

The planning of patent applications and management of procedures before the patent office are prepared for *Swiss Re* with the help of two external patent law firms. For registration and application procedures for US patents and brands, external US patent lawyers are used. Nevertheless, *Swiss Re* will endeavor to be more independent in this area in future: for proceedings before the *European Patent Office*, internal *Swiss Re* employees are increasingly formulating the company's applications.

Cultural aspects. Intellectual property is a new phenomenon in the financial services sector. Up until recently, intellectual property was perceived to be only for technology-intensive sectors, such as mechanical engineering. However, the methods and approaches in these sectors were never transferred to service sectors, such as the banking and insurance industries. For a reinsurance firm like *Swiss Re*, the interaction with intellectual property has been a new and revealing experience. Hence, for many employees, especially mathematicians and engineers, it is difficult to understand why business methods and software applications are no longer just part of regular activities, but are now identified as intellectual property that has to be protected.

Swiss Re's intention is not to elevate the role of intellectual property in its regular employees' every day activities. It will, similar to IT, be seen as a supporting element. Nevertheless, the challenge will be to educate the majority of employees that are not sensitized to or educated about intellectual property. Due to an information overload at work, most workers are not aware of or misinterpret the key information and activities that permeate their day-to-day activities. This makes it difficult for the DIPOs to ask employees to spend 5% of their day undertaking tasks that are not directly related to daily activities in the narrowest sense. For that reason, *Swiss Re* introduced a revised incentive system for inventions. The system includes monetary and non-monetary components. With regard to the monetary award, an inventor receives a monetary lump sum that is dependant on the stage that the invention reaches in the patent application and granting process. For example, an inventor receives a higher sum for the granting of a patent than for the preceding patent application. The steps of the reward process are:

- Decision to patent;
- First filing;
- First grant;

- Technology transfer (license out).

The non-monetary components include:

- Hall of fame on the intranet: Inventors are identified and honored in a special area of *Swiss Re's* intranet;
- Silver dollars;
- Inventor lunches and dinners;
- Letter of appreciation from a member of the senior management;
- Other small gifts.

Swiss Re has focused on establishing an invention culture, with a focus more on non-monetary compensation. At the same time, it is considered important to garner feedback on issues such as perception and recognition. Once a year, a special dinner is held in which all inventors are invited.

Licensing. *Swiss Re* follows an open licensing philosophy and aims to license its technology to third parties. However, within the insurance business and particularly within the reinsurance business, the big players still do not follow an open approach and do not look to adopt a competitor's technology. So, as a first approach, *Swiss Re* has initially focused on making contact with smaller players.

Swiss Re has already gathered various experiences with licensing internal technology to third parties, for example:

- A software solution invented by a *Swiss Re* contractor during his appointment. This was licensed back to his software company so that he could implement it with other clients;
- An artificial intelligence tool invented by a *Swiss Re* colleague and an external scientist. This was licensed back to their software company so they could implement it with other clients;
- A mathematical tool invented by a *Swiss Re* colleague and two *ETH* researchers. It was licensed back to the *ETH* where it should commercialize a software application using the method;
- An e-business application invented by *Swiss Re* colleagues was licensed to the software development company that programmed the implementation, in order to market it to other reinsurance players.

4.5.4 Managing Intellectual Property in R&D Collaborations

If an external third party is involved in a collaboration or R&D project with *Swiss Re*, it requires the signing of a *non-disclosure agreement* (NDA). This especially applies to collaboration projects. This document lays out and regulates any and all potential intellectual property developed during the project. Afterwards, the NDA is examined by the Group Intellectual Property Department.

Swiss Re attempts to justify, in principle, the exclusive ownership of the patents: "The patent should belong to only one party, preferably *Swiss Re*". If it is not possible for *Swiss Re* to be the sole owner of the patent, then it is conceivable that the partner be given sole ownership. Under no circumstances does *Swiss Re* want to share ownership of a patent. The advantages of the sole ownership of a patent for *Swiss Re* are the following:

- *Simplicity:* The administration of patents as well as the patent application process is substantially simplified;
- *Transparency: Swiss Re*'s patent activities can be stated openly and clearly to external and internal stakeholders;
- *Strong position in cases of patent infringement:* If a *Swiss Re* business unit concerned about a patent infringement accusation, the entire patent portfolio can be used, independent of the particular business unit, as an instrument in cross-licensing negotiations;
- *Taxes:* The expected future profit of a larger and more diversified patent portfolio is gained within a tax-favorable area, especially with sole ownership. With the patenting of technologies that are used worldwide by *Swiss Re*, there is a strong potential tax-optimizing source of income.

In return for giving *Swiss Re* patent ownership, partners are often given the opportunity to receive rights of use. *Swiss Re* has a relatively open licensing policy, which means the company wants to use the technology itself, without having to always resort to licensing. A licensing option that is not often mentioned or used, is cross-licensing. The requirement for this option is a strong and diversified patent portfolio. If it were to establish such a portfolio, *Swiss Re* would have a significantly stronger bargaining position in collaborations.

Swiss Re often takes on all patenting costs, which can be an enticing offer, particularly for smaller partners with fewer resources.

The benefits of the licensing go directly to the business unit from which the patent originated.

Swiss Re has been involved in three cases in which patent aspects were regulated. The three partners in these cases were *AlphaSoft*, *CreativeTools*, and *CompuSpec* (Müller 2004). The three collaborations focused on the development of a software solution.

AlphaSoft case. Since *AlphaSoft* developed the product on behalf of *Swiss Re*, the handling of patent ownership presented few problems. *Swiss Re* assumed exclusive patent rights over the computer program.

Swiss Re did, however, offer *AlphaSoft* a basic license. That meant that there was no material, location, or temporal exclusivity. *Swiss Re* could give away as many licenses in this area as it saw fit. It was also negotiated that *AlphaSoft* would have no rights to sub-licenses, but they were allowed to offer basic licenses to the end user. Furthermore, both *Swiss Re* and *AlphaSoft* could use developed versions of the product free of charge, this would also include all subsidiaries of *Swiss Re*.

Given that *Swiss Re* owned the exclusive patent rights to the product, it was assumed that *Swiss Re* would undertake all the patenting costs. Included in these costs would be lawyers' fees, registration costs, and certain maintenance costs. If *AlphaSoft* so chooses, it could register *Swiss Re* granted license rights . But this would normally be done at *AlphaSoft's* expense. However, since *AlphaSoft* is a small company with a minimal budget for patent applications, it was decided that *Swiss Re* would pay these costs. With regard to licensing income, it was agreed that *AlphaSoft* would pay *Swiss Re* a certain percentage per license agreement. This ended up being 35% of the net royalty, with a minimum payment of 2,500 Swiss francs.

CreativeTools case. The intellectual property regulations with *CreativeTools*, as it concerned patent ownership, usage, license rights, costs and other aspects; were almost identical to the *AlphaSoft* case. Therefore, this case is not delved into any deeper separately.

CompuSpec case. The arrangements and contract for the *CompuSpec* case turned out to be much more complicated than in the *CreativeTools* or *AlphaSoft* cases.

Within the context of their collaboration, *CompuSpec* and *Swiss Re* developed a software-based product that analyzed risk. Without contacting the GIP, a project manager from *Swiss Re* coordinated a contract with *CompuSpec* in which the intellectual property aspects were regulated. When the GIP read the contract after the fact, it became evident that *Swiss Re* had delivered on all their rights regarding intellectual property at *CompuSpec*. The GIP initiated another meeting in which *Swiss Re* invited *CompuSpec* to new treaty negotiations.

The patent ownership originally belonged to *CompuSpec*, and during further negotiations it was agreed that *Swiss Re* would eventually gain sole ownership of the patent. Obviously, concessions had to be made in order to make this happen, and they are described below.

CompuSpec received a basic, non-exclusive license in which *Swiss Re* could not stipulate further restrictions of location, matter or time. As long as *Swiss Re* was not involved or threatened by an intellectual property complaint, *CompuSpec* would normally be allowed to license the patent to business partners. *CompuSpec*, however, did not have rights to sub-licenses.

For the symbolic amount of one US dollar, *Swiss Re* took over all patenting costs, including potential process costs during a patent infringement. In order to achieve the licensing benefits, *Swiss Re* had to make compromises to receive sole patent ownership and the corresponding rights. *CompuSpec* did not have to pay any royalties to *Swiss Re*, essentially making their license *royalty-free*. In addition, *CompuSpec* received a portion of *Swiss Re's* licensing receipts. *CompuSpec* receives 30% of *Swiss Re's* license income from third parties outside the *Swiss Re Group* that which are acquired through *Swiss Re* endeavors. Seventy percent of the license income achieved outside the *Swiss Re Group* activities, and directly caused by *CompuSpec*, goes to *CompuSpec*.

InsureWell and SafeFinance cases. A practical possibility for intellectual property regulation, and one that as yet has not been attempted, is one that was tried by another enterprise in the insurance industry. The idea would result in *Swiss Re* examining geographic licensing.

An American insurance company called *InsureWell*, operating within the United States, patented an insurance product in the United States and Europe. At the time of patenting the product, for varying reasons, was considered a flop. At some point, the British direct insurer *SafeFinance* was approached by *InsureWell* about licensing the patent for this product. *InsureWell* gave up its exclusive license, and possibility for sub-licensing, to *SafeFinance*. The British direct insurer placed licenses in Great Britain and sublicenses via subsidiaries throughout Europe. *InsureWell* could thus garner benefits from licensing, while *SafeFinance* found new markets in Europe. The two insurers do not compete with each other due to their different business activities, providing a win-win situation for both parties.

Although, the above example is not based on a real innovation collaboration, it is, however, a collaboration that could be entered into given the current environment of intellectual property protection. Based on this environment, *Swiss Re* can enter into patent collaborations today that will open up new markets that would not have been available without intellectual property protection.

Due to protection of intellectual property, new market growth can be realized by expansion into various niches. Without intellectual property, collaborations within such niches could not be carried out, as there would be the problem of knowledge dilution.

Summary Swiss Re. The world's largest life reinsurer *Swiss Re* is underpinned by a long history of reinsurance business. Even though the company has no typical research and development activities, *Swiss Re* conducts numerous technical projects decentrally, in order to develop information technology solutions. Like all companies in the financial services industry, *Swiss Re* has to cope with a rising risk of third party intellectual property, a large portion of which comes from companies outside the industry sector.

On the one hand, *Swiss Re* aims for research and development collaborations to access new resources and technologies. On the other hand, as a major opportunity, the protection of own technologies through intellectual property enables collaborative market entry into new (niche) markets. Key learnings from *Swiss Re* are:

- Intellectual property is globally and centrally coordinated by a central *Group Intellectual Property Department*;
- The internal awareness of intellectual property is steadily increasing due to a decreasing resistance;
- The *Group Intellectual Property Department* is increasingly involved in the prior clearing of intellectual property rights in research and development collaborations;
- The protection of technology through intellectual property rights enables *Swiss Re* to collaboratively enter into new niche markets;
- Technology transfer is still in its infancy; *Swiss Re* aims to reach further internal acceptance and create a technology transfer market by channeling back incomes into the business units.

5 Typology of Managing Intellectual Property

In the preceding chapter, four individual case studies were presented, namely the information technology company *IBM*, the inter-enterprise software manufacturing company *SAP*, the telecommunication services provider *Swisscom* and the reinsurance company *Swiss Re*. The case studies highlight the practices within the service industry sector with respect to research and innovation, collaborative research and development activities, and intellectual property management as well as with respect to research and development collaborations.

5.1 Cross Case Analysis

Within this section, the four case study companies IBM, SAP, Swisscom and Swiss Re are compared. The cross comparison will assist in gaining new perceptions that cannot be extracted from single case analyses (Eisenhardt 1989).

As the basis for the cross case analysis, the following issues were extracted from the literature review, and the various interviews and industry projects that were conducted with the case study companies as well with other companies (for summarizing overview see Table 15, pp. 131):

Collaborative R&D activities:
- What role(s) do collaborations play in your research and development activities?
- What is the degree and basis of your participation in government-funded projects?

Managing intellectual property:
- Strategy;
- Organization;
- Processes;
- Cultural aspects.

Managing intellectual property in R&D collaborations:
- What is your licensing policy?

- What are your licensing activities (in/out)?
- What success factors apply to you?
- What role does intellectual property play in R&D collaborations?

IBM. *IBM Research* is currently experiencing a shift from science and technology to a focus on customers in R&D collaborations. There are basically three types of constructions, joint programs, service collaborations (ODIS), and so-called *First of a Kind* deals (FOAK). *IBM* distinguishes between three types of 3rd party collaboration partners: commercial partners; non-commercial partners; and partners within government-funded projects.

 IBM has a broad range of patent applications; especially in order to support business-solution-related inventions. Its intellectual property strategy sets targets with respect to:

1. Licensing income;
2. Freedom of action;
3. Reputation;
4. Risk reduction.

 A very strong criterion for invention selection is the potential licensing value of a protection by intellectual property. The majority of patent applications are placed in the United States of America. However, the company

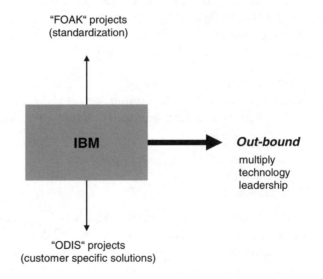

Fig. 29. IBM collaborates to multiply technology

always considers regional content, which could result in patent applications being made in Europe.

IBM has a central intellectual property department with global reach. *IBM Research* is staffed with an internal top-down intellectual property department infrastructure that reports to one central department. Furthermore, there is a global *Intellectual Property and Asset Commercialization Team* to conduct technology transfer and intellectual property licensing deals.

IBM follows clear, visible and easy-access internal processes, such as an on-line patent learning tool that trains R&D staff. For the submission of invention disclosures, *IBM* runs an intranet-based portal *Worldwide Patent Tracking System* (WPTS). An evaluation of inventions, patent applications and patents is conducted through a *Patent Value Tool* (PVT) that helps to assess whether an invention should be filed, published, or disclosed.

IBM offers various monetary and non-monetary invention achievement awards to motivate and reimburse their inventors.

Within *Open Source Software* (OSS) development, *IBM* supports *Linux Technology* and claims to be an active supporter and contributor to OSS. This support is evidenced by the recent donation of 500 patents to the OSS community. However, *IBM* still has to apply various efforts to mitigate internal OSS risks, so as not to dilute their proprietary intellectual property.

IBM follows an open licensing policy. The main licensing goal of *IBM Research* is to commercialize intellectual property. This process is supported and facilitated by an intellectual property asset catalogue.

IBM uses its intellectual property as a basis for establishing technology transfer deals and retaining licensing revenues. The company therefore pursues an *out-bound* focus in collaborations (Fig. 29).

SAP. *SAP Research* currently conducts numerous research collaborations with more than 200 collaboration partners.

Through its intellectual property strategy, the company aims to create:

1. Freedom of action;
2. Establishment of own patent portfolio;
3. Risk reduction;
4. Design access.

Due to the recently confirmed European legislation *SAP* patent applications in Europe focus on software related patent applications with attributed technical effects. *SAP* thereby focuses specific attention on e.g. user-computer interfaces that have a high impact for customer related value creation. The majority of the patent applications are categorized among three sub-classes of the patent classification group *G06F*. *SAP* tends to avoid including coding and algorithms in patent applications, and instead maintains secrecy for these kinds of trade secrets. The most often selected countries for patent protection are the United States, with a significant portion in Europe. *SAP* also seeks protection in Japan. In general the selection of first and second filings depends on the business and legal situation.

The central *Global Intellectual Property Department* takes care of *SAP Research*. In addition, within *SAP Research* there is a legal support function that at times also takes care of intellectual property issues, for example during contracting. The invention protection process starts with idea generation, invention disclosure submission, and search procedure for prior art, followed by drafting, filing and prosecution. For idea submission there is an intranet-based portal for gathering inventions that can be accessed by a wide range of inventors. The prosecution process is largely outsourced.

Within *SAP Research* there is a quantitative target for the research teams per year. Furthermore, there is a monetary incentive system that awards the inventors for filing an invention and for issuance of a patent.

Within R&D collaborations, *SAP* generally provides an open interface for their collaboration partners relating to intellectual property, but ensures to keep own core products proprietary.

SAP looks to develop a large patent portfolio, which thus far has mainly focused on reducing risk, such as patent cross-licensing agreements, e.g. with *Microsoft*. A major goal for *SAP* in conducting collaborations is to in-

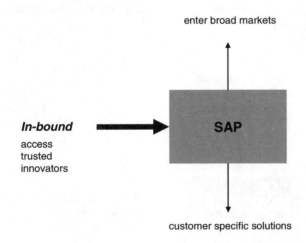

Fig. 30. SAP collaborates to in-source and to get access to new markets

source innovative capacity. Henceforth, *SAP* tries to gain the sole owner-ship rights of collaborative intellectual property within collaborations. *SAP* generally tries to in-source intellectual property on a proprietary level. The company therefore pursues an *in-bound* focus in collaborations (Fig. 30).

Swisscom. In the past, *Swisscom* has conducted R&D collaborations mainly with industry partners in order to implement technologies into its products. However, there have also been collaborations with academia that explored emerging technologies, usability studies, and pre-business cases.

The *Swisscom* intellectual property strategy has the following aims:

1. Freedom of action;
2. Generation of revenue (long-run goal);
3. Exclusivity of self-made innovations;
4. Reputation.

The focus of patent applications is on new technologies that broaden the scope of possible applications of existing technologies in the telecommu-nication market. Application criteria include novelty and potential licens-ing value. *Swisscom* primarily files in Europe; in collaborations, filing in other markets is often left up to the partners.

Swisscom maintains no central intellectual property department. At the group level, however, separate intellectual property departments are re-sponsible for the individual organizational design in managing intellectual property. Therefore, every group company is responsible for the disclosure and progression of its inventions.

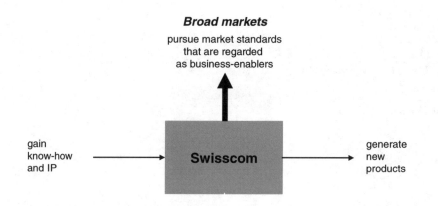

Fig. 31. Swisscom collaborates for standardization

Swisscom follows an open licensing policy, although the whole licensing process still finds itself at an early stage.

Within collaborations, the highest priority remains the generation of new products that can be marketed, mainly with a specific focus on standardization. Other goals include: creation of know-how, observation of recent technological developments, and generation of intellectual property.

Swisscom uses collaborations to establish standards that are regarded as business-enablers. At the same time, collaborations are a useful means through which to gain know-how and intellectual property, and generate new products. The company approaches *broad* market sizes by collaborations (Fig. 31).

Swiss Re. For *Swiss Re*, R&D collaborations are designed and aligned to match the company's long-term perspective philosophy. So far, various collaborations have taken place with a number of partners.

The *Swiss Re* intellectual property strategy has the following aims:

1. Risk reduction;
2. Freedom of action;
3. Establishment of own patent portfolio;
4. Licensing income;
5. Design access.

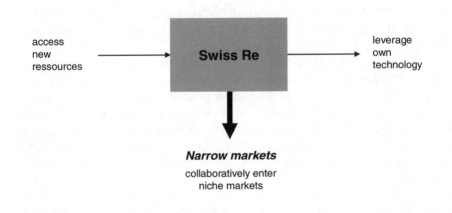

Fig. 32. Swiss Re collaborates to expand into niche markets

The focus for patenting is on business models that run off computer systems, for example the e-business-based reinsurance products. Their characteristics have not necessarily been associated with (re-) insurance products. Whether a patent application is filed or not depends on certain criteria, including novelty, identification of infringement, usefulness for third parties, and relevance to *Swiss Re*. The country selection focuses on Europe, the USA, India, and China; with the latter two being relevant emerging markets with many inhabitants and potential customers.

The *Swiss Re* intellectual property activities are internally organized as central *Group Intellectual Property Department* (GIP). This central entity is supported by decentralized, part-time *Divisional IP-Officers* (DIPO). *Swiss Re* considers it essential to integrate larger projects into the project management organization, which is of paramount importance when seeking inventions. The DIPOs' responsibilities are focused on smaller projects and local development with respect to identification of potential patents and risk of infringements, identification of inventions, and identification of businesses and opportunities. Legal activities are largely outsourced to external law firms.

Swiss Re has an internal patent awareness program with monetary incentives on four levels (disclosure, application, issuance, licensing). As far as remuneration is concerned, there are non-monetary incentives that reflect the inventors' cultural and regional backgrounds.

Swiss Re follows an open licensing policy. The company is becoming very experienced and successful in out-licensing technology to third parties. The first approaches are focused on small external business entities that are interested in in-licensing technology.

For *Swiss Re,* internal intellectual property is often the only guarantee to prevent dilution within collaborative technology development activities; and to secure potential new market segments. An important goal for *Swiss Re* in collaborations is to gain access to new resources, especially new technologies. Due to protection through intellectual property, collaborative growth can often be realized by expansion into various new niche markets. The company expands into *narrow* market sizes through collaborations (Fig. 32).

Summary. Table 15 provides the cross overview of the general data concerning the four case study companies in the service industry sector.

In the next section, the characteristics of the single case studies are retrieved in order to finally deduce the relevant characteristics to extract determinants and to present a typology for managing intellectual property within R&D collaborations.

Table 15. Cross overview of case study companies

Criteria	IBM	SAP	Swisscom	Swiss Re
General company data:				
Industry sector	Business solutions	Software solutions	Telecommunications	Reinsurance
Service typology	Professional Service	Mass Service	Service Factory	Service Shop
Revenue (in bill.)	96"5 $ (2004)	7"5 € (2004)	10"1 CHF (2004)	29"4 CHF (2004)
Net income (in bill.)	8"4 $ (2004)	1"3 € (2004)	1"6 CHF (2004)	2"5 CHF (2004)
R&D expenditures (in mill.)	5,600' $	15' € (only research)	40' CHF (Swisscom Innovations)	n.a.
No. of employees	~319,000	~32,000	~15,500	~8,000
Number of patents / families*	37,000 / 10,000*	750* (patent applications in year 2003)	240 (Swisscom Innovations and Swisscom Mobile)	~52*
Patent applications p.a.	~3.600	~750	<50	~30
Patent activities since	< 1900	1998	1994	2001

5.2 Extraction of Determinants

With the exception of *Swiss Re*, the case study companies have central research departments that are globally diversified, i.e. *SAP Research*, *IBM Research* and *Swisscom Innovations*. These research units build up, maintain and secure know-how, technologies and intellectual property that are relevant for their companies' businesses. At *IBM*, the research group maintains a strong focus on multiplying its technology leadership through transfer and licensing deals.

With the exception of *IBM*, the companies have only started actively taking intensive care of their intellectual property within the last decade. These companies were strongly impacted by external influences that led them to intellectual property strategies that focus primarily on reducing risk exposure with respect to third parties' intellectual property. While *Swisscom* is the most regional of the companies, the other ones run centrally coordinated intellectual property departments that act globally. *Swisscom*, in comparison, runs several intellectual property departments at the business group level that mostly act independently of one another. *Swiss Re* has to put significant effort into identifying valuable inventions due to its lack of a central R&D department and the novelty of intellectual property in general.

All the companies employ various monetary or non-monetary incentives to award process steps, from the submission of invention disclosures, patent applications and issuances through to intellectual property leverage in transfer deals. *SAP* and *IBM* provide intranet portals for a broad range of inventors to submit invention disclosures. *IBM* even employs an evaluation process per invention that is supported by an internal software tool.

The focus of patent applications lies in application-based inventions, and the user-machine-related interfaces that provide good protective leverage. *Swiss Re* looks for opportunities to protect new business models that run on computer systems, e.g. e-business based reinsurance products. Most of the companies in general follow an open licensing policy that must be displayed with regard to potential individual limitations, due to antitrust legislations.

All four companies are involved in R&D collaborations. Intellectual property issues are generally part of the R&D collaborations that are established before the collaborative phase is entered. However, the goals and backgrounds vary from case to case. *SAP* currently handles more than 200 collaboration partners while in-sourcing innovative capacity and establishing customer-specified and broad market fields. *IBM* establishes collaborations with regard to out-licensing and out-transfer technology, know-how and intellectual property. Projects vary from collaboration-partner-specific content to broad range market development. *Swisscom* uses collaborations to establish standards that are regarded as business-enablers. At the same time, collaborations are a useful means with which to gain know-how and intellectual property, and generate new products. *Swiss Re* collaborates to gain access to new resources and leverage their technology. However, collaborations represent good opportunities to enter into and establish new (niche) markets without the burden of first-mover risks.

The cross analysis of the four case study companies has brought up four determinants that vary significantly from case to case as a basis for managing intellectual property in R&D collaborations:

- In-bound;
- Out-bound;
- Narrow;
- Broad.

An overview of these four determinants with respect to the four companies is shown in Table 16. The significance of the characteristics is rated as being high, middle or low.

Table 16. Determinants of managing intellectual property in R&D collaborations

Determinants	IBM	SAP	Swisscom	Swiss Re
In-bound	low	high	middle	middle
Out-bound	high	low	middle	middle
Narrow	middle	middle	low	high
Broad	middle	middle	high	low

Therefore, one can conclude that there are two independent main dimensions for managing intellectual property in R&D collaborations (Fig. 33a/b):

1. The *collaboration focus* dimension: *in-bound* versus *out-bound*;
2. The *market size* dimension: *narrow* versus *broad*.

Within the *collaboration focus* dimension, a partner may have the goal of in-sourcing intellectual property within the R&D collaboration. The in-sourcing serves to obtain access to trusted innovators and to new resources. One can, furthermore, gain know-how and intellectual property.

On the other hand, out-sourcing may enable the generation and market introduction of new products by approving technology leadership and by leveraging own technology.

Within the *market size* dimension, a partner may want to use the R&D collaboration to enter broad markets and standards. Intellectual property therefore assists access to technical standards and functions as a business-enabler to leverage broader markets.

Intellectual property can also be used to narrow market sizes such as niche markets by enabling a collaborative market entry. The main applications are, for example, customer-specific projects and customer-specific solutions.

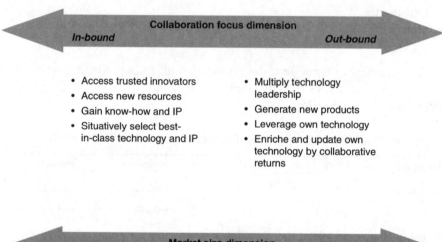

Fig. 33a/b. Characteristic dimensions for managing intellectual property in R&D collaborations

5.3 Assignment of Archetypes

Based on the opposed extremes of the two independent dimensions introduced above, one can therefore differentiate four types of intellectual
property management in R&D collaborations (Fig. 34):

- Multiplicator;
- Leverager;
- Absorber;
- Filtrator.

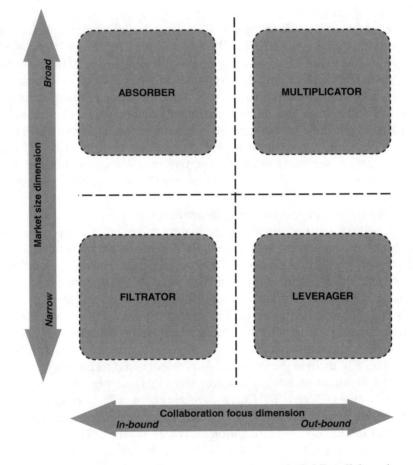

Fig. 34. Typology of intellectual property management in R&D collaborations

5.3.1 Multiplicator

The *Multiplicator a*ims to multiply its intellectual property in R&D collaborations in order to approach broad market sizes. Consequently, the *Multiplicator* needs a strong intellectual property position that, in general, is part of a broad technology leadership. Both form the interdisciplinary basis and act as business enablers for different markets or set a market standard. The *Multiplicator* has to ensure that it reaches and maintains low exposure with regard to other parties' portfolios to prevent itself from being attacked by those parties and their intellectual property. This would result in the *Multiplicator* losing its margin of the collaboration profits, e.g. licensing income and, even worse, risk its credibility with respect to the collaboration partners.

An example of a *Multiplicator* is *BT Exact*, the research, technology and IT operations business of *British Telecom (BT)*. The research group specializes in telecommunications engineering, leading-edge network design, IT system and application, development and has extensive expertise in business consulting and human factors. Its knowledge helps its customers across the *BT Group* and, in selected other businesses, to gain maximum advantage from their investments in communication networks and IT systems, to develop new capabilities and to open new opportunities. *BT Exact* brings together the technological expertise of *BT*'s research laboratories and the operational experience of the teams that design and operate *BT*'s IT systems.

For *BT Exact*, collaboration with other industries is fundamental. A fruitful way of getting research into products and systems is to arrange their transfers to appropriate partners. *BT Exact* uses those partners to help and explore intellectual property. The company also has an open licensing policy. The telecommunication branch is strongly dependent on standardization activities and it would be very difficult to apply exclusivity indefinitely. To optimize its multiplication strength, *BT Exact* uses a general exploitation matrix for structuring and segmenting exploitation fields and as to assist with the steps that should be taken during decision-making. These deals generally include the transfer of knowledge and technology.

The exploitation of intellectual property rights supports the securing of the supply chain. Today, *BT Exact* increasingly uses its licensing activities to grow the market with respect to the upper telecommunication value chain and to support standardization activities where intellectual property is an important asset in strengthening the negotiation position. *BT Exact* seeks an exploitation partner's external help for licensing in North America. *BT* thus aims to speed-up the mining process and to increase engagements.

5.3.2 Leverager

The *Leverager a*ims to leverage its intellectual property in R&D collaborations into narrow market sizes, such as niche markets. Similar to the *Multiplicator*, the *Leverager* needs a strong technology and intellectual property position. For business reasons, e.g. the need to keep a market as exclusive as possible and to not grow competitors, a knowledge, technology and intellectual property transfer might only be considered reasonable to other markets, e.g. to markets with which the *Leverager* itself is not familiar with, or markets that are too small to enter.

The software giant *Microsoft* has developed an intellectual property licensing program as an alternative to its former offensive strategy. This program is called *Microsoft Intellectual Property Ventures* and aims to make the exploitation process of intellectual property more predictable and more transparent (Informationweek Smallbizpipeline 2005). The goal of the licensing program is to further exploit technologies that were developed by *Microsoft* but have remained unused so far (Yahoo News 2005). A *Microsoft* technology that does not expect potential revenues of at least one billion US dollars, or that does not fit into the product portfolio is released to the program (Beck 2005). Currently, there are about 20 *Microsoft* technologies for which a license is being offered, e.g. face recognition software, data visualization tools, biometric ID cards and even the program *XP-Conference* that uses audio, video and network technology for long distance conferences (Informationweek Smallbizpipeline 2005; Yahoo News 2005). Within this program, *Microsoft* offers specific licenses in respect of these technologies to start-ups and small companies. In return, *Microsoft* asks for an equity share in the licensee partner. The licensing conditions are defined on a case-by-case basis, but are not public. In commercial terms they are fair and match the general industry standards. However, licenses are only given on a non-exclusive basis. Through this, *Microsoft* safeguards multiplication opportunities with respect to other potential licensees (Yahoo News 2005).

If the *Leverager* has a strong position, it might be able to commercialize its intellectual property without establishing an R&D collaboration, i.e. to just license the intellectual property that might still be enriched with know-how and technology. However, the difficulty with pure licensing deals is to receive a sufficient back-license option, including technology and know-how access, to maintain technology leadership.

Eastman Kodak follows three core business activities: *Photography*, *Health Imaging* and *Commercial Imaging*. About 3,000 scientists work in its corporate research organization at 14 different R&D centers in six countries. *Eastman Kodak* interacts with industrial partners. They invest relatively high efforts to understand and clarify each other's businesses and responsibilities. All parties have to understand every detail before an agreement is signed. However, it is also a question of negotiation power.

Eastman Kodak has proved to be a strong player, even when it comes to leveraging technology leadership into non-core niche markets: In 2004, *Kodak* sued *Sun* on the basis that *Sun's Java* language infringes certain object-oriented patents that *Kodak* acquired when it bought *Wang*'s imaging unit. The claim sought more than a billion dollars in damages, basically half of the operating profits *Sun* made from January 1998 to June 2001 by selling its servers and storage units. The companies finally settled the case with *Sun* paying 92 million dollars for the *Kodak* technology license.

Eolas versus Microsoft: Moving from being a Leverager to being a Multiplicator. Due to a patent infringement decision in August of 2003, *Microsoft* must pay more than a half billion US dollars. A US Federal Court awarded Chicago-based *Eolas Technologies* and the *University of California* upwards of 520 million US dollars (460 million euro); Microsoft subsequently appealed. In its defence *Microsoft* said the patent was invalid because it was pre-empted by the *Viola* web browser of which two versions were publicly available in the early 1990s. *Microsoft* further claimed that *Eolas* founder Michael Doyle knew about the *Viola* browsers but did not reveal this to the *USPTO*.

The court found that *Microsoft* had infringed a patent in its browser Internet Explorer, which had been co-developed between *Eolas'* CEO and single employee Michael Doyle and the *University of California*. In essence, the case concerns a technology, one that enables access to interactive programs imbedded in web pages. *Eolas* was established in 1994, specifically to distribute the software on which the University had an appropriate patent. *Eolas* and the *University of California* accused *Microsoft* of having integrated their technology into Windows.

Eolas' victory over *Microsoft* and its Internet Explorer browser sent shockwaves through the web and the software industry. *Microsoft* has vowed to fight the judgment, although the standards body the *World Wide Web Consortium* (W3C) is not waiting for the appeal. The W3C is investigating whether the venerable *Hypertext Markup Language* (HTML) is also an infringement. It seems that the 'object' and 'embed' tags in HTML may fall under the wording of the *Eolas* patent. It is thought that the W3C is on the verge of funding a "patent advisory group" to determine if there is a problem. *Eolas* certainly thinks there is: "If you read the trial testimony, you'll see references several times to experts who testified that browsers that support the 'embed' and 'object' tags are covered by the patent," according to Doyle (Edittech International, 24.09.2003).

Two years after the *USPTO's* director ordered a reexamination, the *Eolas* patent's validity was reaffirmed by the Office in 2005, which is likely to affect the outcome of litigation that will decide whether or not *Microsoft* is liable for patent infringement (MIP Week 03.10.2005).

5.3.3 Absorber

The *Absorber* aims to absorb outside intellectual property in R&D collaborations on a broad market size level. In order to do so, the *Absorber* must be an attractive collaboration partner, e.g. due to its strong market presence, or as a valuable purchaser.

Collaboration with an Absorber: The *Siemens Information and Communication Mobile Group (ICM)* operates in a market in which close inter-firm collaboration is required to survive due to mobile phones' high complexity and the converging media (voice, data, graphics), chip, software, network and micro technology.[17] Hence, collaborative innovation processes are likely to form a vital part of the mobile industry and to take place on a horizontal, vertical and diagonal level.

In this market segment, network providers usually act as *Absorbers*. The network provider (*Absorber*), e.g. does research on *ICM's* patents in a specific field, in order to discover its related competencies and competitive position. Another common practice is to publish an invitation to bid and then choosing the partner that can best fulfill the requirements. Unlike cellphone manufacturers, network providers are fewer in number and consequently have strong negotiation power. They are therefore able to select their partners carefully, and to dictate conditions, if necessary. For technology providers like *ICM*, this means developing innovative capabilities consequently and always being at the forefront of development in order to gain competitive advantage and be an attractive partner for other companies. Appropriate protection, e.g. publication, patents, and secrecy, also plays an important role in this context. Once a partner has been chosen, a collaboration contract is signed, which normally includes intellectual property rights and licensing agreements.

As a mobile phone manufacturer, *ICM*'s interest is obviously to produce as many similar phones as possible in order to achieve economies of scale. To reach this goal, the company needs the market leader as its partner, or needs to have the possibility to deliver products to other network providers as well. On the other hand, *ICM* would like to be the exclusive supplier of a certain technology and not allow its partner to order other mobile phones with the same features. However, the network provider is interested in a unique position regarding specific services and might therefore claim exclusive rights himself. *ICM* would consequently lose a significant market, while competitors could soon provide similar solutions in conjunction with the network provider. In the presence of all these conflicting interests, an agreement between equal partners, e.g. different manufacturers, would

---

[17] *Siemens* sold its *ICM Group* to the Taiwanese electronics enterprise *BenQ* in 2005.

most likely look as follows: the intellectual property rights are allocated in accordance with common law, while full exploitation rights are granted to each partner. However, the unequal power between network providers and mobile phone manufacturers leads to rather varying agreements: it is quite possible that, in some cases, the ownership rights are fully awarded to the network provider partner, while *ICM* only obtains the right to use the intellectual property resulting from the R&D collaboration. Because each case is unique to a certain extent, the allocation of rights is always decided case-by-case. The quantity and quality of the intellectual property of a mobile phone manufacturer, like *ICM*, remains an important issue that can improve the company's negotiation power significantly.

Furthermore, the *Absorber* has to take care of keeping an adequate back-currency for the absorbed intellectual property and technology, e.g. market access or even its own intellectual property.

Another example is *Microsoft,* whose CEO Steve Ballmer emphasized the high relevance of intellectual property portfolio management during the 2005 Venture Capital Conference. He announced that *Microsoft* would sometimes spend more money on acquiring or generating intellectual property than on developing the specific technology (Beck 2005). *Microsoft* has accumulated more than 11,000 patents and patent applications in 15 ECLA patent classification categories.

Patent infringement complaints in the software industry have become more prevalent, particularly in the United States. This is particularly true in respect of large organizations: *Microsoft* has filed more than three dozen patent infringement complaints since 1988 and has received more than 30 from other parties. Companies often settle judicial proceedings, such as *Time Warner* and *Netscape* did with *Immersion*, and with *AT&T*. *Microsoft* paid out 1.95 billion US dollars to *Java*-based *Sun Microsystems*. Nor can small companies escape the world of patent law, as evidenced by the Santa Clara-based (California) *Inter Trust Technologie*. The company filed a suit pertaining to a set of 30 patents relating to DRM Technology (Digital Rights Management) against *Microsoft in* 2001. The result of this suit was a 440 million US dollars payout by *Microsoft* to *Inter Trust Technologies*, and a user license for the patent portfolio for *Microsoft* and the end users of Windows operating systems.

Perhaps as a result of these experiences, *Microsoft's* intellectual property strategy focuses on efforts to reduce its own exposure to third parties' intellectual property. What ever the case may be, *Microsoft* is looking for cross licensing agreements that give the company access to valuable and intellectual property portfolios that could perhaps otherwise be problematic (Beck 2005). So far, *Microsoft* has signed cross licensing agreements with *Cisco Systems*, *Hewlett-Packard*, *IBM*, *SAP*, *Siemens*, *Sun Microsystems*, *Unisys* and *Xerox* (Informationweek Smallbizpipeline 2005).

5.3.4 Filtrator

The *Filtrator* aims to filter-in missing and complementary intellectual property within R&D collaborations while approaching narrow market sizes to gain access to trusted innovators and to gain collaborative, customer-specific projects. The *Filtrator* has to be capable of selecting a suitable collaboration partner, i.e. a suitable source of intellectual property and technology for the specific niche market. The *Filtrator* also has to ensure that its rights concerning the in-sourced intellectual property are good enough, both generally and specifically, whether the collaboration is concluded in a normal way or aborted; in failing to do so, the *Filtrator* risks becoming dependent on the intellectual property collaboration partner. If the *Filtrator* has a strong position, e.g. as a solution provider owning a strong market brand, it might be possible to take over control, thereby preventing a drain via the delivering collaboration partner to competitors.

Even though the German logistics and financial services enterprise *Deutsche Post World Net* clearly focuses on service innovations, it is an apt example because its range of services depends heavily on a technical backbone. By pursuing an active intellectual property management, the company filters-in best-in-class technical content from outside, while realizing consequent cost cuts to secure its leadership with regard to other international competitors. Earlier, *Deutsche Post World Net* might not have gone to great efforts to receive adequate access to the fruits from its interfirm R&D collaborations, i.e. the intellectual property when, e.g., co-developing automated letter and parcel distribution machines. But this policy led to a larger knowledge drain than the enterprise found necessary. Today, this has clearly changed: *Deutsche Post World Net* even bought various companies to secure market, technology and intellectual property access in order to accelerate its businesses in the fields of letters, express, logistics and financial services.

The consumer goods manufacturer *Henkel* manages to successfully collaborate with partners. The company has developed the following approach for its specific branch segment: *Henkel* no longer insists on entirely obtaining all intellectual property rights that are derived from collaboration. The collaboration partner may keep, e.g., the patents, utility models and trademarks that result from its collaboration work. *Henkel* might even support the partner with its own know-how. The advantage for *Henkel* is that it has become very attractive for suppliers to collaborate with *Henkel* and that the collaborations have reached a high level of mutual trust. As *Henkel* is a rather small company compared to some of its competitors, it is important for them to maintain relationships with the best suppliers and other potential partners. In return, *Henkel* receives, e.g., an exclusive purchase agreement for a specific period of time. A typical exclusivity time frame is two years.

Summary. Table 17, p. 143, provides an overview of the characteristics of the four types of managing intellectual property in R&D collaborations.

In the next chapter, the four types will be further enriched by a theoretical basis based on the literature review. By cross comparison with the case study companies from the preceding chapter, several hypotheses are formulated to create an empirically grounded theoretical model for managing intellectual property in R&D collaborations.

Table 17. Characteristics of intellectual property management types

	Multiplicator	Leverager	Absorber	Filtrator
Collaboration focus	out-bound	out-bound	in-bound	in-bound
Market size	broad	narrow	broad	narrow
Description	Multiplicates IP into broad markets on a collaborative basis to set standards which are regarded as business-enablers.	Leverages own IP to enable collaborative market entry into niche markets and customer-specific projects.	Absorbs broad IP sources on a collaborative basis to enrich own IP and to gain access to standards.	Filtrates IP sources to gain access to trusted innovators and to gain collaborative, customer-specific projects.
Strengths	Strong in technology and IP position; low exposure.	Strong in technology and IP position within a certain market/technology.	Strong market presence, e.g. valuable purchaser.	Strong in market-specific niche market.
Weaknesses	Danger of being attackable by third party IP with regard to own technology and products.	Dependency on collaborative improvements and relating IP.	Need for adequate back-currency to license IP, e.g. market access or own IP.	Need for own competence and IP to fully satisfy customer needs on its own.
Opportunities	Value of own technology can be multiplied by participating in third parties' business opportunities while profiting from technological improvements through back-licenses.	Participate in other market business opportunities; bind suppliers or customers to develop leading-edge technology.	Get access to valuable IP without market restrictions; reduce own exposure.	Situational selection option for best-in-class collaboration partner; gain customer-specific projects.
Threats	Risk to loose credibility as technology leader and source for valuable IP.	Risk of not being in the position to keep/receive the collaborative improvement, i.e. the IP.	Risk of being attacked by third parties due to large exposure and due to few own IP.	Risk of being too dependent of IP suppliers or loosing market segments to them.

6 Theoretical Implications

6.1 Derivation of Propositions

Based on the literature review in chapter two several anticipated *core components* for managing intellectual property in the early stages of R&D collaborations can get extracted.[18] With respect to the findings for characterizing collaborations (Kale, Singh and Perlmutter 2000), these core components are structured into the three categories for managing intellectual property in R&D collaborations (Table 18): *motivation*, *structure* and *performance*. Based on the core components derived from theory, propositions are induced. These propositions are proven in a second step by means of an in-depth comparison with the case studies presented in chapter four to formulate hypotheses (Eisenhardt 1989).

Table 18. Categories and core components for managing intellectual property in R&D collaborations

Motivation-related core components
▪ Main goal of collaboration;
▪ Prior experience with collaborations;
▪ Information asymmetry, trust and power.

Structure-related core components
▪ Strategic compatibility;
▪ Implementation capability;
▪ Complementary commercialization capability.

Performance-related core components
▪ Collaboration formation capability;
▪ Intra-firm relationship capability;
▪ Legalization capability (policy process).

---

[18] The term *core components* describes the constitutive elements for forming an overall comprehensive concept (Enkel 2005).

6.1.1 Motivation

(1) Main goal of collaboration. Intellectual property can be generated internally or externally (Ernst 2002a). It is therefore an important issue for a collaborating company to know whether the collaborative activities will create intellectual property. This could also depend on the company's general attitude to in-bound and out-bound licensing. The anticipated patenting output depends, however, on the sectoral partnering and patent intensity and finally on the sectoral strength of the intellectual property (Hagedoorn 2003).

During the early stages of R&D collaborations, it is the technologies that matter most. At these stages, the acquisition of intellectual property is often of secondary importance. However, intellectual property often turns out to be the final outcome of such collaborations. The longer a collaboration project lasts, the more tangible the outputs become.

Proposition 1:

The collaboration partners make use of inter-firm R&D collaborations to generate new intellectual property.

(2) Prior experience with collaborations. The capability of knowing when it is the best time to enter a collaboration, of selecting highly fitting collaboration partners, and of administrating a collaboration relies strongly on prior experience with inter-firm R&D collaborations (Anand and Khanna 2000). The quality of this process also depends on the capability to scan and monitor third party intellectual property to find and evaluate a suitable collaboration partner (Abraham and Moitra 2001). The overall ability to manage intellectual property in collaborations depends on intellectual property management skills and is therefore dependant of the level of prior experience with a joint patenting process (Hagedoorn, van Kranenburg and Osborn 2003).

Proposition 2:

Prior experience within inter-firm R&D collaborations influences the capability of the collaboration partners to manage related intellectual property issues.

(3) Information asymmetry, trust and power. In general, the collaborating partners must accept that they may not know everything about their partner. However, during the early stages it is essential for the potential partners to clearly understand the reciprocal interests of the participating collaborative partners (Chiesa, Manzini and Toletti 2002). The number of collaboration partners influences the extent of the collaboration partners' knowledge of one another (Becker and Dietz 2004). Even though experts from patent departments might support the collaboration procedure by identifying open issues and recommending solutions, information asymmetry can also occur due to other influences. One example is the difficult issues that are often faced due to uncertainty resulting from anti-trust legislations, which is a major issue within the car manufacturing industry. Very relevant in the partnership decision is the level of trust between partners (Chiesa, Manzini and Toletti 2002).

Proposition 3:

Information on intellectual property that is publicly available and enriched with specific R&D collaboration know-how reduces information asymmetry and fosters trust between the collaboration partners.

6.1.2 Structure

(1) Strategic compatibility. Companies that collaborate generally do so because of a lack of resources or competencies, which are necessary to form an autonomous standard. From their research, Chiesa, Manzini and Toletti (2002) concluded that there were three bases of motivation for a standardization procedure in the form of a development collaboration. The first is to reduce the risks and costs of standardization, the second is to increase and complement the available skills and competencies, and the third is to increase the market power favoring the introduction of the technology to the market. Another important selection criterion for choosing partners is determining if the shared resources are complementary (Nooteboom 1999; Miotti and Sachwald 2003). Therefore, strategic fit greatly depends on the level of the competitiveness between the collaboration partners.

Proposition 4:

Partner selection depends on the complementarity of the collaboration partners' resources, including the intellectual property.

(2) Implementation capability. Inter-firm collaborations based on joint R&D is one of the most significant reasons for forming alliances, especially in high-tech industries and in the emerging technical industry sectors (Mowery 1988; Mytelka 1991; Hagedoorn 1993; Arora and Gambardella 1994; Colombo 1995). But even in other industries, such as manufacturing, R&D collaborations may have a positive effect if there is sufficient absorptive capacity (Veugelers 1997). With respect to the information and communication technology industry sector, the more alike the technological portfolios of the collaboration partners, the easier it is to mutually absorb each other's capabilities (Santangelo 2000).

Successful collaborating parties therefore agree to exchange specific information about intellectual property rights before, during and even after the collaboration. During the finalization of contracts, the most difficulties often occur while resolving content-related issues. These difficulties can include trying to solve which party should receive which rights of use.

Proposition 5:

The level of joint R&D within inter-firm R&D collaborations influences the level of joint intellectual property.

(3) Complementary commercialization capability. Another important part of the partnership decision process is assessing the coalition's market power (Chiesa, Manzini and Toletti 2002). However, it is common practice to split patent ownership and rights of usages according to the collaboration partners' business models, as the partners might like to use the intellectual property in different markets beyond the scope of the collaboration. In those cases, the partners will need to agree to bilateral conditions. Another reason why exclusivity might be preferred is that both partners want to avoid situations where the competitors can easily obtain access to their collaboration results and thereby reduce their competitive advantage. Another possibility is to agree to time-limited exclusivity, or to declare certain market sectors exclusive, for example the high end or low end of the market. However, the value of exclusivity needs to be established with respect to product volume and the value versus cost ratio for customers.

Proposition 6:

The individual collaboration partners' business models influence the level of exclusivity, e.g. of ownership rights, rights of use and licensing rights.

6.1.3 Performance

(1) Collaboration formation capability. In order to be able to form a collaboration, the collaboration partners have to undergo a process of collective identity building. The collaboration partners thus rely on three elements when collaborating: the willingness to collaborate, means of communication and a common purpose to justify the collaboration (Segrestin 2005). However, during the collaboration process formation, finding the right moment to broach intellectual property issues is crucial, especially during the early collaboration stages or standardization procedures (Bekkers, Duysters and Verspagen 2002).

Another practical issue deals with deciding whether intellectual property issues should be involved at all. If the decision is positive, it should not be dealt with too late in the early stages of the R&D collaborations.

Proposition 7:

The collaboration partners' expectations concerning intellectual property influence the set-up of the inter-firm collaboration.

(2) Intra-firm relationship capability. Within a company, there are several factors that influence the company's capability to handle collaboration processes. A main factor is the managers' experience in handling people and relationship issues early in the collaboration stages (Kelly, Schaan and Joncas 2002). As a prerequisite for successful collaborations, top-management should clearly support the collaborations' reciprocal goals. The companies' intellectual property departments often need to deal with the inherent problem of researchers' preferences for disclosing information as soon as possible. It is thus important to understand that early in the collaboration formation phase researchers already often anticipate who their partners are likely to be. Legal staff is often only involved much later and are regularly only asked to handle unpleasant situations.

An increase in the number of new R&D collaborations towards the end of a fiscal year is important for firms in order to quickly invest the remaining allocated budgets. This puts pressure on the legal staff, as they need to conduct several negotiations and finalize contracts within a limited period of time. Intellectual property departments strive to proactively inform and educate their R&D and marketing people about the procedures necessary to maintain an adequate level of quality and security. Those responsible for concluding the collaboration are then able to operate in a goal-oriented manner, while simultaneously knowing the essential do's and don'ts. It has been found that internal patent awareness committees, formed by participants from various departments and functions, form a key basis for internal training and inter-communication.

Proposition 8:

Firm-internal procedures and processes influence the capability to successfully handle intellectual property issues concerning inter-firm R&D collaborations.

(3) Legalization capability. There is evidence that legal procedures play a dominant role, as formal rules and legal devices have often proved tangible instruments for a collaboration's cohesion. Furthermore, legal instruments define the conditions of entry into or exit from a collaboration as well as defining the results or opportunities and analyzing the sharing procedures or risk and opportunity assumption (Segrestin 2005). It is common practice, especially in large enterprises, to maintain a selection of standardized contract samples for various situations. The onus is then placed on the other parties involved to change any element of the contract. However, it is evident that dealing with intellectual property processes in collaborations can rarely be standardized, since most situations faced must be handled on a case-by-case basis.

Proposition 9:

Standardized goals, processes and contractual intellectual property elements influence the ability to handle intellectual property issues when forming a collaboration.

6.2 Induction of Hypotheses

6.2.1 Motivation

(1) Main goal of collaboration. Contrary to all other kinds of collaborations, the generation of intellectual property forms the core of any research collaboration for *IBM*. Therefore, *IBM* treats intellectual property aspects as a crucial part of most agreements, especially as these aspects can lead to major disputes or even prevent collaborative activities. The whole point of intellectual property, the appropriate level of protection and allocation of rights is to maintain *freedom of action*. Once an agreement is achieved, the intellectual property is usually no longer subject to major disputes. This process might take years, though. At *IBM*, the Business Development function specifically assesses whether the planned collaborations are reasonable regarding in respect of the strategic and technical aspects as well as the core technologies. If the technology in question is considered strategically important and a potential future core technology, *IBM* tries to contract the technology and abstain from collaboration. In such a case, *IBM* could develop the technology in-house, or order or buy the development and therewith obtain the rights.

SAP maintains strong partnerships with various universities, e.g. *University of Karlsruhe* and various customers, e.g. *BP*. The research collaborations are based on the belief that customers do not strategically consider the impact, opportunities and risks of new technologies. Therefore, *SAP's* main goal for collaborative research is to find a way to gain new customers and to motivate the existing customer base to join into the research projects.

SAP always tries to find suitable partners. While universities fill the role of basic knowledge suppliers, industrial partners tend to provide business scenarios that are expected to influence product development.

The current collaboration projects are often established with a technology research perspective. However, the business perspective is becoming increasingly important. Collaboration provides the opportunity to work with both partners and potential customers.

SAP often takes the lead in its collaborations as project coordinator. Very profound and trustful relationships form the basis for partner selection with various research institutes and universities.

Swisscom's main goal for entering collaborations is the generation of new technology and products that can be broadly marketed. Other important goals include gaining know-how, the observation of recent technological developments and the generation of intellectual property.

Swiss Re still copes with two emotions within the company: On the one hand there is the traditional open attitude, while on the other hand there is the residual internal focus on independence and the self-development of products. In the past, product developments stemming from collaborations were of lesser importance. Marcel Bürge, Head Risk Engineering & Training, feels that the old paradigm is still important for individual employees who think that self-development is better than developments in collaborations with external partners.

The learning culture within *Swiss Re* is slightly more conspicuous than in other firms in the financial services industry. The *Swiss Re* guidelines state (Swiss Re 2003): "We share our information with others, and pass on our knowledge. We constantly promote the development and dissection of knowledge. We encourage a culture of learning in the company. We are open to new situations."

Hypothesis 1:

The higher the expected outcomes of an inter-firm R&D collaboration, the more important the individual intellectual property exploitability of the collaboration partners becomes.

---

(2) Prior experience with collaborations. Based on a good deal of experience with respect to the benefits and issues of collaboration projects, *IBM* evaluates three critical issues before entering a collaboration: generation of tangible value; freedom of action; and protection of the competitive advantage. At *IBM*, a case-by-case attitude still forms the basis for the process according to which intellectual property from collaborations is handled. The limited exclusivities of certain exploitation rights illustrate this practice.

SAP currently conducts research collaborations with about 200 partners from different industries and research organizations and often takes the lead as project coordinator in its collaborations.

As a former monopolist, *Swisscom* generally needs to take care of antitrust legislation when entering collaborations. *Swisscom* has some experience concerning collaborations with academia that were targeted at the exploration of emerging technologies, usability studies and the set-up of pre-business cases. More importantly, *Swisscom* mainly experienced innovation collaborations with industry partners on a project basis in order to push the market introduction of new technologies. Although intellectual property does not play a major role in this type of collaboration, it should not be neglected. Therefore, *Swisscom* developed an informal pattern of pre-entering checks to try to avoid inefficient and ineffective collaborations.

Swiss Re has had collaborations with a number of partners in the past. Essentially, the common invention mindset of both parties has played a supporting role in these partnerships. *Swiss Re* has so far not yet signed licensing contracts with more than one party at any given time.

152 Theoretical Implications

Innovation collaborations led *Swiss Re* to work with their partners up to a certain point. This solution is obvious, since a larger number of partners requires a more complex set of contract rules, resulting in a substantial increase in costs for *Swiss Re*.

Hypothesis 2:

The more experience a collaboration partner has gathered with intellectual property issues in inter-firm R&D collaborations, the better this partner is able to establish and realize its interests concerning intellectual property.

---

(3) Information asymmetry, trust and power. At *IBM*, trust is considered a main factor that influences the choice of a collaboration partner. Although small companies might be impressed by *Big Blue* and therefore see power as an important factor in collaborating with *IBM*, power is usually not of great importance at the research level at *IBM* itself. Therefore, *IBM* tries to build up trust through balanced contracts to ward off an imbalance of power.

SAP's experience has proved that very profound and trustful relationships form the basis for partner selection for collaborations with academia, technology partners and customers.

Swisscom focuses on the possible potential of combining knowledge from otherwise separate technology fields. At *Swisscom*, the partner's complementary knowledge and therewith the information asymmetry are regarded as the central motivational factors which might lead to radical new products. Other aspects like trust are only regarded as additional dimensions that play a major, but secondary role.

Donat Bischof, an intellectual property manager at *Swiss Re*, recently noted: "*Swiss Re* always shows its cards, and maintains honest, up-front dealings with current and potential partners in order to create clarity and trust".

On the other hand, *Swiss Re* expects a similarly open, communicative approach from its partners. Within the first few meetings with representatives from the other company, *Swiss Re* can determine the appropriateness in this regard.

However, it must be noted that in its collaboration with *CompuSpec*, there had been some difficulty during the contract negotiations. Specifically, it was felt that *CompuSpec* might not have always been upfront, forcing *Swiss Re* to handicap certain elements of the collaboration to protect their rights, while still saving the collaboration. Afterwards, it was established that some of those rights could be recovered if an admission or concession was made regarding some of the prior dealings.

The collaborations with *AlphaSoft* and *CreativeTools* were conducted on a smaller scale with smaller partners, in contrast to the collaboration with a larger partner like *CompuSpec*. However, the size of partners is irrelevant to *Swiss Re*, as it looks for the best situations and partners irrespective of size and power. In the collaboration negotiations with the smaller partners, the emphasis was placed on finding commonalities, and ensuring that the license agreement was a win-win situation for both sides.

Hypothesis 3:

The more open the information exchange philosophy of the collaboration partners, the more likely it is that balanced collaboration contracts with respect to intellectual property can be closed.

6.2.2 Structure

(1) Strategic compatibility. Concerning the compatibility of collaboration partners, *IBM* specifically focuses on an equal level of know-how and skills from which both partners can benefit. These requirements concern the collaborating teams' know-how and less the partners' general knowledge. Over the years, the company has had very good experiences with a *symmetric* model in joint research and development as well as with joint patenting. Based on these experiences, *IBM* is convinced that both a mutual contribution to the project is a good starting point, and that any agreements that might hinder one of the partners after the collaboration, are disadvantageous for learning and innovation. Consequently, *IBM* does not usually sign any contracts that restrict its capability to exploit potential outcomes, for example, regarding certain companies, regions or markets.

At *SAP*, the selection of collaboration partners is based, on the one hand, on existing relationships. On the other hand, an overall fit must also be reached. In partly government-funded projects this means to determine the ideal firm size and country portfolio. At *SAP Research*, partner selection criteria could follow any of the following strategic aspects: reaching potential *SAP* customers that are interested in collaborating with *SAP* on research level; approving research relationships; and contributing to own research and business agenda. But it also has to find good answers for these questions: the business activities into which the collaboration topic really fits; the form the intended consortium takes; the European Union's acceptance of the research proposal; how to find win-win-situations, while staying within the core competencies; how to avoid that partners do not significantly enter into each other's core competencies; and how achieved research results shall be divided between the collaboration partners. Non-government funded projects normally are based on similar research road maps between the research partners.

An example is *MobileCorp's* search for mobile phone based applications. On the one hand, *MobileCorp* and *SAP* have a similar research road map and their collaboration makes sense. On the other hand, there is the risk that *MobileCorp* might be getting too much access to *SAP's* software competences. This differs from the general case where customers such as hardware companies hand over some of their hardware to be used by *SAP* for software development and testing. Both parties would not fear any overlap of competencies. *SAP* would not expect the hardware partner to move into software applications and vice versa. Under these circumstances the clients approach *SAP* for such a collaboration.

Swisscom enters collaborations with partners from outside the telecommunications industry (non-competitors) and partners that are located in their value chain. Strategic compatibility is therefore not of crucial importance, as the collaboration partners may have different objectives, which do not harm each other. An excellent illustration of this is the collaboration of *Swisscom Mobile* with *Atrua Technologies* in which both partners reached an excellent fit of their company business models.

As an internationally active enterprise, *Swiss Re* has entered into collaborations with a wide array of partners worldwide. For the most part, collaborations are formed with universities and research institutes. There are also collaborations with competitors, but those arrangements are dependent on the decision of each respective department within *Swiss Re*.

Of all of the innovation partnerships, all but three partners were from Switzerland and were not in direct competition with *Swiss Re*. The partnerships with *AlphaSoft* and *CreativeTools* can be characterized as contract collaborations, with *Swiss Re* being the contractor. Both partners are noticeably smaller than *Swiss Re*. The collaboration with *CompuSpec*, a company larger than *Swiss Re*, is in the form of an R&D collaboration.

Hypothesis 4:

The better the strategic, compatible fit between the collaboration partners, the more likely it is that a balanced intellectual property model can be found for the R&D collaboration partners to support learning and innovation.

---

(2) Implementation capability. *IBM* does not have an accurately defined procedure for the allocation of rights on entering collaborations, as the company treats every collaboration as an individual case. *IBM* therefore usually suggests a fairly easy solution to its partners, although the agreements reached may vary from case to case (Fig. 35). For example, an evaluation agreement might be reached for testing prototypes. Nevertheless, when *IBM* wishes to exchange confidential information, it will aim at a *non-disclosure agreement* or an *agreement for exchange of confidential information*. Without such an agreement, the partners risk obtaining too much confidential information at a stage when there is still uncertainty regarding the collaboration itself.

IBM generally enters into a *joint research agreement*, or into a *joint development agreement* when undertaking collaborative R&D activities. Joint research agreements are usually agreed on to protect *IBM's* intellectual property and confidential information from publication. Joint development agreements often aim at jointly developing certain product components. The latter agreements also comprise licensing issues to enable development. A mutual balance of know-how and exchanged information is essential in this case, since no payment is due or owing by any party to any other party under a joint development agreement.

Collaboration activities can either have a product-related character or an explorative character. Product-related activities are mainly organized between *IBM* and Japanese industries. Licensing and charging aspects depend on the specific project. Such activities are more difficult to organize and need more arrangements to handle possible difficulties like potential bankruptcy or the exit of the collaborating partner.

During the explorative activities in respect of a technological transfer, the collaboration's focus is on the enlargement of technical competencies, skills and potentials as well as the mutual gain of knowledge. In such explorative collaborations, the implementation of the freedom of action is driven by simple and clear arrangements aimed at agreeing and entering the partnership. Each partner and its subsidiaries have gratuitous rights to use the project-related know-how and intellectual property that evolve from the collaboration, although inventions are not generally shared. The rights of use only consider foreground knowledge, which is knowledge developed during the collaboration. Background knowledge, which is each partner's pre-existing knowledge, is protected in advance and can be licensed. This *IBM* approach has proven to be very practical and has never led to serious disputes or misunderstandings among the industries involved. The rules simply state that whoever makes the invention also gets the ownership rights, similar to most patent laws.

Know-how generated through collaboration can be licensed without the agreement of the partner, as mutually generated know-how is considered free and independently available for use by each of the involved parties. This regulation does not yet apply to marketable products. Joint innovations establish joint patenting rights, for which both partners generally receive full exploitation rights. After analyzing the potential risks or financial consequences of such an approach, *IBM* sometimes does not include the related paragraphs in the agreement in order to avoid intellectual property disputes and further time-consuming negotiations. The increased harmony in national patent laws allows this behavior, which is, moreover, often appreciated by the counterparts, especially small companies. The possibility of co-applicants or co-inventions is generally not useful, as both parties would have to apply, translate and register. This requires significant time and effort for the administrative coordination from both parties.

Typical characteristics of *SAP's* collaborative research projects are: duration of two to three years; competency augmentation through diverse con-

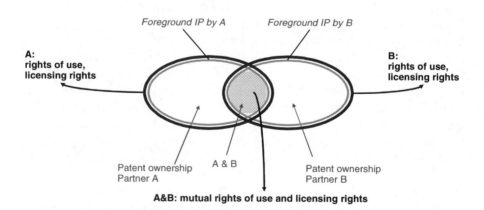

Fig. 35. Allocation of intellectual property rights at IBM (standard solution)

sortia; risk sharing through cost sharing and joint applications for partly governmental funding. *SAP* insists in collaborative research projects that intellectual property belongs to the inventor, while joint intellectual property is shared.

Swisscom clearly focuses on industrial partnerships whose target is to push the market introduction of new technologies. Based on its desire to yield results, *Swisscom Mobile* has developed a four-step selection process from the intellectual property perspective. These four steps include: an analysis of potential partners' patent portfolios, the definition of complementary intellectual property, the identification of potential benefits and the decision to enter a collaboration or drop out. *Swisscom* generally handles collaborations and intellectual property issues case-by-case. Where intellectual property is developed mutually, costs and profits are shared. However, *Swisscom* often manages to take ownership of later patents and therewith becomes responsible for all related costs. A non-exclusive right of use is then granted to the partner. If a collaboration were to result in any products, each partner would be responsible for any associated fees and costs.

In the *Atrua Technologies* case, the resulting technology was patented. *Atrua Technologies* holds the patent for the biometric sensor that identifies the user's fingerprint, and *Swisscom Mobile* holds the patent for one special feature implemented in the device: the ability to communicate with a mobile phone's SIM card, governing the resulting data stream. *Swisscom Mobile* now plans to license this technology by generating a related market, thereby earning royalties on the jointly developed technology.

Swiss Re has only been involved in a few licensing agreements so far. Nonetheless, the company strives to learn: "We have made some mistakes, and will likely make more, but this will lead to successful and sustainable licensing agreements".

The constant focus on intellectual property in collaborations requires much time and commitment on the part of many employees, something that increases costs significantly. However, based on patenting, certain partnerships are possible that could not otherwise have taken place.

Hypothesis 5:

The more concrete ownership rights, rights of use and licensing rights have been aligned by the inter-firm R&D collaboration partners, the better intellectual property and joint intellectual property can be handled by the collaboration partners.

(3) Complementary commercialization capability. There are no standards without exceptions. *IBM* too made some compromises, especially regarding joint intellectual property. A typical situation is when the *IBM* partner is a company operating within a niche of minor importance to *IBM*, which minimizes *IBM's* potential risk. Such agreements include, for example, the allocation of technical inventions' ownership rights with respect to components or systems, and exploitation rights regarding different geographical regions. In general though, markets are not subject to related arrangements and a fragmentation of the rights of use and licensing rights will therefore only occur as an exception. However, the pharmaceutical industry is a good illustration of this practice. Long research periods for testing and prototyping products normally cause high investments for pharmaceutical companies. To regain these investments, they might need to ensure the most exclusive position in respect of their development outcomes. In such a case, *IBM* might have to abandon the right to use the intellectual property required by the pharma-related foreground and leave it to the partner (Fig. 36). This condition might even turn out to be a prerequisite of the pharmaceutical partner for entering the collaboration. The foreground intellectual property will then be divided between *IBM* and the partner as it relates to each market. Other fragmentations are always possible, but are rare exceptions.

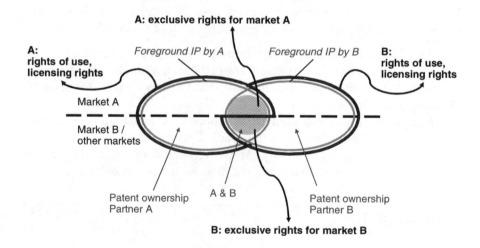

Fig. 36. Allocation of intellectual property rights at IBM (exceptional solution)

At *SAP*, the compatibility between the partners depends on the anticipated deliverables of each partner, and their compatibility. It is important to ensure that there is no overlap in the usage of research results post-collaboration. At this stage, there is a need to have a look into technical content and details. Very often strong efforts have to be taken to jointly develop an agreement that mutually ensures each others interests and defines suitable exit criteria for the case of an earlier termination of the agreement. In principle, each partner may use the joint research results, but only on basis of its own research contribution and intellectual property.

Swisscom considers commercialization capability as a crucial criterion in collaborations. As a result of the enforcement of implementation capability, *Swisscom's* collaborations mostly need to result in saleable products. From a financial perspective, both intellectual property and cross-license agreements have only recently gained attention in the telecommunications services industry. A first external licensing contract was recently signed with *idQuantique*.

For *Swiss Re*, collaborations are designed and aligned to the company philosophy, taking a long-term perspective. A long-term, intensive partnership often results in a win-win situation for both sides.

The locked-in licensing agreement with *AlphaSoft* has a duration of four years, the agreement with *CreativeTools* lasts around three years. There is a tacit agreement in both cases that allows the contracts to be extended by a year. The contract with *CompuSpec* runs for the life of the patent, which is up to a maximum of 20 years. However, there is no set agreement between the parties beforehand that establishes a long-term relationship. Instead, that decision is made in each specific situation.

Costs, which can be decreased through the protection of intellectual property, also play an important role. The easily imitable (re–) insurance products, which could not be fully protected in the past, can take on greater importance through possible intellectual property protection. Thereby, licensing income from patents can be a good source of income.

Hypothesis 6:

The lower the anticipated overlap of the collaborative intellectual property is, the more realistic it is that a mutual fit can be found to use and exploit the collaboration results, including the intellectual property.

6.2.3 Performance

(1) Collaboration formation capability. If collaboration is foreseen by *IBM*, the actual partner selection is usually left to the scientists. The most important factors that influence the start of a collaboration are former experiences with this partner, common interest in the subject, proper communication and information exchange. Usually it is a scientific decision whether or not to collaborate at all. Yet the kind of collaboration is determined more by the scientists with their high specialization in certain research domains, and within a small worldwide network of scientists.

At *SAP*, a Research Business Development Team initiates collaborative research projects. For *SAP*, patents play a relatively important role within collaboration projects. The quantity of achieved invention disclosures has even become an indicator of project success. *SAP Research* sets a quantitative invention goal measured per project, which is included in personal target agreements and effects salary bonuses.

Swisscom has neither formal limitations nor numerical restrictions on the choice of potential collaboration partners. Due to *Swisscom's* history as a monopolist, the company has to take care when collaborating with direct competitors to avoid possible cartel structures. Therefore, long-term collaborations with competitors have not as yet been taken into consideration, especially not in the same geographical market.

Right at the initial phases of a collaboration, when partners get to know each other and the first bits of information are shared, it is essential for *Swiss Re* to identify the implicit knowledge within their own firm. Importantly, any new knowledge developed in collaborations must be identified before it enters the public domain.

At *Swiss Re*, funded patent analyses of (re–) insurance activities are underway. The aims of these analyses will be to detect market trends, prevent patent infringements, and assist in choosing the appropriate collaboration partner. A first step towards this goal was reached with the introduction of a multi-functional search and classification instrument in the spring of 2003. This will make it possible to conduct verifiable analyses in future.

Hypothesis 7:

The clearer a collaboration partner has defined its goals and needs concerning the collaboration's intellectual property outcomes, the clearer it can evaluate the anticipated benefits of the inter-firm R&D collaboration in advance.

---

(2) Intra-firm relationship capability. Especially during the early stages of collaborations, *IBM* is sometimes confronted with internal difficulties due to conflicting perspectives between the collaborating level and the negotiating level. Whereas the latter still negotiates with the partners' attorneys, the collaborating level might already be working with the partners' scientists. Language and cultural aspects may also play a role, as researchers generally communicate in a different way than attorneys do. Whereas researchers act in a solution-driven and technology-orientated way, lawyers have to consider the worst cases. To diminish this gap, attorneys inform the researchers about the risks and advantages of good contracts and good documentation.

At *IBM*, the legal department reviews all contracts and in the case of a non-standard contract, it employs the intellectual property department to examine the relevant intellectual property issues. In this *IBM* matrix-organization, the *IBM* patent attorneys of both the research and intellectual property organization work together in order to smooth their various interests. To enable the researchers to work freely and independently, *IBM* strives towards closing good contracts: "A good contract is a contract you never have to look at again".

At *SAP*, in the corporate *Global Intellectual Property Department* the patent professionals have dedicated internal customers and follow a specialization in various fields. Consequently, technical expertise is backed by a constant contractual and legal expertise, ensuring that there is an internally harmonized and continuous representation of *SAP's* corporate interests.

Swisscom's top-management is willing to support collaborations, especially as innovation that might be strengthened by patents is important to the company. The research group *Swisscom Innovations* that is the main developer of intellectual property, acts as a link between the group companies and monitors potential synergy effects.

There is no explicit R&D department within *Swiss Re*. As a rule, research and development activities are carried out in practically every business unit, yet there is no central R&D department. It is a known fact that there are researchers, of varying numbers, in each of the departments. This *Swiss Re*-specific peculiarity does not mean that they do not enter into R&D collaborations. Rather, they do so without the coordination and involvement of a central R&D department.

It is not only difficult to account for which business group takes on the most collaborations, but also what innovation collaborations are being conducted in the individual business groups at any time. Within the realm of financial services, there have been only some patents thus far. However, it is anticipated that more patents will be created in this area, along with more external partnerships. These undertakings highlight the ever-increasing importance of financial services and innovation collaborations. The current innovation collaborations can be characterized as R&D collaborations.

Hypothesis 8:

The more accepted the collaboration partners' intra-firm relations between internal stakeholders, e.g. intellectual property department, legal department, R&D department, are, the more efficient and effective the evolution of the collaborative intellectual property decision-making processes and procedures.

---

(3) Legalization capability. *IBM* basically considers all collaboration models as a possibility, and therewith shows great readiness to negotiate fair and appropriate agreements. Yet, certain alternative models turn out to be impractical, for example, the unclear definition of criteria and appropriate allocations is regarded as risky by *IBM* and a potential cause of future disputes. The *symmetric* standard solution is therefore usually applied and is intended to provide enough incentives to reach the collaborative goals. The majority of the partners perceive the symmetric model, in which they are mostly free to license the collaborative outcomes, as mutually fair. Nevertheless, there are partners who do not perceive this as enough, and who would also like to gain a share of the revenues that *IBM* generates with its licensing policy. This is not practical, due to *IBM's* numerous and complex licensing contracts and is thus refused by *IBM*. Moreover, *IBM* fails to see why the partner should additionally benefit from *IBM's* successful practices.

Based on long years of practice, *IBM* attempts to keep its negotiated contracts relatively short, clear, and practical. Like many other large companies, *IBM* attempts to enforce its standard contract paragraphs when negotiating a bilateral agreement.

SAP generally insists on its own standard agreements for collaborative projects. *SAP* makes a distinction between pre-existing knowledge and collaborative knowledge. Pre-existing intellectual property is kept exclusive within collaboration agreements. The only exception is that of open interfaces. For collaborative intellectual property, *SAP* seeks single patent ownership, although joint inventions are shared.

Swisscom has a high interest in applying clear regulations and guidelines to intellectual property issues in R&D collaborations. The partitioning of employees' activities in respect of collaboration and for *Swisscom* exclusively is, e.g., subject to intellectual property allocation agreements during the set-up phase. Also classification agreements help to prevent intellectual property that is developed in collaborations from diffusing into the involved collaboration partners before property rights are defined.

At *Swiss Re*, collaborations, which were once regulated on the basis of patent aspects, are now explicitly regulated using licensing agreements. In general, parties often enter into collaborations without fully understanding the intellectual property component. In a *normal* collaboration, therefore, a basic agreement is often enough to get things started. However, "as soon intellectual property gets involved, things become more complicated".

Hypothesis 9:

The sounder the combination of goals, processes and standardized elements on intellectual property issues, e.g. contract paragraphs, as well as on an individually decided case-by-case basis, the less negotiations on intellectual property issues hinder the start of an inter-firm R&D collaboration.

---

7 Managerial Implications

After having analyzed the case studies to deduce an intellectual property management typology in chapter five, a cross case analysis was applied in chapter six to analyze the theoretical implications of managing intellectual property in R&D collaborations by deriving hypotheses. On basis of the aforementioned findings, the managerial implications are discussed in this section to arrive at a typology-based management model for managing intellectual property in R&D collaborations.

The implications with respect to managing intellectual property in R&D collaborations will be described according to four major views:

- Scope of contract;
- Terms of contract;
- Procedural aspects;
- Collaborative settings.

First, the *scope of contract* is presented with respect to the related content and the resulting value of the R&D collaboration. Second, the *terms of contract* are analyzed with regard to the different legal issues addressed in collaborative agreements. Third, the *procedural aspects* of managing intellectual property are derived with respect to pre- and post-conditions within R&D collaborations. Fourth, the *collaborative settings* are analyzed with regard to the dynamization of intellectual property management.

Finally, based on the typology of intellectual property management, the theoretical implications are reduced to practice by developing a conceptional model for intellectual property management in R&D collaborations.

7.1 Scope of Contract

As described in Fig. 37, the scope of contract varies with respect to the further values that are included in an R&D collaboration:

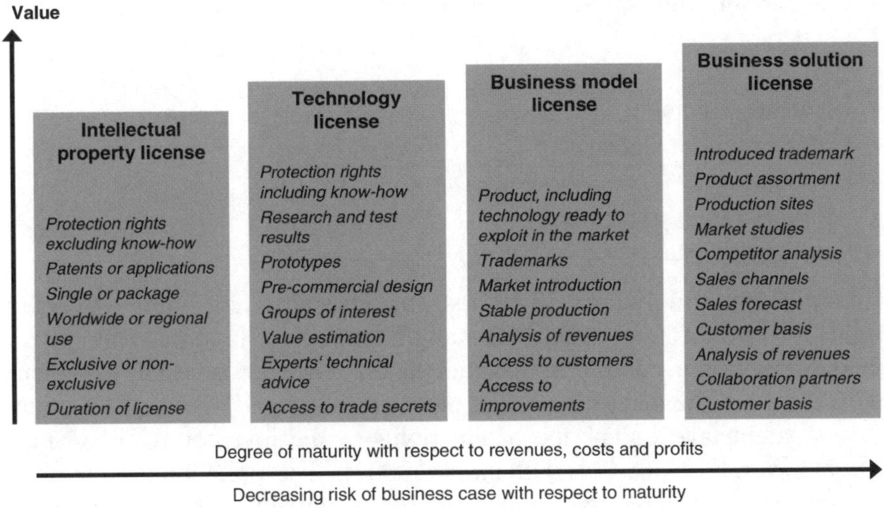

Value

Fig. 37. Scope of contract in R&D collaborations

- Intellectual property license;
- Technology license;
- Business model license;
- Business solution license.

A purely intellectual property license includes only legal rights and leaves technology and market risks entirely to each of the collaboration partners. Conversely, a business solution license at least includes an almost ready market with an existing customer basis and therefore involves a much higher degree of maturity with respect to revenues, costs and profits.

7.2 Terms of Contract

Collaborations are generally characterized by a high degree of mutual dependence. At the very beginning, the partners need to make extra efforts to develop a common vision. The parties can substantiate this vision by formally agreeing upon subjects such as benefits, ownership, costs and resources. The purpose of conducting these negotiations is not only to establish a clear legal basis, but also to maintain and support the common vision. Based on our research on intellectual property rights, the following issues need to be addressed with regard to R&D collaborations:

- Inventorship rights;
- Ownership rights;
- Rights of use;
- Licensing rights;
- Enforcement of rights;
- Prosecution;
- Administration of rights;
- Sharing of costs.

Inventorship and ownership rights. Inventorship rights and ownership rights are two different aspects in many national legislations. While inventorship rights are commonly granted to the inventor, national laws vary with regard to the determination of patent ownership. For example, United States patent law assigns the patent rights to the inventor (United States patent law 35 U.S.C. 111; Dillahunty 2002). The collaboration partners should therefore agree upon who gets the ownership rights by taking the relevant national legislation into account. In this context, the partners should clarify the matter of joint inventorship, i.e. inventions with inventors from both partners. If this issue is not explicitly resolved, ownership of the patent is in principle and by default solely determined by the ownership of the invention. The problem is that in such cases each collaboration partner will try to make as many inventions as possible without the involvement of the other. At the same time, each partner will try to get rights to the inventions made by the other partner. This results in severe mistrust on a working level. Instead of collaborating and synergizing, collaborators tend not to work together and eventually separate.

Collaboration partners can avoid this problem by delinking the ownership rights from the inventorship rights. Ownership could be determined according to the area to which the invention relates, e.g., system-related

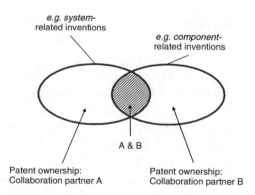

Fig. 38. Patent ownership according to content of invention

inventions might be assigned to partner *A* and component-related inventions might be assigned to partner *B*, irrespective of which partner's inventors were involved. Joint inventions could result in joint ownership (Fig. 38).

Alternatively, all the rights to inventions could be assigned to one collaboration partner, or the rights to all the inventions could be assigned jointly to all the collaboration partners (Fig. 39a/b). This might be useful for optimizing the patent prosecution process and for avoiding state of the art disputes. The partners can also agree to share or redistribute the patents after their issuance. This could be done by the above-mentioned method. This might be relevant where cultural differences play a role, like in Japan (Nakano 2000).

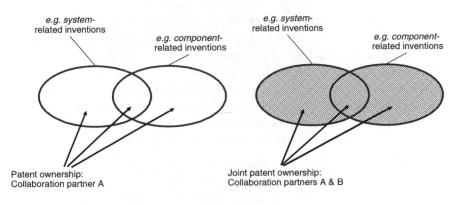

Fig. 39a/b. Single or joint patent ownership

Rights of use and licensing rights. The rights of use and the licensing rights can be apportioned in accordance with the distribution of the ownership rights (Fig. 40). However, jointly owned intellectual property might cause problems in some legislations. In the United States of America, each patent owner of a jointly owned patent has the right to use and give licenses to others without the permission of the co-owner (O'Reilley 2000). This can result in negative competition and can have cannibalizing effects on the collaboration partners' business. On the other hand, in Great Britain, Japan and Malaysia, a patent owner may give a license only with the permission of the co-owner (Brown 2000; Nakano 2000; Siaw 2000). The partners can agree to share the licensing revenues of jointly owned patents.

One drawback of the above-mentioned solution is that it might not sufficiently take individual collaboration partners' key motivational factors into account, e.g., a component-producing collaboration partner might like to sell its components not only to its system collaboration partner, but also to others. Likewise a system collaboration partner might like to acquire components not only from the collaborating component collaboration partner, but also from a second source.

One solution to address collaboration partners' different concerns is to agree upon the exclusivity of markets and areas of use to the collaboration partners, e.g. market A versus market B. Or it could be all other markets, but market A (Fig. 41).

Where the first alternative is viable, the jointly owned intellectual property can be used and licensed exclusively in market A by collaboration partner A and in market B by collaboration partner B.

The second alternative is to extend this idea to all intellectual property, i.e. to exclusively and jointly owned patents: collaboration partner A can exclusively use and license the collaboration intellectual property in market A and partner B in market B (Fig. 42).

The advantage of the second solution is that collaboration partner A can give a license for use to a second source supplier within its market A. Collaboration partner B can acquire further customers and give them an extended license for use outside the market A (Fig. 43a/b).

Enforcement of rights. Enforcement of rights depends strongly on national law. Questions that need to be answered during the early stages of collaboration agreements deal with how a collaboration partner needs to be involved so that he can enforce intellectual property rights in respect of an infringer. If national law requires the involvement of all partners, this should be part of their collaboration agreement and need to be agreed upon in advance according to the above-mentioned rights of use and licensing rights.

Litigation against third parties may be conducted jointly, which would result in the sharing of costs and recovery payments. If one party wishes to litigate on its own, there is an obligation to ask the other partner whether it wishes to join. If not, the costs and recovery payments belong to the litigating party.

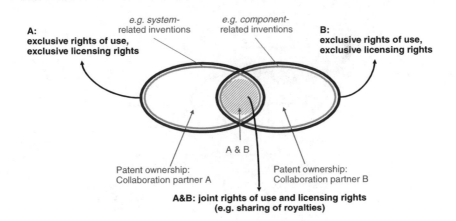

Fig. 40. Rights to use and licensing rights

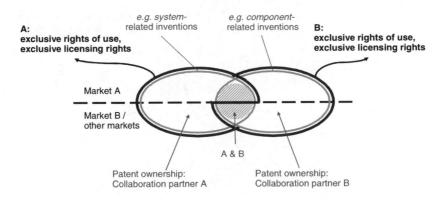

Fig. 41. Separating jointly owned rights of use and joint licensing rights

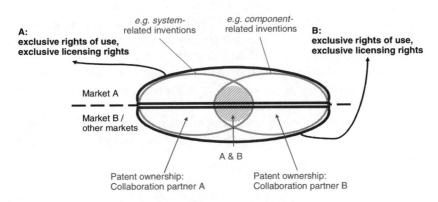

Fig. 42. Market-defined, exclusive field of use and licensing rights

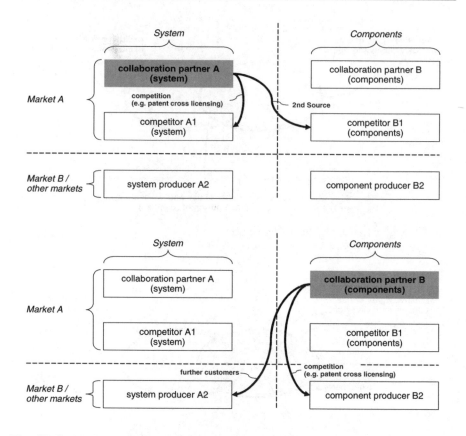

Fig. 43a/b. Market-defined, exclusive licensing rights

Prosecution, administration of rights and sharing of costs. In the early stages, the partners can also agree upon who should be ultimately responsible for the administrative process of drafting, filing and applying for the patent. They can also agree upon the decision-making process, e.g. to decide on which inventions should be selected for further processing and in which countries, on the administrative process that needs to be followed to reach these decisions and, if needed, the kind of outside counsels that should be sought in the latter case.

Finally, the sharing and apportionment of costs incurred in the procedures described above also need to be decided in advance by the collaborating parties.

7.3 Procedural Aspects

Collaborations are generally characterized by a high degree of mutual dependence. During the early stages of a collaboration, partners need to make an extra effort to establish a common vision. Parties can substantiate this vision by formally agreeing upon subjects such as benefits, ownership, costs and resources. The purpose of conducting these negotiations is not only to establish a clear legal basis, but also to maintain and support the common vision.

Within this research work, motivation-, structure- and performance-related core components for managing intellectual property in R&D collaborations have been extracted. However, collaborating partners should not focus only on the collaboration phase, but must look at the prerequisites and post collaboration stage. The value of a collaboration's outcome for each of the partners also depends greatly on the value of the relevant knowledge and the intellectual property rights that are not directly part of the collaboration as such. When the collaboration partners intend to exploit the fruits of the collaboration on their own, they might be especially dependent on the resources of the other partner.

Therefore, it is important to identify the relevant intellectual property rights that were created before, during, outside and after the collaboration time frame. These can be classified as *background*, *foreground*, *sideground*, and *postground* intellectual property as well as *residual information* (Fig. 44). Very often a collaboration partner requires more specific rights than just the *foreground* intellectual property that is created during the collaboration. Moreover, those rights are needed to create a second source of knowledge, or to acquire a new customer and derive a practical benefit from a license to use. For these reasons, to a further extend relevant intellectual property should also be considered early and become part of the collaboration agreement.

Considering the clear and simple contribution of rights, especially as demonstrated by the *IBM* case, the collaboration has to be seen in the context of time. The most important decisions and negotiations for the project are especially made during the early stages. Confidentiality during that period plays a major role in ensuring that secrets are kept in-house while the collaboration is still uncertain. If an exchange of confidential information is necessary for the negotiations, two developments are likely: the partners are either likely to sign a collaboration agreement, or they need further information for their negotiations. In the first case, the exchange of confidential information could be described in an actual collaboration agreement, e.g. in a joint development agreement. In the second case, further negotia-

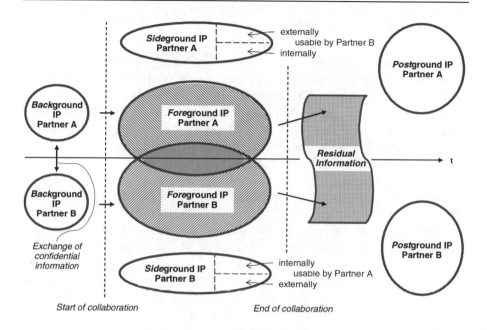

Fig. 44. Procedural aspects of managing intellectual property in R&D collaborations

tions are probably necessary. The exchange of confidential information could be determined in a separate agreement such as an agreement on the exchange of confidential information, or a non-disclosure agreement.[19] As seen in Fig. 44, at this point the project-related *background* intellectual property is mutually shared and may be used for any internal purpose by either party. Internal means no disclosing, publishing or disseminating exchanged information to any third party.

Once the collaboration has started, the use of certain in-licensed *background* intellectual property might be divided into royalty bearing and royalty-free parts. These obligations will be specifically determined on a case-to-case basis, except for joint development agreements that usually do not contain any royalty obligations. The *foreground* intellectual property developed by one or both parties will be shared and is considered free and independently available for use by either party as described above. *Sideground* intellectual property developed during the collaboration period, but in not-project-related activities, should be classified according to the form in which it will be used in future. It can also be divided into confidential

---

[19]   An example for a model agreement for the exchange of confidential information is given in the appendices, pp. 229.

and non-confidential sideground intellectual property. Difficulties obviously only occur if the intellectual property is regarded as confidential. It might be used internally in research activities or in explorative activities, or externally within other projects. If it is used internally, no critical confidentiality questions occur, unless it is published or disseminated. For external use, which means third parties might have access to that information, one partner needs to obtain permission for the disclosure to a third party in written form from the other partner. If this partner is not willing to agree to the request, the information has to be kept confidential, as agreed upon in the collaboration agreement.

After termination of the collaboration, the information related to the project activities and kept in the memories of the participants, such as ideas, concepts, know-how and techniques, is defined as *residual information*. *Residual information* represents an intangible volume and is difficult to evaluate. It should be clearly defined whether any obligations are imposed on this information. Usually it may be used freely, unless confidential, and can be disclosed, published or disseminated. New intellectual property that is created during a certain period after the termination of the collaboration, such as five years, might still be classified as *postground* intellectual property. Both partners may consider to grant each other certain rights, for example rights of use, to cover various improvements developed and applied by one or the other partner after the termination of the R&D collaboration.

7.4 Collaborative Settings

There are three different main collaborative settings in R&D collaborations as shown in Fig. 45a/b/c: bilateral, multilateral and collateral. While bilateral and multilateral collaborations are based on bidirectional relations, collateral collaborations have a higher complexity and especially demand attention when managing the intellectual property. The management of intellectual property in a collateral setting environment is therefore further described as follows:

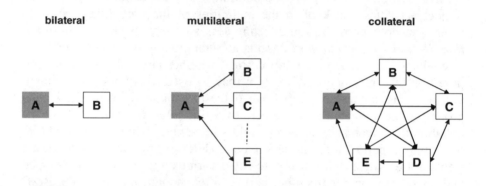

Fig. 45a/b/c. Different collaborative settings of R&D collaborations

Access to intellectual property. As indicated in Fig. 46, party *A* could receive access to the intellectual property and pre-existing intellectual property of the other partners *B* to *E*. Access will depend on the nature of the project, and, if granted, it means they would not have to pay royalties. After the collaboration, however, only the intellectual property created during the collaboration may be used for internal or non-commercial research. If access to pre-existing intellectual property is necessary, party *A* has to apply for a license. The other partners cannot repudiate this application as long as party *A* does not use its part of the collaboration results without using the license.

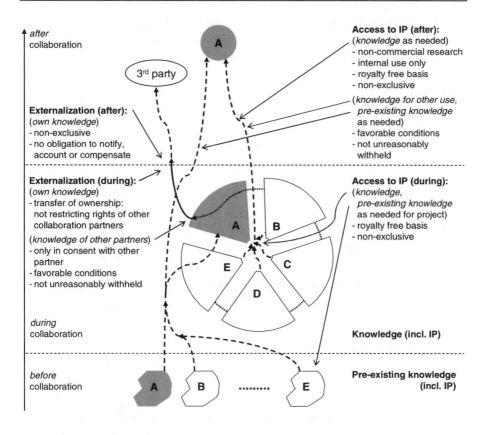

Fig. 46. Access to intellectual property in R&D collaborations

Externalization. Party *A* may *grant access rights* for its pre-existing and intellectual property to third parties (*3rd party*) outside the collaboration. They can do so without having to notify, account for, or compensate the other parties. Furthermore, *ownership of rights* cannot be transferred to third parties, unless there is no limitation of the rights of the other collaboration partners. Party *A* may even *externalize* the access to the rights of the collaborative intellectual property of its partners *B* to *E* to third parties (*3rd party*). This would be necessary if party *A* seeks to use the intellectual property within other research activities, to enter into other technical collaborations, or if the licensing arrangements and the affected owners *B* to *E* agree.

Dynamizing collaborative activities. There might be certain risks in using collaborative results from a former project, if the contract is only open for the formerly selected partners. New substitute partners might then not be able to use the exclusive project results of the former collaboration at all. And the re-selected partners might only be able to do so after having requested a license that they might not be able to receive on a royalty-free basis by the former but not re-selected partners (Fig. 47).

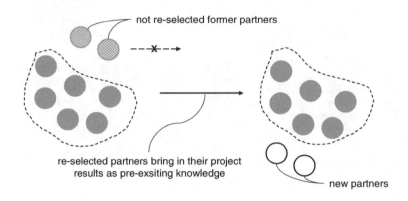

Fig. 47. Problems with additive partner selection

7.5 Reduction of Theoretical Implications to Practice

In this section, the hypotheses of chapter six are reduced to practice[20] by linking them to the typology model in chapter five, on the basis of the previously introduced and described four views of managing intellectual property in R&D collaborations.

Hypothesis 1: The higher the expected outcomes of an inter-firm R&D collaboration, the more important the individual intellectual property exploitability of the collaboration partners becomes.

This hypothesis is relevant with respect to the view of *procedural aspects*: On the one hand, it is the collaboration target dimension that influences the management of intellectual property with respect to the procedural aspects of the R&D collaboration. A collaboration partner whose focus is on out-bound licensing has to ensure that he can still participate in

---

[20] *Reduction to practice:* Technical term in patent language to describe the manifestation of an idea becoming an invention and that refers to the actual construction of the invention in physical form.

improvements and further developments that are applied by the other collaboration partner. Furthermore, he has to assure that the in-bound collaboration partner's other intellectual property rights will not be used against him at a later stage and therefore has to include a back-license in the collaboration agreement. While the *Multiplicator* needs the back-licenses in general, the *Leverager* may only need them outside the other collaboration partner's niche market.

On the other hand, an in-bound collaboration partner has to make sure that the relevant intellectual property is included in the collaboration and that the remaining residual intellectual property provides enough space for an independent operation. As the out-bound collaboration partner may request back-licenses that include improvements to the in-bound intellectual property, the in-bound collaboration partner should also try to participate in improvements made by the out-bound partner's other collaboration partners. While the *Absorber* needs general rules with respect to the market size dimension, the *Filtrator* can be satisfied with limitations concerning its niche market.

Another aspect for the in-bound collaboration partner is a pre-collaborative option agreement term for extending possibly time-limited rights of use or licensing rights with respect to the residual intellectual property.

Hypothesis 2: The more experience a collaboration partner has gathered with intellectual property issues in inter-firm R&D collaborations, the better this partner is able to establish and realize its interests concerning intellectual property.

This hypothesis is relevant with respect to the view of *scope of contract*: It is important to be aware of the own individual needs as well as that of the collaboration partner to understand what tangible values will be generated, what the partners' level of freedom will be before, during and after the collaboration and how competitive advantages can be achieved through the collaboration and be protected by intellectual property. *Multiplicator*, *Leverager*, *Absorber* and *Filtrator* are dependent on their experiences to realize their interests concerning the management of intellectual property within a collaboration.

Hypothesis 3: The more open the information exchange philosophy of the collaboration partners, the more likely it is that balanced collaboration contracts with respect to intellectual property can be closed.

This hypothesis is relevant with respect to the view of *terms of contract*: The collaboration partners have to balance the contracts with respect to and to counter imbalance of power. The *Multiplicator* and the *Leverager* have to ensure that the return of the licensee collaboration partner to the licensor collaboration partner is balanced with its business scope and related risks and opportunities. The *Absorber* and the *Filtrator* should offer enough information to their licensor collaboration partner to make that one truly understand the business model and the value of the collaboration-related intellectual property for the licensee collaboration partner, i.e. the *Absorber* or the *Filtrator* respectively.

Hypothesis 4: The better the strategic, compatible fit between the collaboration partners, the more likely it is that a balanced intellectual property model can be found for the R&D collaboration partners to support learning and innovation.

This hypothesis is relevant with respect to the view of *collaborative settings*: The collaboration partners should also focus on the skills and the know-how of the collaboration team to estimate future outcomes and to create a win-win situation to balance the intellectual property model. This is applicable to the *Multiplicator* and the *Leverager* with regard to back-licenses, but also concerning the ability of the other collaboration partner to adequately value and enrich the out-bounded intellectual property. The *Absorber* and *Filtrator* depend on the licensor collaboration partner's intellectual property's out-bound capacity.

Hypothesis 5: The more concrete ownership rights, rights of use and licensing rights have been aligned by the inter-firm R&D collaboration partners, the better intellectual property and joint intellectual property can be handled by the collaboration partners.

This hypothesis is relevant with respect to the view of *terms of contract*: *Multiplicator, Leverager, Absorber* and *Filtrator* should focus on clarifying and setting the terms of the collaboration as thoroughly as possible before entering the collaboration. Otherwise, the *Multiplicator*, and to a certain degree the *Leverager*, risk suddenly becoming dependant on the collaborative intellectual property of the collaboration partner, e.g., due to the collaboration partner's intellectual property's overlap with the own activities. The *Absorber*, and to a certain degree the *Filtrator*, risk still being heavily dependent on the collaboration partner's intellectual property after the collaboration has ended.

Hypothesis 6: The lower the anticipated overlap of the collaborative intellectual property is, the more realistic it is that a mutual fit can be found to use and exploit the collaboration results, including the intellectual property.

This hypothesis is relevant with respect to the view of *scope of contract*: The collaboration partners have to understand one another's business model and the role of the background, foreground, sideground and postground intellectual property, as well as the residual information for each of the collaboration partners. If one collaboration partner wants to access a niche market only, the other partner might be able to agree to an exclusive rights package, even on joint intellectual property as long as that niche market is not exceeded.

Concerning exclusivity terms, the *Multiplicator* has to be careful with exclusive licenses, as there is the interest in respect of maximum general own freedom of action without market restrictions, and continuing own licensing activities. The *Leverager*, however, may be able to offer exclusivity within the niche market to reach better collaborative returns. The *Absorber* has to be careful with insisting on an exclusive use of collaborative outcomes, as this might be a deal-breaker for the other collaboration partner. Finally, the *Filtrator* should try to achieve exclusivity for its niche market segment to gain maximum competition advantages from the collaborative intellectual property.

Hypothesis 7: The clearer a collaboration partner has defined its goals and needs concerning the collaboration's intellectual property outcomes, the clearer it can evaluate the anticipated benefits of the inter-firm R&D collaboration in advance.

This hypothesis is relevant with respect to the view of *collaborative settings*: In order to evaluate the performance expectations, the collaboration partners need experienced staff within the early stages of the collaboration process. A very relevant expertise with respect to the collaboration partner selection process is technical expertise, i.e. from scientific experts. The *Multiplicator* and the *Leverager* need to select best fitting collaboration partners with enough competence to provide high prospects of intellectual-property-related returns. This issue is especially important for the *Absorber* and the *Filtrator* to evaluate the in-bound perspectives of the collaboration.

Hypothesis 8: The more accepted the collaboration partners' intra-firm relations between internal stakeholders, e.g. intellectual property department, legal department, R&D department, are, the more efficient and effective the evolution of the collaborative intellectual property decision-making processes and procedures.

This hypothesis is relevant with respect to the view of *procedural aspects*: The collaboration-partner-specific, internal process between the negotiating and collaborating levels has to be setup and optimized, i.e. the researchers and the legal level in general. This is advisable for all types, i.e. the *Multiplicator, Leverager, Absorber* and *Filtrator*.

Hypothesis 9: The sounder the combination of goals, processes and standardized elements on intellectual property issues, e.g. contract paragraphs, as well as on an individually decided case-by-case basis, the less negotiations on intellectual property issues hinder the start of an inter-firm R&D collaboration.

This hypothesis is relevant with respect to the view of *procedural aspects*: The collaboration partners have to take deal with the various stages of collaboratively generated intellectual property, e.g. by distinguishing pre-existing and collaborative intellectual property. The *Multiplicator* may setup standard contracts that, e.g., are reviewed by legal departments and are used and applied by researchers. The *Leverager* should implement a process to adapt standard contracts to specific situations, e.g., by involving the intellectual property department. The *Absorber* should try to implement its own standard contract philosophy. Finally, the *Filtrator* has to focus on the adaptation process to the specifics of its niche market segment to optimize its in-bound results with respect to collaborative intellectual property.

Summary. The foregoing hypotheses-based, managerial implications are summarized in Table 19, pp. 181, with respect to the intellectual property management types on the basis of the four management views *scope of contract*, *terms of contract*, *procedural aspects* and *collaborative settings*.

A summarizing conceptional management model for managing intellectual property in R&D collaborations is presented in Fig. 48, p. 183.

Table 19. Hypotheses-based and type-specific views of managing intellectual property in R&D collaborations

	Multiplicator	Leverager	Absorber	Filtrator
Scope of contract	Understand the individual needs and positions of the collaboration partners and how competitive advantages can be reached through the specific, collaboration-related intellectual property:			
	Understand value of IP for collaboration partner.		*Understand value of self-generated IP for collaboration partner.*	
	(in general)	*(in niche)*	*(in general)*	*(value of niche contribution)*
	Understand the collaboration partner's business model and the role of collaborative IP for it:			
	Be careful with exclusive licenses.	*Check possibility of exclusive license for niche market segment.*	*Be careful with exclusive licenses as they might be a deal-breaker.*	*Check possibility for an exclusive license for own niche market.*
Terms of contract	Focus on clarifying and setting the terms of the collaboration as clearly as possible before entering the collaboration:			
	Calculate the impact of the overlapping IP on own activities.		*Figure out dependency of the collaborative IP after the collaboration has ended.*	
	(in general)	*(value of niche contribution to own focus)*	*(in general)*	*(in niche)*
	Balance the contracts to counter imbalance of power:			
	Balance returns of licensee to licensor collaboration partner with respect to business scope and risks.		*Offer sufficient authentic information to licensor collaboration partner about business objectives.*	
	(in general)	*(in niche)*	*(in general)*	*(in niche)*
Procedural aspects	Make sure that a back-license on collaborative improvements and further developments is given.		Secure the relevant intellectual property to have enough space for operating independently post collaboration.	
	(in general)	*(at least for own market segments)*	*(in general)*	*(at least for own market segments)*
	Deal with the various stages of collaboratively generated IP, e.g. by distinguishing pre-existing and collaborative IP:			
	Form standard contracts, e.g. reviewed by legal department and are used by researchers.	*Implement a process to adapt standard contracts to specific situations, e.g. IP department.*	*Form standard contracts, e.g. reviewed by legal department and are used by researchers.*	*Implement a process to adapt standard contracts to specific situations, e.g. IP department.*
	Setup and optimize the (internal) process between the collaborating and negotiating levels, i.e. between the research and legal level.			

	Multiplicator	**Leverager**	**Absorber**	**Filtrator**

Collaborative settings

Focus on the skills and the know-how of the collaboration team to create a win-win situation, rather than the collaboration partners' general knowledge:

Make sure that the collaboration partner is able to value und enrich the out-bound IP.

Be aware of the dependency on the IP out-bound capacity of collaboration partner.

Deploy experienced staff for the collaboration selection process; i.e. technical experience from expert scientists. The analysis of the partner's IP strength and potential is based on a scientific view:

Select the most suitable collaboration partner with high potential for valuable returns.

Evaluate in-bound perspectives of collaboration with respect to IP.

(in general) *(value of niche contribution to own focus)* *(in general)* *(in niche)*

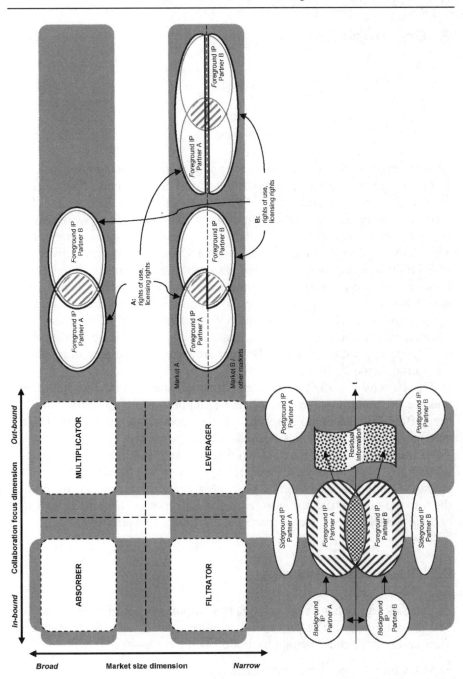

Fig. 48. Summarized model for managing intellectual property in R&D collaborations with respect to terms of contract and procedural aspects

8 Conclusions

This research work has focused on investigating the management of intellectual property in R&D collaborations. As a core element, four in-depth case studies were conducted of the service innovation companies *IBM*, *SAP*, *Swisscom* and *Swiss Re* (chapter four). The companies were selected based on their level of contribution to labor intensity and customer contact as well as the customization of the service solutions that they deliver. The case study research was conducted on three iterative and refining levels: in-depth interviews with various internal company experts and managers, long-term intellectual property best practice workshop series, a bilateral project and a benchmarking research project in which all the case study companies participated. The practical findings of the case studies were used to set up a typology of intellectual property management in R&D collaborations (chapter five).

The currently available findings from the literature review have been analyzed (chapter two) to extract core components and to derive propositions. Based on these, the propositions have been tested with respect to the case study findings to induce hypotheses (chapter six).

Furthermore, four views of managing intellectual property in R&D collaborations have been described and applied to the findings of the case studies. Finally, the hypotheses have been reduced to practice by linking them to the intellectual property management typology to form a typology- and view-based conceptional management model (chapter seven).

8.1 Theoretical Résumé

As introduced in chapter six, nine core components for managing intellectual property in R&D collaborations were extracted from the literature review and structured according to the following categories:

- Motivation-related core components;
- Stucture-related core components;
- Performance-related core components.

Based on the core components, nine propositions were derived. Those propositions were then compared to the findings from the in-depth case studies to finally induce nine hypotheses that are summarized as follows:

Motivation-related core components. The motivation-related core components are:

- Main goal of collaboration;
- Prior experience with collaborations;
- Information asymmetry, trust and power.

Hypothesis 1: The higher the expected outcomes of an inter-firm R&D collaboration, the more important the individual intellectual property exploitability of the collaboration partners becomes.

Hypothesis 2: The more experience a collaboration partner has gathered with intellectual property issues in inter-firm R&D collaborations, the better this partner is able to establish and realize its interests concerning intellectual property.

Hypothesis 3: The more open the information exchange philosophy of the collaboration partners, the more likely it is that balanced collaboration contracts with respect to intellectual property can be closed.

Structure-related core components. The structure-related core components are:

- Strategic compatibility;
- Implementation capability;
- Complementary commercialization capability.

Hypothesis 4: The better the strategic, compatible fit between the collaboration partners, the more likely it is that a balanced intellectual property model can be found for the R&D collaboration partners to support learning and innovation.

Hypothesis 5: The more concrete ownership rights, rights of use and licensing rights have been aligned by the inter-firm R&D collaboration partners, the better intellectual property and joint intellectual property can be handled by the collaboration partners.

Hypothesis 6: The lower the anticipated overlap of the collaborative intellectual property is, the more realistic it is that a mutual fit can be found to use and exploit the collaboration results, including the intellectual property.

Performance-related core components. The performance-related core components are:

- Collaboration formation capability;
- Intra-firm relationship capability;
- Legalization capability (policy process).

Hypothesis 7: The clearer a collaboration partner has defined its goals and needs concerning the collaboration's intellectual property outcomes, the clearer it can evaluate the anticipated benefits of the inter-firm R&D collaboration in advance.

Hypothesis 8: The more accepted the collaboration partners' intra-firm relations between internal stakeholders, e.g. intellectual property department, legal department, R&D department, are, the more efficient and effective the evolution of the collaborative intellectual property decision-making processes and procedures.

Hypothesis 9: The sounder the combination of goals, processes and standardized elements on intellectual property issues, e.g. contract paragraphs, as well as on an individually decided case-by-case basis, the less negotiations on intellectual property issues hinder the start of an inter-firm R&D collaboration.

8.2 Managerial Résumé

Typology of intellectual property management in R&D collaborations. Based on a further in-depth analysis of the four case studies, the characteristics for managing intellectual property in R&D collaborations were extracted (chapter five). These characteristics are based on two dimensions:

1. The *collaboration focus* dimension: *in-bound* versus *out-bound*;
2. The *market size* dimension: *narrow* versus *broad*.

Consequently, a typology including four types of intellectual property management in R&D collaborations were assigned (Fig. 49; see also chapter five, Fig. 34, p. 135):

- *Multiplicator:* The Multiplicator type manages intellectual property in inter-firm R&D collaborations in order to enable and to gain access to broad markets. It thereby multiplicates intellectual property into broad markets on a collaborative basis that includes setting standards, which are regarded as business-enablers.

- *Leverager:* The Leverager type manages intellectual property in inter-firm R&D collaborations to enable collaborative projects in specific markets. It leverages its intellectual property into narrow markets whereby the collaboration partner benefits from the Leverager's intellectual-property-based technology leadership.

- *Absorber:* The Absorber type in-sources intellectual property to gain access to broad markets on a collaborative basis. The in-sourcing helps to broaden and enriching the Absorber's own intellectual property's foundation. An Absorber may consequently prefer to favor collaboration partners that are willing to contribute or share their intellectual property.

- *Filtrator:* The Filtrator type conducts inter-firm R&D collaborations to in-source selected external intellectual property in order to gain access to specific narrow markets. The Filtrator usually looks for valuable and trustworthy innovators to gain collaborative, situatively selected best-in-class technology and intellectual property.

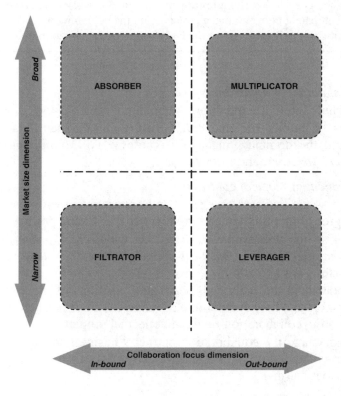

Fig. 49.   Typology of intellectual property management in R&D collaborations

Success factors for managing intellectual property in R&D collaborations. By reducing the hypotheses to practice, managerial implications were extracted on the basis of four views of managing intellectual property in R&D collaborations. Furthermore, next to the typology-specific managerial implications for managing intellectual property in R&D collaborations,[21] six additional success factors are presented based on the analyses and findings of this research work (Table 20):

Table 20. Success factors for managing IP in R&D collaborations

Success Factors R&D Collaborations
1. Determination of dominant typology;
2. Assessment of scope of contract;
3. Establishment of terms of contract;
4. Incorporation of procedural aspects;
5. Consideration of collaborative settings;
6. Demarcation from existing intellectual property;
7. Regular communication;
8. Invention checks at early milestone markers in the innovation process;
9. Efficient patent portfolio management from the beginning on;
10. Definition of exit strategies at the early stages of the collaboration.

1. *Determination of dominant typology:*
   - Include future use intentions at the initial stages of the collaboration;
   - Assess *market size* and *collaboration focus* dimensions to understand the dominant managing typology, i.e. *Multiplicator, Leverager, Absorber*, and *Filtrator*.

2. *Assessment of scope of contract:*
   - Assess the business case risks and opportunities with respect to the degree of maturity concerning revenues, costs and profits;
   - Define the collaboration scope, i.e. *intellectual property license; technology license; business model license; business solution license;*
   - Understand the individual needs and positions of the collaboration partners and how competitive advantages can be reached through the specific, collaboration-related intellectual property;
   - Understand the collaboration partner's business model and the role that collaborative intellectual property plays for it to decide on exclusivity terms.

---

[21] See overview given by Table 19, pp. 181, chapter seven.

3. *Establishment of terms of contract:*
   - Mutually reflect and fully address the following issues with respect to content and legal approval, i.e. *inventorship rights; ownership rights*; *rights of use*; *licensing rights*; *enforcement of rights*; *prosecution*; *administration of rights*; *sharing of costs*;
   - Focus on clarifying and setting the terms of the collaboration as clearly as possible before entering the collaboration;
   - Calculate the impact of the overlapping intellectual property on own activities and the own dependency on collaborative intellectual property after the collaboration has ended;
   - Balance the contracts to counter an imbalance of power by taking into account anticipated returns, business scope and risks, and offering the collaboration partner sufficient information about the business objectives.

4. *Incorporation of procedural aspects:*
   - Consider the mutual contribution and the aspect of the use of rights in the context of time, i.e. *background intellectual property*; *foreground intellectual property*; *sideground intellectual property; postground intellectual property*; *residual information;*
   - Ensure that a back-license on collaborative improvements and further developments is given;
   - Secure the relevant intellectual property to have enough space to operate independently after the collaboration has ended;
   - Deal with the various stages of in- and out-bounded and collaboratively generated intellectual property, e.g. by distinguishing pre-existing and collaborative intellectual property;
   - Setup and optimize the (internal) process between the collaborating and negotiating levels, i.e. between the research and legal level.

5. *Consideration of collaborative settings:*
   - Assure that each collaboration party has a clear view of the access rights to and needs for the later externalization of rights that are deemed necessary for future research and business activities, i.e. with respect to *bilateral*, *multilateral* and *collateral* constellation;
   - Focus on the skills and the know-how of the collaboration team to create a win-win situation, rather than on the collaboration partners' general knowledge;
   - Deploy experienced staff for the collaboration selection process; i.e. technical experience from expert scientists; the analysis of the collaboration partner's intellectual property strength and potential is based on a scientific view.

6. *Demarcation from existing intellectual property:*
   Before entering a collaboration, ensure the safety and integrity of own inventions and intellectual property as thoroughly as possible.

7. *Regular communication:*
   - Internally communicate between the different involved experts and negotiation stakeholders;
   - Early integrate internal and external patent experts;
   - Communicate consistently between the collaboration partners.

8. *Invention checks at early milestone markers in the innovation process:*
   Ensure to get hold of valuable ideas and inventions as early as possible for further refinement and prosecution.

9. *Efficient patent portfolio management from the beginning on:*
   Develop a concise and effective intellectual property portfolio with a rational value-cost ratio throughout the collaboration time frame.

10. *Definition of exit strategies at the early stages of the collaboration:*
    Develop a clear view of how to exit in order to have a pre-defined exit and to avoid destructive side effects if the collaboration is terminated on purpose or enforced.

Success factors for managing intellectual property in the service industry sector. Based on the in-depth case studies, the following success factors for managing intellectual property, with a particular emphasis on the service industry sector, can still be amended (Table 21):

Table 21. Success factors for managing IP in the service industry sector

Success Factors Service Industry Sector
1. Support from top and middle management;
2. Awareness program;
3. Incentive systems for inventions;
4. Identification of inventions;
5. Local investigative and discovery partners;
6. Legal protection of value position;
7. Establishment of defense position;
8. Sustainability of intellectual property activities and sufficient budget;
9. Use of external expert know-how.

1. *Support from top and middle management:*
   While support from the top management and the patent department is vital, much depends on the interactions that middle managers and employees have with third parties. If these parties are dedicated and loyal to the company's intellectual property, inventions can be protected before secrets reach the general public.

2. *Awareness program:*
   A sensitization with regard to the topic of intellectual property is necessary. A well-arranged awareness program, one that reaches as many employees within as many years as possible, can create this awareness. Such measures should be implemented unconditionally over the long term. This is due to the fact that in industries such as the service industry sector with dominantly only a short tradition or ignorant of patents, active interaction must be launched for counteraction.

3. *Incentive systems for inventions:*
   The introduction of an incentive system for inventions is a proven aid to help support a patent department's activities. An important point here is that in order to assess the workforce's view of inventions, it is necessary to understand their underlying perceptions. Without an effective incentive system, or a proper perspective on inventions, there is a danger that inventions will not be declared or will be done so too late. This can happen even if there is a general understanding at the firm about the importance of intellectual property.

4. *Identification of inventions:*
   The identification of knowledge residing in employees' minds will largely depend on the presence of informal contacts within the organization. Subsidiaries can use integrated processes and mechanisms to support projects, which helps to facilitate their identification.

5. *Local investigative and discovery partners:*
   Another important area of knowledge identification comes from middlemen, e.g. the DIPOs at *Swiss Re*, who are found between the business units and the patent department. There should be a set of criteria established for this position, including: interactions with employees, market knowledge, understanding of intellectual property issues, and sensitivity towards innovation and inventions. In organizations where there is no concentrated R&D department and potential inventors are scattered throughout the company; companies like *Swiss Re* rely on decentral intellectual property officers to identify and isolate *hot spots* within the organization.

6. *Legal protection of value positions:*
   Analyze thoroughly service innovations with respect to service components' leverage in the value chain and with regard to their legal protect-
   ability – independently of constraints concerning national differences in
   patentability.

7. *Establishment of defense position:*
   A large and widely diversified patent portfolio is the best defense
   against intellectual property attacks from third parties. One's bargaining
   position can be greatly strengthened and enhanced with such an arsenal.
   There is, for example, the option to conclude cross license agreements.

8. *Sustainability of intellectual property activities and sufficient budget:*
   The establishment of an internal intellectual property portfolio is a time-
   consuming and complicated matter; especially in the service industry
   sector. Therefore, it is advantageous if the intellectual property department can absorb some of the operating costs, and takes a leadership role
   in the application and process phases of the patent application process.

9. *Use of external expert know-how:*
   The presence of skilled and experienced external patent agents is vital,
   especially for those organizations that have little experience in dealing
   with intellectual property.

8.3 Limitations and Scope for Further Research

Several limitations that leave space for further research activities apply to
this research that has focused on formal inter-firm research and development collaborations within the early innovation phase and with respect to
the early collaboration stage:

- The selected case data were gathered with a clear focus on *research and
  development collaborations* that have proved to generate most technology-based innovations and are therefore a main basis of intellectual
  property. In other types of collaborations, e.g. for distribution, other factors could be more dominant than the question of how to manage intellectual property.

- There was a focus on the *early innovation phase* of the collaborative innovation process by mainly examining the research departments of the
  case study companies. During the later, and much more focused, project
  management innovation process there is less uncertainty and collaboration results can be estimated much clearer. The collaboration outcomes

can therefore be narrowed down more easily and contract evolution can occur with fewer risks and a higher degree of success.

- Even though the research results should probably be extended to non-formal collaborations, e.g. due to oral agreements, the focus of this research has been on *formal collaborations* based on fixed contracts as a result of an early negotiation stage. This results in there being much pressure on the collaboration partners to find solutions to and to manage intellectual property even before they start collaborating. An informal process might improve the start of the collaboration, but would very likely be confronted with a risk of failure due to problems that arise later and are then unsolvable.

- Intra-firm and non-inter-firm collaborations were excluded due to the collaboration partners' different situation and motivation when compared to *inter-firm* research and development collaborations, and because collaborations between companies need the highest level of professionalism in dealing with collaborations in general and intellectual property in particular. Research collaborations between universities and industry in general serve as an example as the two parties often have different financial and political backgrounds. However, one can assume that the theoretical and managerial implications can be extended to these fields of activities.

- The *unit of analysis* of this research is the formal inter-firm R&D collaboration, i.e. the joint project as described from one of the collaboration partner's point of view. This results in the *early stages* of collaborations being emphasized, i.e. the stages before the start of the collaborative operation, which is the most difficult stage for the partners as they are not yet fully aware of the impact that the arising intellectual property might have on them. This limitation results in this research only having a minor focus on the collaboration process and its success rate as such.

- The cases have mainly been described from the *perspective of one collaboration partner*, therefore omitting the other's view. However, at this point it should be emphasized that the business of managing intellectual property in general is considered highly sensitive and it has been very difficult to obtain research results from companies that they were happy to have published as the basis for this research analysis.

- In considering intellectual property, there was a strong focus on the legal instruments of *patents* and *utility models*. Other intellectual property rights, such as design models, trade dress, trademarks and copyrights might, however, still specifically reveal further management dimensions that were not fully investigated during this research.

- The analyzed case study companies were intentionally selected within the *service industry sector*. There might be various limitations with respect to other industry sectors. Furthermore, the chosen companies are all considered large companies with various human and financial resources. Small and medium enterprises might be confronted with different problems due to their lesser complexity but higher inter-dependency, especially when collaborating with big partners.

- Finally, the theoretical implications, i.e. the hypotheses, have been formulated on the basis of a qualitative, exploratory research design and are open to further verification, e.g. through quantitative research methods.

8.4 Outlook on Future Challenges

The ability to generate innovations has become a key factor for success. However, it is becoming increasingly evident that only in few cases product innovations could be handled by companies themselves, especially in the service industry sector. This means that the boundaries of enterprise and industry innovation processes must be opened in order to actively gain access to external sources. Various large enterprises have quite early recognized that integration of external ideas and sources of knowledge into their innovation process leads to competitive advantages. The advantage of specialization and focusing as well as the synergies attainable through alignment of the R&D activities outweigh the fear of one-sided dependence.

This innovation process, which large companies are already actively practicing, will also reach small and medium sized enterprises soon. Those companies that are dependent on external partners are especially challenged, because strategic positioning and suitable innovation development demand a great deal from an enterprise acting alone. Projects that are run by a single company could even endanger it's survival if they fail. Companies are therefore increasingly accessing sources outside their firms' boundaries and no longer rely on getting everything done internally. Important external sources of innovation are customers, suppliers and competitors as well as universities and research organizations.

The current trend is intriguing: competitive advantages attainable through patent and trademark innovations are further intensified by service innovations and innovation collaborations between industrial firms. The enhancement of the innovation process in the form of open innovation trends has influenced the surrounding intellectual property environment: Organizations are more willing to share and propagate intellectual property. The initial position of an innovation collaboration focuses on the intentions of the future use of the intellectual property; along with its future peripheral and post-collaborative use. A clear entry strategy is the hidden key to collaboration success: Be clear at the start concerning which party has what rights at the conclusion of the collaboration, especially if the relationship were to sour. Here, the art of negotiation is to create a solid legal basis, while not jeopardizing the common vision and spirit of collaboration. Otherwise, there is a real danger of both sides losing out.

From a wider perspective, the overall importance of intellectual property for companies should be understood and well communicated. In the service industry sector and particularly in the (re–) insurance and banking industry sector, software solutions and business practices have a strong business relevance. Only time will tell what the current various differences in legal protection for processes, business methods and software-related inventions in Europe, Japan and the United States will lead to in practice.

The security of a company's research and development investments in intellectual property will become of increasing strategic importance for companies in the service industry sector. Increasingly protected service innovations will lead to imitation and second-mover advantages being reduced if not terminated. Furthermore, legal protection instruments anticipate the potential for service-oriented enterprises to open up new markets, specifically if based on collaborative industry efforts. One could thus expect that it might still take some time for patent portfolios to grow, but that technology transfer and licensing models will find entrance to the financial services industry sector (Swiss Re Global IP Group 2005).

However, the protection of service innovations is a relatively new phenomenon, especially for the European service industry sector. Currently, this industry is confronted with prospects and risk scenarios relating to legal business protection instruments, specifically patents. Furthermore, own investigations have revealed that US companies are already much more aggressive in protecting their intellectual property rights than their European counterparts, not only on their home turf, but also in Europe (Fig. 50). Especially Anglo-American and Japanese entities serve as examples of predecessors that incorporated intellectual property into business activities. At the *European Patent Office* 75% of patent applications in the bank and (re–) insurance industries originate from companies in Anglo-Saxon countries like the United States, Canada, and Great Britain.

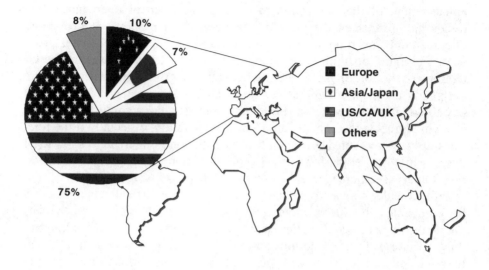

Fig. 50. Patent applications in the financial services industry sector in Europe

The result is that although the *European Patent Office* and various national patent offices such as those in Germany or the United Kingdom are bound to a much more restrictive granting procedure policy, wealthy US-based firms have managed to strengthen their positions by looking for numerous software and business-model-related patent applications in Europe. To a large extent, European companies within the service industry sector have neither recognized the major risks relating to intellectual property, nor have they taken countermeasures or actions to protect their own prospects.

Companies that are looking to take initiative and seize the opportunities present in the service industry sector should, however, first obtain some advice as, in general, technologies are characterized by too few patents and too many trade secrets, too little understanding of technology-related business models, and too few success stories to demonstrate feasibility. In an industry sector that does not handle intellectual property in an expedited manner, sustainability and cultural factors inside the firm will play determining roles in the success of an intellectual property management program. The qualities of those working in the intellectual property area of a firm should not only include solid technical knowledge, but they should be able to handle a collaborative work environment and thrive in it.

This research affirms that intellectual property management in collaborations already plays an important role in the early stages of collaboration processes. The findings recommend that agreements have to be made on business plans and legal issues that govern the anticipated fruits of the collaboration, including intellectual property. It is vital to establish an early and explicit agreement between partners in order to determine how to share the ownership, rights of use and exploitation rights of the resulting intellectual property. This requires a clear exit strategy that will answer: Who has ownerships of and access to what rights after the collaboration has ended? The main reason for the difficulty in answering this question is that at the start, the partners do not know the final relevant markets and competitors to the full extend that will be present throughout the collaboration's duration and beyond. At best, the partners can attempt to approximate the future situation – in other words: They try to divide a cake before it is even baked.

9 Executive Summary

In highly industrialized countries, innovation and technologies account for about half of economic growth. Intellectual property management plays a crucial role in managing innovation by providing legal protection, especially when supporting factual protection strategies that enable profits from temporary monopolies. Due to an increase in complexity, shortened innovation cycles as well as the higher risks and costs of generating innovation, companies are forced to focus on core competencies. Simultaneously, customers' demands for extensive solution concepts drive companies to fill gaps by opening up their boundaries and collaborating with additional, external sources of innovation. Consequently, the results of collaborative innovation, which largely also includes intellectual property, have become a critical issue.

Legal protection strategies are a novelty in emerging business fields, such as the service industry sector, as innovation and value creation are shifting towards service innovations. Managing intellectual property in such an environment is therefore the subject of this work.

An explorative, case-study-based research approach was chosen due to the novelty of managing intellectual property in inter-firm research and development collaborations as an empirical phenomenon. By analyzing selected service innovation companies, namely *IBM*, *SAP*, *Swisscom* and *Swiss Re*, a typology for managing intellectual property in research and development collaborations is compiled, resulting in a Multiplicator, Leverager, Absorber and Filtrator type with respect to the collaboration focus dimension and the market size dimension.

Starting with the findings from the literature review, core components are extracted to derive propositions. These theoretically derived propositions are tested in practice with respect to the case study outcomes to induce hypotheses. Finally, by analyzing the impact of the theoretical findings on the above-mentioned types, typology-specific management implications are deduced and structured according to four views to form a hypotheses- and typology-based conceptual model for managing intellectual property in research and development collaborations.

This elaboration concludes with managerial success factors and an outlook on future challenges.

Appendices

Questionnaire

General philosophy:
The intention of the benchmarking is not to exchange trade secrets or other non-disclosable information but to share methods and processes that can be mutually exchanged and help the participants to improve their own processes.

Basic company and intellectual-property-related information:
- General data about company: industry, size, markets, history, organizational structure;
- Information about your general intellectual property activities (as disclosable, e.g. size of intellectual patent department, central/local activities, key activities, organizational involvement, interfaces, meetings/boards).

Questions about the research and innovation process:
Research activities:
  - Strategy?
  - Organization?
  - Processes?
  - Culture?
  - Finance?
    (How do you finance your research? Is it seed money, are you charging for development? Any external funding?)
  - Reimbursement (via technology, products, royalties)?
- How do you stimulate idea creation?
- How is your idea evaluation and selection process?
- Do you obtain inventions from your ideas? If yes, how is this done?

Transfer to organization:
- How do you transfer the research results (internally, externally)?
- Do you sell IP to outside organizations?

Partnering:
- Under what circumstances do you partner with third parties?
- How do you select your partners?
- What expectations do you have concerning the collaboration outcome?
- How do you share the research results?
- Do you have university partnerships? How does the model work?

Questions about the role of intellectual property:
- How do you handle foreground, background, sideground and post-ground IP in R&D collaborations (co-development/research with external firms or universities) with respect to
  - ownership issues?
  - exploitation rights issues?
  - costs, prosecution and administration issues?
  - government funding?
- What is the degree and basis of your participation in government-funded projects?
- How and due to what activities and instruments do you stimulate inventing and the submission of invention disclosures (push/pull)?
- What methods do you use to determine where to file patent applications?
- Do you patent business methods and why – what are your success factors?
- What is your attitude to participation in standardization groups?
- What is your attitude to open source software (flow in /out)?

Questions about managing intellectual property in R&D collaborations:
- How does your (central) R&D process work?
- Are your research activities based on collaborations with external partners (companies, universities)?
- If yes, what is your motivation for collaborating and how and on what basis do you share the results?
- What is the general process of multiplying results from research and development into your organization and/or of commercializing them outside?
- … and with respect to collaboration results?

Questions about multiplication activities:
- What are your licensing activities (in/out)?
- What success factors apply to you?

Model Agreements

Technology License Agreement[22]

THIS AGREEMENT, dated as of March 10, 1997 ("Effective Date"), by and be-tween *INTERNATIONAL BUSINESS MACHINES CORPORATION*, a New York corporation ("IBM"), and *UNIPHASE CORPORATION*[23], a Delaware corporation ("LICENSEE");

WHEREAS, pursuant to an agreement of purchase and sale of even date herewith among IBM, LICENSEE, and a Subsidiary of LICENSEE (the "Purchase Agreement"[24]), LICENSEE or its Subsidiary is acquiring certain assets located in Zurich, Switzerland relating to the design, testing and manufacture of certain components (such operations being hereinafter referred to as the "Laser Opera-tions"); and

WHEREAS, LICENSEE desires to utilize *IBM's* information and know-how associated with the Laser Operations at the Facility (defined below), and *IBM* desires to provide such a license subject to the terms and conditions hereinafter set forth;

NOW, THEREFORE, in consideration of the premises and mutual cove-nants contained herein, the parties hereto agree as follows:

Section 1.0 Definitions

"Authorized Locations" shall mean the Facility and the Second Source.

"Employees" shall have the meaning set forth in the Purchase Agreement.

---

[22]   *Source: http://cobrands.contracts.findlaw.com/agreements/uniphase/ibm.techlic. 1997.03.10.html (18.11.2004).*

[23]   *JDS Uniphase* was founded in 1999 from the merger of *JDS Fitel*, Canada, and the American *Uniphase Corporation*. The enterprise is a worldwide leader in optical tech-nology and designs and manufactures products for fiber optic communications. With its headquarter being in San Jose, California, USA, it employs about 6,000 people world-wide. *Uniphase* reported a total sales of approximately 636 million US dollars in fiscal year 2004, while investing approximately 100 million US dollars for research and de-velopment including 647 employees. The company runs 14 manufacturing sites, eight of which lay throughout the United States, fourin China, and one of each in Canada, Singapore and Indonesia. *Uniphase* was able to reduce their net loss by 88% from 934 million US dollars in 2003 to 115 million US dollars in 2004, at a stable revenue level. *Source: 10-K report, JDS Uniphase Corporation, 16.09.04, http://www.jdsu.com, sub page: Investors/SEC Filings.*

[24]   For *"Purchase Agreement"* see http://contracts.corporate.findlaw.com/agreements/uni-phase/ibm.purch.1997.03.10.html, incl. *"Schedules"*, e.g. *"Services Agreement"* and *"Lease Agreement"*.

"Facility" shall mean the manufacturing location in Zurich, Switzerland where the Laser Operations are occurring on the Effective Date and any subsequent location in Europe or the US where LICENSEE shall determine after the Effective Date to relocate the Laser Operations, subject to any restrictions in the Purchase Agreement.

"Full Wafer Technology" shall mean a batch processing chlorine-assisted ion beam etching technique capable of producing more than one edge emitting semiconductor ridge waveguide laser having a gallium arsenide quantum well active region.

"*IBM* Improvement Patents"'" shall mean all patents issued or issuing on patent applications entitled to an effective filing date prior to five (5) years after the Effective Date that are: (i) licensable at any time by *IBM* or any of its Subsidiaries, and (ii) derived from or constitute improvements to the Licensed Patents and/or the Licensed Technical Information.

"LICENSEE's Patents" shall mean all patents issued or issuing on patent applications entitled to an effective filing date prior to five (5) years after the Effective Date that are: (i) licensable at any time by LICENSEE or any of its Subsidiaries, and (ii) derived from or constitute improvements to the Licensed Patents and/or the Licensed Technical Information. LICENSEE's Patents also include foreign counterparts to such patents, if any, and any divisions, extensions, continuations or continuations-in-part thereof.

"Licensed Patents" shall mean the patents listed in Exhibit A and *IBM* Improvement Patents (and their foreign counterparts, if any) and any divisions, extensions, continuations or continuations-in-part thereof.

"Lasertron Agreement" shall mean the license agreement dated August 1, 1994, between *IBM* and *Lasertron, Inc.*

"Licensed Business Information" shall mean any and all business information used prior to the Effective Date in the conduct of the Laser Operations, such as customer information, pricing and cost information, strategic product plans and the like, which relates to Licensed Products. Licensed Business Information may be in tangible or intangible form.

"Licensed Information" shall mean Licensed Business Information and Licensed Technical Information.

"Licensed Products" shall mean R-F Products and R-B Products.

"Licensed Technical Information" shall mean any and all *IBM* technical information, mask works, data, formulas, knowledge, processes and/or trade secrets developed or acquired by *IBM* relating to the design, testing and manufacture of Licensed Products which is used by *IBM* in the conduct of the Laser Operations and which includes, without limitation, the *IBM* technical information described in the documents listed in Exhibit B. Licensed Technical Information does not include any computer programs.

"Red Lasers" shall mean indium gallium phosphorus/ aluminum gallium indium phosphorus/ aluminum gallium arsenide semiconductor laser chips emitting red light at about 670nm, and having an ordered phase quantum well, dry etched ridge-type structure and aluminum gallium arsenide cladding layers.

"Royalty-Bearing Products" or "R-B Products" shall mean Red Lasers, 1300nm Lasers and any other semiconductor laser chips made using Full Wafer Technology.

"Royalty-Free Products" or "R-F Products" shall mean semiconductor laser chips comprising a gallium arsenide substrate and an active region composed of gallium indium arsenide, gallium arsenide or gallium aluminium arsenide.

"Second Source" shall mean a single manufacturing location, other than the Facility, which is: (i) located in the US or Europe and (ii) wholly-owned by LICENSEE.

"Selling Price" shall mean the actual selling price to unaffiliated customers, and the greater of actual selling price or fair market value in sales to affiliated customers; provided that in either case the Selling Price shall be reduced for discounts, taxes, transportation fees and other unreimbursed charges paid by LICENSEE or its Subsidiaries in connection with the sale of Licensed Products.

"Subsidiary" shall mean a corporation, company or other entity:

(a)   more than fifty percent (50%) of whose outstanding shares or securities (representing the right to vote for the election of directors or other managing authority) are, now or hereafter, owned or controlled, directly or indirectly, by a party hereto, but such corporation, company or other entity shall be deemed to be a Subsidiary only so long as such ownership or control exists; or

(b)   which does not have outstanding shares or securities, as may be the case in a partnership, joint venture or unincorporated association, but more than fifty percent (50%) of whose ownership interest representing the right to make the decisions for such corporation, company or other entity is, now or hereafter, owned or controlled, directly or indirectly, by a party hereto, but such corporation, company or other entity shall be deemed to be a Subsidiary only so long as such ownership or control exists.

"1300nm Lasers" shall mean indium phosphide/ indium gallium arsenide phosphide semiconductor laser chips emitting light at about 1300nm, having a simple double heterostructure with a thin active layer, and a self-aligned ridge structure made by the GRUNT process.

Section 2.0 License Grants

2.1   Subject to Sections 2.5 and 2.9, *IBM* grants to LICENSEE and its Subsidiaries, to the extent that it has a right to do so, a nonexclusive right and license to use the Licensed Information to: (i) make and have made Licensed Products only at the Authorized Locations and sell such products worldwide; (ii) to use and make any apparatus (other than the E2 prototype tool) required to manufacture Licensed Products only at the Authorized Locations; and (iii) improve, modify and enhance the Licensed Information and to use and incorporate any such improvements, modifications and enhancements in the exercise of the license rights pursuant to clause (i) and (ii) and Section 2.11 below. Subject to the last sentence of Section 2.3 hereof, the foregoing license rights shall include the right to sell and distribute any product that includes a Licensed Product as a component or subassembly thereof. Providing *IBM* receives the payment specified in Section 4.1, the license granted in this Section 2.1 with respect to R-F Licensed Products shall be royalty-free and fully paid-up. The license granted in this Section 2.1 with respect to R-B Licensed Products shall be royalty-bearing as provided in Section 4.2.

2.2   Subject to licenses granted to third parties prior to the Effective Date and a license retained by *IBM* for itself and its Subsidiaries to use, copy, modify and distribute internally, IBM hereby transfers, assigns and conveys to LICENSEE all of *IBM's* right, title and interest in and to those computer programs used at the Facility and identified in Exhibit C-1 hereto. *IBM* hereby grants to LICENSEE, to the extent it has a right to do so, a nonexclusive, paid-up and royalty-free license under copyrights, or other similar rights for computer programs, to use, execute, reproduce, modify, and prepare derivative works based upon the additional computer programs listed in Exhibit C-2, only at the Authorized Locations.

2.3   Providing *IBM* receives the payment specified in Section 4.1, *IBM* hereby grants to LICENSEE a nonexclusive, paid-up and royalty-free license under the Licensed Patents to make and have made R-F Licensed Products at the Authorized Locations and to use, offer to sell, sell and import R-F Licensed Products worldwide. The foregoing license shall not extend to any infringement of *IBM* patents not licensed hereunder resulting from the combination of Licensed Products with other products not licensed herein. The term of the license granted in this Section 2.3 shall be for a period of five (5) years from the Effective Date, unless LICENSEE exercises the option granted in Section 2.6 and makes the payment specified therein, in which event the term of the license shall be extended to the date of expiration of the last to expire of the Licensed Patents.

2.4   Except as specifically granted in this Section 2.0, no license or other right is granted, either directly or indirectly, by implication, estoppel or otherwise, to LICENSEE with respect to any patents or patent applications, trademarks, copyrights, trade secrets, computer programs, know-how, mask works or other intellectual property rights of *IBM*.

2.5   The license to have Licensed Products made by another manufacturer granted in Sections 2.1 and 2.3 to LICENSEE shall only apply when the specifications for Licensed Products were created by LICENSEE (either solely or jointly with one or more third parties); and shall not apply to any Licensed Products in the form manufactured or marketed by said other manufacturer prior to LICENSEE furnishing said specifications.

2.6   *IBM* grants to LICENSEE an option to obtain a fully paid-up extension of the term of the patent license granted in Section 2.3 with respect to R-F Licensed Products to cover the period extending to the date of expiration of the last to expire of the Licensed Patents. This option may be exercised at any time prior to five (5) years from the Effective Date by LICENSEE paying to *IBM* the sum of nine million US dollars ($9,000,000) and giving written notice of the exercise of the option in accordance with Section 7. Communications.

2.7   LICENSEE hereby grants to *IBM* an irrevocable, worldwide, nonexclusive, paid-up and royalty-free license under LICENSEE's Patents to make, have made, use, offer to sell, sell and import R-F Licensed Products. *IBM* shall have no right to grant sublicenses under LICENSEE's Patents, except to its Subsidiaries.

2.8   In the event that LICENSEE identifies in writing to *IBM* any patents licensable by *IBM* which are necessarily infringed by the exercise of the license granted in Section 2.1 with respect to R-F Licensed Products being manufactured at the Facility on the Effective Date, and *IBM*, after a good faith analysis, agrees with LICENSEE's position, then upon *IBM's* written notification, Exhibit A shall be automatically amended to include such additional patents without further charge to LICENSEE. In the event that *IBM* shall determine for any reason that such infringement will not occur as to a licensable *IBM* patent, *IBM* shall thereafter be estopped from making any claims of infringement against LICENSEE, its Subsidiaries or its customers as to such *IBM* patent for any exercise by LICENSEE of its rights under Section 2.1 above.

2.9   Notwithstanding anything to the contrary, the license granted in Section 2.1 shall not include rights to use any designs or other information which are used exclusively to manufacture products for *IBM*.

2.10   Subject to the restrictions limiting the license rights to Authorized Locations, LICENSEE shall have the right to exercise any license rights granted hereunder through any Subsidiary, and any reference in this Section 2 and Section 3 below to LICENSEE shall be deemed to refer to any Subsidiary through which LICENSEE shall so exercise such license rights.

2.11   LICENSEE shall have the further right to use the Licensed Technical Information relating to Royalty Free Products in the development and manufacture of any semiconductor laser chips and to exercise the license rights specified in Section 2 as to any such semiconductor laser chips without payment of any royalty pursuant to Section 4.2 hereof, subject to the limitations and restrictions contained in this Agreement and the payment of any patent royalties, as applicable.

2.12   For so long as *IBM* continues to manufacture the E2 Prototype Tool (the "E2 Tool") for sale to any third party, *IBM* agrees to sell to LICENSEE E2 Tools on terms no less favorable than *IBM* has sold E2 Tools during the preceding twelve (12) months to any other non-*IBM* customer purchasing equivalent quantities of the E2 Tool as LICENSEE. Such most favored terms shall include price, production allocation, functionality of the E2 Tool and payment terms and shall be granted to LICENSEE upon the condition that LICENSEE accept all material terms upon which such most favored customer purchased the E2 Tool. In the event such most favored terms shall not apply, *IBM* agrees to sell E2 Tools to LICENSEE on commercially reasonable terms.

Upon written request by LICENSEE and in the event that *IBM* is no longer in the business of supplying E2 Tools to third parties, *IBM* shall provide LICENSEE with component part drawings and any other technical information, including all improvements, necessary for the manufacture and operation of E2 Tools, to the extent *IBM* can provide such information without violating any obligations to third parties, at a reasonable cost invoiced to LICENSEE to cover associated procurement expenses, and LICENSEE shall have the nonexclusive right to manufacture E2 Tools for LICENSEE's internal use and that of its Subsidiaries. Any manufacture of the E2 Tool, or any portion thereof, by LICENSEE may require additional patent licenses which the parties agree to negotiate in good faith.

IBM shall make a good faith effort to notify LICENSEE of its intention to stop manufacturing E2 Tools to third parties at least three (3) months prior to the date it plans to stop such manufacture, and agrees to promptly respond to all reasonable written requests from LICENSEE as to whether it intends to stop such manufacture.

2.13   *IBM* disclaims any common law trademark rights that it may have acquired through the use of the "E2" designation. To the extent that *IBM* has acquired any common law trademark rights in the "Laser Enterprise" or "LE" designation, *IBM* hereby assigns all such rights to LICENSEE, together with all goodwill pertaining thereto.

2.14   In the event that IBM now or hereafter obtains any patents which would necessarily be infringed by the assembly by LICENSEE's customers of Royalty-Free Products into an Erbium Doped Optical Fiber Amplifier ("EDFA") configuration or EDFA architecture compliant package, *IBM* agrees to make a license under such patents available to LICENSEE's customers in accordance with *IBM's* licensing practices at such time.

Section 3.0 Confidentiality

3.1   For a period of ten (10) years from the Effective Date, LICENSEE agrees to use the same degree of care and discretion, but at least a reasonable level of care and discretion, to avoid any disclosure, publication, or dissemination of any part or all of the Licensed Information outside of LICENSEE, and its Subsidiaries, as LICENSEE employs with information of its own which it regards as confidential and which it does not desire to publish, disclose or disseminate. If any Licensed Information of a third party requires a different standard of care or different period of confidentiality than that specified above, LICENSEE agrees to protect such third party's Licensed Information in accordance with the terms of the agreement under which such information was received by *IBM*.

3.2   Disclosure of Licensed Information shall not be precluded, if such disclosure is:

(a)   in response to a valid order of a court or other governmental body; provided, however, that LICENSEE shall first have given notice to *IBM* and made a reasonable effort to obtain a protective order requiring that the information and/or documents so disclosed be used only for the purposes for which the order was issued;
(b)   otherwise required by law;
(c)   reasonably necessary to establish rights under this Agreement (but only to the extent necessary to do so); or
(d)   reasonably necessary to exercise LICENSEE's license rights hereunder and such disclosure is made to an entity or other person that is bound as to the nondisclosure of such Licensed Information by a written agreement that is no less restrictive than this Section 3.

3.3   No obligation of confidentiality shall attach to:

(a)   any information that LICENSEE already possesses without obligation of confidentiality;
(b)   any information LICENSEE rightfully receives from another without obligation of confidentiality; or
(c)   any information that is, or becomes, publicly available without breach of this Agreement.

3.4   In the event that LICENSEE discovers any *IBM* confidential information in the possession of Employees that is unrelated to the Licensed Products, it will promptly return such information to *IBM*.

3.5   *IBM* agrees not to disclose the trade secret information described in (Information redacted and filed separately.) for a period of three (3) years from the Effective Date subject to Sections 3.2(a) & (b). *IBM* agrees not to disclose the trade secret information relating to the process (Information redacted and filed separately) for a period of two (2) years from the Effective Date subject to Sections 3.2(a) & (b). Notwithstanding the above, neither (i) the inherent disclosure of such information in *IBM's* products, nor (ii) the disclosure of such information as part of a disclosure of process information relating to products other than Royalty-Free Products and Royalty-Bearing Products shall be deemed to be a violation of this Section 3.5.

Section 4.0 Consideration

4.1   As partial consideration for the licenses granted by *IBM* to LICENSEE in Sections 2.1, 2.2 and 2.3 with respect to R-F Products, LICENSEE shall pay *IBM* the amount of twenty-seven million US dollars (US $27,000,000), on the Effective Date, which sum is nonrefundable, in accordance with instructions to be provided by *IBM* prior to such date.

4.2   As partial consideration for the licenses granted by *IBM* to LICENSEE in Sections 2.1 and 2.2 with respect to R-B Products, LICENSEE shall pay *IBM* a royalty of five percent (5%) of Selling Price. LICENSEE acknowledges that any royalties owing for patents covering R-B Products shall be payable in addition to the royalty specified herein, pursuant to a separate patent license agreement between the parties.

4.3   LICENSEE shall bear and pay all taxes (including, without limitation, sales and value added taxes) imposed by any national, provincial or local government of any country in which LICENSEE is doing business as a result of the existence of this Agreement or the exercise of rights hereunder; provided, that the foregoing shall not obligate LICENSEE to pay any tax based on the income, gross receipts or property of *IBM*.

4.4   LICENSEE shall be liable for interest on any overdue payment or royalty, commencing on the date such payment or royalty was due and ending upon payment by LICENSEE, at an annual rate which is the greater of ten percent (10%) or one percentage point higher than the prime interest rate as quoted by the head office of Citibank N.A., New York, at the close of banking on such date, or on the first business day thereafter if such date falls on a non-business day. If such interest rate exceeds the maximum legal rate in the jurisdiction where a claim therefore is being asserted, the interest rate shall be reduced to such maximum legal rate.

4.5   Royalties shall accrue when an R-B Licensed Product, with respect to which royalty payments are required by this Agreement, is first sold or otherwise transferred to a party other than LICENSEE or its Subsidiaries (including, except as otherwise agreed in writing by *IBM*, sold or otherwise transferred to *IBM* or any of its Subsidiaries). To the extent an R-B Licensed Product is incorporated as a component, subassembly or subsystem in another product, the Selling Price shall be determined based on the published list price (or if no such published list price exists, the fair market value) of such R-B Licensed Product exclusive of any other portion of such product.

4.6   LICENSEE shall pay all royalties and other payments due hereunder in United States dollars. All royalties for an accounting period computed in other currencies shall be converted into United States dollars at the exchange rate for bank transfers from such currency to United States dollars as quoted by the head office of Citibank N.A., New York, at the close of banking on the last day of such accounting period (or the first business day thereafter if such last day shall be a non-business day).

4.7   LICENSEE's accounting period shall be semiannual and shall end on the last day of each June and December during the term of this Agreement. Within sixty (60) days after the end of each such period LICENSEE shall furnish to IBM a written report containing the information specified in Section 4.8 and shall pay to *IBM* all unpaid royalties accrued hereunder to the end of each such period. Such payments will be nonrefundable.

4.8   LICENSEE's written report shall be certified by an officer of LICENSEE and shall contain the following information:

(a)   for each type of R-B Licensed Product upon which royalty has accrued: a description of said R-B Licensed Product, the quantity sold or otherwise transferred during the accounting period, and the sum of the Selling Price for such quantity; and

(b)   the aggregate amount of all royalties due.
    In the event no royalties are due, LICENSEE's report shall so state.

4.9   LICENSEE shall keep records in accordance with generally accepted accounting principles and in sufficient detail to permit the determination of which products are subject to royalty payments under this Agreement, the royalties due *IBM*, and the accuracy of the information on LICENSEE's written reports. Such records shall include, but not be limited to, detailed records supporting the information provided under Section 4.8. Such records shall be kept for six (6) years following the due date for the report relating to the reporting period to which such records pertain.

Upon *IBM's* written request for an audit, LICENSEE shall permit auditors designated by *IBM*, together with such legal and technical support as *IBM* deems necessary, to examine, during ordinary business hours, records, materials, and manufacturing processes of LICENSEE for the purpose of determining royalties due *IBM*.

Such audit shall be restricted to an audit of those records, materials, and manufacturing processes related to R-B Licensed Products. Such records and materials shall be deemed to include general financial information to provide a cross-check for the amount of royalties reported.

LICENSEE shall provide its full cooperation in such audit. Such cooperation shall include, but not be limited to, providing sufficient time for such examination and convenient access to relevant personnel andrecords.

Each party shall pay the charges that it incurs in the course of the audit. However, in the event that the audit establishes underpayment greater than or equal to the lesser of: five percent (5%) of the royalties which should have been paid for the accounting periods being audited or the cost of the audit, then LICENSEE shall reimburse *IBM* for the costs *IBM* incurred in conducting such audit. However, such costs shall not include salaries paid to *IBM* employees associated with such audit and such reimbursement shall not exceed the amount of underpayment.

4.10   In the event an audit under the provisions of Section 4.9 identifies an underpayment of royalties by LICENSEE, LICENSEE shall pay an amount equal to the sum of such underpayment, any interest due under the provisions of Section 4.4, and any reimbursement to IBM for the costs *IBM* incurred in conducting such audit as specified by Section 4.9, within sixty (60) days of *IBM's* written request. Reimbursements due for costs shall also be subject to interest under the provisions of Section 4.4.

4.11   *IBM* agrees that any statements or audit results furnished or otherwise made available to or obtained by *IBM* pursuant to this Section 4.0 shall be subject to equivalent confidentiality restrictions set forth in Section 3 and shall not be disclosed by *IBM* for a period of three (3) years from the date of disclosure.

Section 5.0 Term; Termination and Assignability

5.1   The licenses granted in Sections 2.1 and 2.2 with respect to Licensed Products shall remain in effect unless terminated in accordance with this Section 5.0. The patent license granted in Section 2.3 with respect to R-F Licensed Products shall remain in effect for a period of five (5) years from the Effective Date, unless terminated in accordance with this Section 5 or extended pursuant to the option granted in Section 2.6. The patent license granted to *IBM* in Section 2.7 shall remain in effect for a period of five (5) years from the Effective Date.

5.2   If LICENSEE is in material breach of its obligations hereunder with respect to R-B Licensed Products and IBM provides written notice to LICENSEE specifying the nature of such breach, LICENSEE shall either cure such breach or produce a plan for such cure reasonably acceptable to *IBM* within sixty (60) days after such written notice. If LICENSEE does not provide a plan for cure, or comply with a plan reasonably acceptable to *IBM*, *IBM* shall have the right to terminate the licenses granted to LICENSEE with respect to R-B Licensed Products under this Agreement by giving written notice of termination to LICENSEE. For purposes of this Section 5.2, a material breach by LICENSEE shall mean and be limited to:

(i)   an intentional and continuing breach of its obligations under Section 3 hereof or of the license restrictions in Section 2 hereof with respect to Licensed Information relating to R-B Licensed Products;

(ii)   LICENSEE being more than fifty thousand dollars ($50,000) in arrears on its payment obligations herein that are not otherwise subject to a good faith dispute between *IBM* and LICENSEE; or

(iii)   the failure by LICENSEE to submit reports or permit audits as specified in Section 4.

5.3   If LICENSEE is in material breach of its obligations hereunder with respect to R-F Licensed Products and *IBM* provides written notice to LICENSEE specifying the nature of such breach, LICENSEE shall either cure such breach or produce a plan for such cure reasonably acceptable to *IBM* within sixty (60) days after such written notice. If LICENSEE does not provide a plan for cure, or comply with a plan reasonably acceptable to *IBM*, *IBM* shall have the right to terminate the licenses granted to LICENSEE with respect to R-F Licensed Products under this Agreement by giving written notice of termination to LICENSEE. For purposes of this Section 5.3, a material breach by LICENSEE shall mean and be limited to an intentional and continuing breach of its obligations under Section 3 hereof or of the license restrictions in Section 2 hereof with respect to Licensed Information relating to R-F Licensed Products.

5.4   In addition, in the event that LICENSEE engages in or suffers any of the following events of default:

(a)   becomes insolvent, is dissolved or liquidated, files or has filed against it a petition in bankruptcy, reorganization, dissolution or liquidation or similar action filed by or against it, is adjudicated as bankrupt, or has a receiver appointed for its business; or
(b)   has all or a substantial portion of its capital stock or assets expropriated or attached by any government entity; then LICENSEE shall promptly notify *IBM* in writing that such event has occurred. If any default as specified above in this Section 5.3 is not cured, or an acceptable plan for such cure is not proposed within ninety (90) days after written notice from *IBM* specifying the nature of the default, *IBM* shall have the right to terminate this Agreement by giving written notice of termination to LICENSEE.

5.5   This Agreement and any rights or licenses granted herein are personal to the parties and neither shall assign or sublicense any of its rights or privileges hereunder. Any attempted act in derogation of the foregoing shall be considered void. Notwithstanding the foregoing, in the event of a transfer by LICENSEE of all or substantially all of its assets or those of the Laser Operations, LICENSEE shall have the right to assign this Agreement to the purchaser of such assets, provided: (i) such purchaser agrees in writing to be bound by all terms and conditions hereof, (ii) in the event that such purchaser and *IBM* are involved in any intellectual property dispute at the time of such transfer, such purchaser shall resolve such dispute to *IBM's* satisfaction; both as conditions precedents to the effectiveness of such assignment.

5.6   No failure or delay on the part of *IBM* in exercising its right of termination hereunder for any one or more causes shall be construed to prejudice its right of termination for such causes or any other or subsequent causes.

5.7   Upon termination of this Agreement, all licenses granted in Section 2 will automatically terminate, and LICENSEE shall promptly return to *IBM* or destroy all tangible information containing Licensed Information. The confidentiality obligations of Section 3 will remain in effect beyond any termination for the time period stated in Section 3.1.

Section 6.0 Representations and Warranties

6.1   *IBM* represents and warrants that:

(a) it has the full right and power to grant the licenses set forth in Section 2, that there are no outstanding agreements, assignments, or encumbrances inconsistent with the provisions of said licenses or with any other provisions of this Agreement;

(b) in the last two years it has not received any written claim or written notice from any third party alleging infringement or unauthorized use of any intellectual property rights owned by such party in relation to the Laser Operations;

(c) to the personal knowledge of the four most senior level executives among the Employees, as expressed to LICENSEE prior to the signing of this Agreement during due diligence, they do not believe the operation of the Laser Enterprise, as operated by *IBM* immediately prior to the Effective Date, infringes or makes unauthorized use of any intellectual property rights of any third party;

(d) subject to LICENSEE's compliance with all limitations and/or conditions contained in this Agreement and any of the other agreements relating to the sale of assets relating to the Laser Enterprise, LICENSEE shall be entitled to continue the operations of the Laser Enterprise, as being conducted by *IBM* on the Effective Date, without claim of infringement or other misappropriation of intellectual property rights by *IBM* or any of its Subsidiaries as to patent, copyrights, trade secret or other intellectual property rights owned by or licensed to IBM or any of its Subsidiaries; and

(e) to the personal knowledge of the most senior level executive among the Employees, *IBM* has not since March 1, 1995, licensed any improvements to the Licensed Technical Information relating to the Royalty-Free Products to any third party which was licensed by *IBM* prior to said date to manufacture Royalty-Free Products.

6.2   EXCEPT AS PROVIDED IN SECTION 6.1, NEITHER PARTY MAKES ANY OTHER REPRESENTATION OR WARRANTY, EXPRESS OR IMPLIED, INCLUDING, BUT NOT LIMITED TO, THE IMPLIED WARRANTIES OF MERCHANTABILITY AND FITNESS FOR A PARTICULAR PURPOSE, NOR DOES EITHER PARTY ASSUME ANY LIABILITY IN RESPECT OF ANY INFRINGEMENT OF PATENTS OR OTHER RIGHTS OF THIRD PARTIES DUE TO THE OTHER PARTY'S OPERATION UNDER THE LICENSES HEREIN GRANTED.

6.3   *IBM's* liability for breach of any of the representations and warranties set forth above shall be subject to Section 7.2 of the Purchase Agreement.

Section 7.0 Communications

7.1   All payments due after the Effective Date shall be made by electronic funds transfer. Any notice or other communication required or permitted to be made or given to either party hereto pursuant to this Agreement shall be sent to such party by facsimile or by registered airmail (except that registered or certified mail may be used where delivery is in the same country as mailing), postage pre-paid, addressed to it at its address set forth below, or to such other address as it shall designate by written notice given to the other party. Payments shall be deemed to be made on the date of electronic funds transfer. Notices or other communications shall be deemed to have been given or provided on the date of sending. The addresses are as follows:

(a)   For electronic funds transfers of payments:
      IBM Director of Licensing
      The Bank of New York
      48 Wall Street
      New York, New York 10286
      United States of America
      Credit Account No. 890-0209-674
      ABA No. 0210-0001-8

(b)   For mailing to *IBM*:
      Director of Licensing
      International Business Machines Corporation
      500 Columbus Avenue
      Thornwood, New York 10594
      United States of America

(c)   For facsimile transmission to *IBM*:
      (914) 742-6737

(d)   For mailing to LICENSEE:
      Director, Intellectual Property
      Uniphase Corporation
      163 Baypointe Parkway
      San Jose, CA 95134

(e)   For facsimile transmission to LICENSEE:
      (408) 954-0540

Section 8 Applicable Law

8.1   This Agreement shall be construed, and the legal relations between the parties hereto shall be determined, in accordance with the internal laws of the State of New York, United States of America, applicable to agreements made and to be performed entirely within such state, without regard to the conflicts of laws principles of such state.

8.2   Each of the parties waives its right to a jury trial and consents to the jurisdiction of any state or federal court located within the State of New York. Each of the parties hereby:

(i)   waives trial by jury,

(ii)   waives any objection to venue of any action instituted hereunder and

(iii) consents to the granting of such legal or equitable relief as is deemed appropriate by any aforementioned court.

Section 9 Miscellaneous

9.1   This Agreement may be executed by the parties hereto in one or more counterparts, each of which shall be an original and all of which shall constitute one and the same instrument.

9.2   Nothing contained in this Agreement shall be construed as conferring any right to use in advertising, publicity, or other promotional activities any name, trade name, trademark, trade dress or other designation of either party hereto (including any contraction, abbreviation or simulation of any of the foregoing), save as expressly stated herein. Each party hereto agrees not to use or refer to this Agreement or any provision hereof in any promotional activity associated with apparatus licensed hereunder, without the express written approval of the other party.

9.3   LICENSEE agrees not to export or re-export, or cause to be exported or re-exported, any technical data received hereunder, or the direct product of such technical data, to any country or person which, under the laws of the United States, are or may be prohibited from receiving such technical data or the direct product thereof.

9.4   This Agreement will not be binding upon the parties until it has been signed herein below by or on behalf of each party, and in which event it shall be effective as of the Effective Date. No amendment or modification hereof shall be valid or binding upon the parties unless made in writing and signed as aforesaid. This Agreement embodies the entire understanding of the parties with respect to the subject matter hereof and merges all prior discussions between them, and neither of the parties shall be bound by any conditions, definitions, warranties, understandings or representations with respect to the subject matter hereof other than as expressly provided herein.

9.5   The headings of the several Sections are inserted for convenience of reference only and are not intended to be a part of or to affect the meaning of interpretation of this Agreement.

9.6   If any Section of this Agreement is found by competent authority to be invalid, illegal or unenforceable in any respect for any reason, the validity, legality and enforceability of any such Section in every other respect and the remainder of this Agreement shall continue in effect so long as the Agreement still expresses the intent of the parties. If the intent of the parties cannot be preserved, this Agreement shall be either renegotiated or terminated.

9.7   In the event that Lasertron, Inc. requests *IBM* to provide any wafers pursuant to the Lasertron Agreement within one (1) year from the Effective Date, LICENSEE agrees that it will enter into suitable arrangements with *IBM* to provide such wafers under the terms and conditions set forth in the Lasertron Agreement, which terms and conditions are appended as Exhibit D.

IN WITNESS WHEREOF, the parties hereto have caused this Agreement to be duly signed as of the date first written above.

UNIPHASE CORPORATION

By: Danny E. Pettit
Name: Danny E. Pettit
Title: Vice President,
        Finance & CFO

INTERNATIONAL BUSINESS
MACHINES CORPORATION

By: Suzanne C. Lewis
Name: Suzanne C. Lewis
Title: Business Development
           Consultant

EXHIBIT A

LICENSED PATENTS
Issue or File

Patent/Application Number	Date (DD/MM/YY)
5,154,333	13/10/92
5,305,340	04/19/94
5,311,539	10/05/94
5,391,036	21/02/95
5,301,202	05/04/94
5,498,973	12/03/96
4,995,539	26/02/91
5,029,555	09/07/91
5,063,173	05/11/91
5,144,634	01/09/92
5,059,552	22/10/91
5,171,717	15/12/92
4,805,179	14/02/89
5,185,289	09/02/93
5,280,535	18/01/94
5,319,725	07/06/94
5,376,582	27/12/94
5,414,293	09/05/95
5,516,727	14/05/96
5,594,749	14/01/97
Appl. 721072	26/09/96
PCT/IB97/00055	27/01/97

EXHIBIT B

LICENSED TECHNICAL INFORMATION

I LICENSED TECHNICAL INFORMATION FOR ROYALTY FREE PRODUCTS

Process

Documentation, as is, for each process used in the development and fabrication of the following royalty free laser products and the detailed procedure for carrying out each step of the fabrication. Descriptions identify the tools and equipment used, and specifies the in-process tests that are performed.

QUALIFIED	IN QUALIFICATION	UNDER DEVELOPMENT
* 980 nm L-N series (narrow stripe lasers) - 120mW (linear power) - 150mW - 180mW - 210mW	* 980 nm lasers for submarine (70mW) * 956 nm broad area lasers (0.5 Watt)	* 980 nm narrow stripe laser (300mW) * 920...1020 nm narrow stripe lasers (150...210mW) * 910...980 nm broad area lasers (1W, 4W)

Process Materials

Documentation, as is, for all materials used when making *IBM's* royalty free laser products, including information concerning vendors, material grades, and part numbers,

Process Tools

Documentation, as is, for tools employed when making *IBM's* laser chips. This information comprises drawings and/or blueprints for jigs and tools such as the barhandler, facet coater, and bar tester, vacuum chuck, as well as details concerning the tools for lithography, etching and deposition, tools for material characterization and so forth.

Video Tapes

Tapes illustrating various process steps.

Reliability Database

Reliability data on *IBM's* royalty free products in computer readable form. Mask Set used for royalty free laser products processing

1) Laser – Development ZRL
        CSP Groove
        CSP NAM
        CVWAFMAP
        FUWA1
        FUWA2
        INP1
        LASER1
        LASER1P
        LASER2 (NEXUS)
        LASER3
        LASER4 (KORINTH)
        LASERX
        PULSE1
        REDARRAY
        SEGLASER
        SCLLD1
        PASSAGE
        VELNAM
        T2V2
        T3V1
        T13V1
        T14V1
        SOF1
        KOKIPHOT

2) Laser – Rests from EF
        RUESCHLIKON5170-5178
        FUWA113
        T2 LASER
        RS
        EPNPB
        PROTECT
        GOT2
        RUSHT2
        PULSE
        PAIRARC
        PASSAGE
        INP TO
        LASERX
        TTRNRN
        TNMETRP

TVIAPR-VIA
RIDGE LASER
METALR
TRIDRP
TPMETRN
TPMETRP
RID2CN
RID2CP
G2 PRIME

E2 Prototype Tool

Documentation, as is, for operation/maintenance of E2 Tool
- Assembly drawings, schematics, commercial components, spare parts
- Set-up manuals

II LICENSED TECHNICAL INFORMATION FOR ROYALTY BEARING PRODUCTS: *Documentation, as is, for:*

- Full Wafer Technology_A batch processing technique capable of producing more than one edge emitting semiconductor lasers simultaneously.
- Red Lasers_Indium gallium phosphorus/aluminum gallium indium phosphorus/aluminum gallium arsenide semiconductor laser chips emitting red light at about 670nm, and having a quantum well ridge-type structure and aluminum gallium arsenide cladding layers.
- 1300nm Lasers_Indium phosphorus/indium gallium arsenide phosphorus semiconductor laser chips emitting light at about 1300nm and having a double heterostructure or quantum well structure.

EXHIBIT C

NON-COMMERCIAL COMPUTER PROGRAMS USED AT THE FACILITY

C-1 ASSIGNED PROGRAMS

1)   Autobar Tester Software (BT2MESS and BT2ANA, home build)
2)   Waveguide/optical simulation (MODE, home build)
3)   Laser Lifetest (home build)
4)   Thermal device simulation (HEAT, home build)
5)   Heat flow modeling (HETMOD, home build)
6)   Device simulation (MONTE on AIX)
7)   Waveguide simulation (WAGSI)
8)   Epi software for running the MBE and CBE system (home build)
9)   Software for ESCA system (home build)
10)   Quick turnaround Device test software (QTAT, home build)
11)   [intentionally left blank]
12)   Photo Luminescence software (home build)

C-2 LICENSED PROGRAMS

ISP Laser Cleaver Tool Program

EXHIBIT D

Exhibit G to the *Lasertron* Agreement follows this page.

EXHIBIT G

WAFER MATERIAL

Till end of 1996 *IBM* will provide qualified and non-qualified epitaxially grown wafers to *LT*. Non-qualified epitaxially grown wafers are wafers out of specification. *IBM* is not committed to sell more than the maximum number of wafers given in the below tables. In 1997, epitaxially grown wafers will be sold to *LT* only if *LT* placed an order in 1996, such that *IBM* is able to grow those wafers in 1996. Such an advanced order shall include any information on the specification and structure necessary to grow the wafers as well as the number of wafers needed by *LT*. *IBM* is not committed to sell any wafer material in 1998 and later. The terms and conditions of this bridge offering are as follows:

Qualified epitaxially grown wafers (3 quarters per wafer)

Year	Price per wafer (0 – 25 wafers)	price per wafer (26 – 50 wafers)	maximum number/year
1995	(*)	(*)	(*)
1996	(*)	(*)	(*)
1997 (1)			(*)

(1) Subject to order by *LT* in 1996: price on request only.
*   Information redacted and filed separately with the SEC.

Non-qualified epitaxially grown wafers (2) (3 quarters per wafer)

Year	Price per wafer (0 – 20 wafers)
1995	(*)
1996	(*)
1997 (3)	

(2) Will be sold on the base of availability only.
(3) Subject to order by *LT* in 1996: price on request only.
*   Information redacted and filed separately with the SEC.

Patent License Agreement[25]

PATENT LICENSE AGREEMENT ("Agreement") with an Effective Date of March 10, 1997 between *INTERNATIONAL BUSINESS MACHINES CORPORATION*, a New York corporation (*"IBM"*), and *UNIPHASE CORPORATION*, a Delaware corporation ("LICENSEE").

Contemporaneously with the execution of this Agreement, the parties have entered into a Technology License Agreement which includes, in part, a license under certain technology owned by *IBM* to manufacture and sell Royalty-Bearing Products (as defined in such "Technology License Agreement"). The exercise of such technology license by LICENSEE may require a license under the *IBM* patents listed in Exhibit 1 (the "Licensed Patents"). LICENSEE desires to acquire a nonexclusive license under the Licensed Patents for such Royalty-Bearing Products.

In consideration of the premises and mutual covenants herein contained, *IBM* and LICENSEE agree as follows:

Section 1. Definitions

1.1 "Patented Portion" shall mean that portion of a Product which:

(a) embodies or uses all the elements or steps recited in any one Claim of one Licensed Patent; or
(b) is manufactured by use of all the steps recited in any one Claim of one Licensed Patent.

1.2 "Products" shall mean semiconductor laser chips other than Royalty-Free Products (as defined in the Technology License Agreement).

1.3 "Selling Price" shall mean the actual selling price to unaffiliated customers, and the greater of actual selling price or fair market value in sales to affiliated customers; provided that in either case the Selling Price shall be reduced for discounts, taxes, transportation fees and other unreimbursed charges paid by LICENSEE or its Subsidiaries in connection with the sale of Products.

1.4 "Subsidiary" shall mean a corporation, company or other entity:

(a) more than fifty percent (50%) of whose outstanding shares or securities (representing the right to vote for the election of directors or other managing authority) are, now or hereafter, owned or controlled, directly or indirectly, by a party hereto, or
(b) which does not have outstanding shares or securities, as may be the case

---

25   http://contracts.corporate.findlaw.com/agreements/uniphase/ibm.patentlic.1997.03.10. html (28.11.2004).

in a partnership, joint venture or unincorporated association, but more than fifty percent (50%) of whose ownership interest representing the right to make the decisions for such corporation, company or other entity is now or hereafter, owned or controlled, directly or indirectly, by a party hereto, but such corporation, company or other entity shall be deemed to be a Subsidiary only so long as such ownership or control exists.

1.5 "Claim" shall mean an allowed claim under a Licensed Patent that has not expired or been adjudicated invalid.

Section 2. License

2.1 *IBM* grants to LICENSEE and its Subsidiaries a nonexclusive license under the Licensed Patents to make, use, import, offer to sell, sell and otherwise transfer Products. The license as to any Subsidiary shall terminate on the date such Subsidiary ceases to be a Subsidiary. Additionally, subject to Section 2.4, *IBM* grants to LICENSEE and its Subsidiaries a nonexclusive license under the Licensed Patents the right to have LICENSEE's Products made by another manufacturer for the use and/or lease, sale or other transfer only by LICENSEE and its Subsidiaries. Such license shall further include the right to incorporate Products as components, subassemblies or subsystems in other products manufactured and/or sold by LICENSEE and its Subsidiaries.

2.2 No license is granted pursuant to Section 2.1 with respect to any particular Product, unless:

(a) a Licensed Patent defines a Patented Portion of said Product;
(b) said Licensed Patent is identified in a report as covering said Product, if required by Section 4.5; and
(c) either the royalty attributable to said Product is paid as required by Section 4.2, or a late payment of said royalty is made and accepted by *IBM* pursuant to Section 4.4.

2.3 No license, immunity or other right is granted under this Agreement, either directly or by implication, estoppel, or otherwise:

(a) other than under the Licensed Patents;
(b) with respect to any item other than a Product notwithstanding that such other item may incorporate one or more Products; or
(c) to parties acquiring any item from LICENSEE or its Subsidiaries for the combination of such acquired item with any other item, including other items provided by LICENSEE or its Subsidiaries, or for the use of any such combination even if such acquired item has no substantial use other than as part of such combination.

2.4 The license to have Products made granted in Section 2.1 to LICENSEE:

(a) shall only apply when the specifications for LICENSEE's Products were created by LICENSEE (either solely or jointly with one or more third parties);

(b) shall only be under Claims of Licensed Patents, the infringement of which would be necessitated by compliance with such specifications;

(c) shall not be under Claims for a method or process unless such method or process is based upon technology created by LICENSEE (either solely or jointly with one or more third parties) or otherwise licensed by *IBM* to LICENSEE; and

(d) shall not apply to any Products in the form manufactured or marketed by said other manufacturer prior to LICENSEE furnishing said specifications.

Unless LICENSEE informs *IBM* to the contrary, LICENSEE shall be deemed to have authorized said other manufacturer to make LICENSEE' Products under the license granted to LICENSEE in Section 2.1 when the condition specified in Section 2.4(a) is fulfilled. In response to a written request identifying a Product and a manufacturer, LICENSEE shall in a timely manner inform *IBM* of the quantity of such Product, if any, manufactured by such manufacturer pursuant to the license granted in Section 2.1.

2.5 LICENSEE shall have the right to exercise any license rights granted hereunder through any Subsidiary, and any reference in this Section 2 to LICENSEE shall be deemed to refer to any Subsidiary through which LICENSEE shall so exercise such license rights.

Section 3. Payment

3.1 LICENSEE, on behalf of itself and its Subsidiaries, shall pay a royalty for each Product which contains a Patented Portion at a rate computed at the following percentages of Selling Price of such Product:

Number of Licensed Patents Covering the Product	Percentage of Selling Price
1	1%
2	2%
3	3%
4	4%
5 or more	5%

For the purposes of this Section 3.1, a Licensed Patent and its corresponding patents in other countries, listed in Exhibit 1, shall be deemed to be one Licensed Patent.

Royalties shall only be payable on one occasion for each Product manufactured and sold by LICENSEE or its Subsidiaries. To the extent a Product consisting of a semiconductor laser chip, which is subject to LICENSEE's royalty obligations pursuant to this Section 3.1, is incorporated as a component, subassembly or subsystem in another product, the Selling Price shall be determined based on the published list price (or if no such published list price exists, the fair market value) of such semiconductor laser chip exclusive of any other portion of the product that does not contain Patented Portions.

3.2 Subject to Section 3.4, no royalties shall be paid by LICENSEE with respect to Products which LICENSEE purchases from a third party licensed under all of the Licensed Patents to sell such Products, and for which Products a royalty or other consideration was paid to *IBM*.

3.3 If LICENSEE purchases from a third party portions of a Product and combines such portions with each other and/or with other portions such that the combination is itself a Product which includes a Patented Portion not fully included in any individual purchased portion, then royalty shall be due for the combination in accordance with this Section 3, whether or not said third party is authorized by *IBM* to sell said purchased portions.

3.4 Any semiconductor laser chip that would otherwise be subject to LICENSEE's royalty obligations pursuant to this Section 3 shall not be subject to such royalty obligations if such chip is sold by LICENSEE (or any Subsidiary of LICENSEE authorized to exercise LICENSEE's license rights hereunder pursuant to Section 2.5 hereof) to a customer that is licensed by *IBM* at the time of such sale as to the Patented Portion that would otherwise give rise to such royalty obligation; provided such customer notifies LICENSEE, in writing at or prior to the time of such sale, that it is exercising its own "have made" rights as to such Patented Portion, and LICENSEE notifies *IBM*, of its intention to excercise such exclusion from its royalty obligation in the royalty report for such reporting period.

Section 4. Accruals, Records, Reports and Other Information

4.1 Royalties shall accrue when a Product, with respect to which royalty payments are required by this Agreement, is first sold or otherwise transferred (including, sold or otherwise transferred to *IBM* or any of its Subsidiaries), or first used in each country of use, by or for LICENSEE or any of its Subsidiaries.

4.2 LICENSEE's accounting period shall be semiannual and end on the last day of each June and December during the term of this Agreement. Within sixty (60) days after the end of each such period, LICENSEE shall furnish to *IBM* a written report containing the information specified in Section 4.5 and shall pay to IBM all unpaid royalties accrued hereunder through the end of each such period.

4.3 LICENSEE shall pay all royalties and other payments due hereunder in US dollars. All royalties for an accounting period computed in other currencies shall be converted into US dollars at the exchange rate for bank transfers from such currency to US dollars as quoted by the head office of Citibank N.A., New York, USA, at the close of banking on the last day of such accounting period (or the first business day thereafter if such last day is a non-business day).

4.4 *IBM* may accept a late payment provided such payment includes all overdue royalties or other payment plus interest. The interest on any overdue royalty or other payment shall be calculated commencing on the date such royalty or other payment became due, using an annual rate which is the greater of ten percent (10%) or one percentage point higher than the prime interest rate as quoted by the head office of Citibank N.A., New York, USA at the close of banking on such date, or on the first business day thereafter if such date falls on a non-business day. If such interest rate exceeds the maximum legal rate in the jurisdiction where a claim therefore is being asserted, the interest rate shall be reduced to such maximum legal rate.

4.5 LICENSEE's written report shall be certified by an officer of LICENSEE and shall contain the following information:

(a) a description of each type of Product, the quantity sold or otherwise transferred during the accounting period, and the sum of the Selling Prices for such quantity;

(b) identification of each Licensed Patent covering each such Product. However, if LICENSEE pays royalties for the use of five (5) or more Licensed Patents, LICENSEE shall have no obligation to identify the Licensed Patents for that Product;

(c) the amount of royalties due for each type of Product; and

(d) the aggregate amount of all royalties due.

In the event that any of Sections 4.5(a) through 4.5(d) does not apply to an accounting period, LICENSEE shall so indicate. In the event no royalties are due, LICENSEE's report shall so state.

4.6 For the purpose of determining obligations under *IBM* patents, LICENSEE shall, within thirty (30) days of a written request by *IBM*:

(a) provide to or make available for inspection by *IBM* or its designee any Product or a copy of any materials relevant to any Product identified by *IBM*;

(b) sell, license or otherwise transfer and deliver to *IBM* any Product at any time offered for sale or transferred by LICENSEE; and

(c) provide to *IBM* or its designee access to those manufacturing processes used by LICENSEE in the manufacture of Products.

4.7 LICENSEE shall keep records in accordance with generally accepted accounting principles and in sufficient detail to permit the determination of royalties due to *IBM*. Such records shall include, but not be limited to, detailed records supporting the information provided under Section 4.5. Such records shall be kept for six (6) years following the submission of the related report.

Upon written notice for an audit, LICENSEE shall permit auditors designated by *IBM*, together with such legal and technical support as *IBM* deems necessary, to examine, during ordinary business hours, records, materials, and manufacturing processes of LICENSEE for the purpose of verifying compliance with this Agreement.

Each party shall pay the costs that it incurs in the course of the audit. However, in the event that the audit establishes underpayment greater than five percent (5%) of the royalties due, LICENSEE shall reimburse *IBM* for the cost of the audit; provided, however, such reimbursement shall not exceed the amount of the underpayment.

4.8 *IBM* agrees that any statements or audit results furnished or otherwise made available to or obtained by *IBM* pursuant to this Section 4.0 shall be subject to equivalent confidentiality restrictions set forth in Section 3 of the Technology License Agreement and shall not be disclosed by *IBM* for a period of three (3) years from the date of disclosure.

Section 5. Term; Termination

5.1 The license granted herein shall remain in effect for a period of five (5) years from the Effective Date, unless earlier terminated under the provisions of this Agreement.

5.2 LICENSEE may terminate the license granted herein, in whole or as to any specified Licensed Patent by giving notice in writing to *IBM*; provided, however, that termination of the license as to any specified Licensed Patent shall include termination of the license as to all corresponding Licensed Patents in other countries. Any such termination shall be irrevocable.

5.3 *IBM* shall have the right to terminate this Agreement, or the license granted hereunder, if LICENSEE is more than fifty-thousand dollars ($50,000) in arrears in its payment obligations or if LICENSEE fails, at any time to:

(a) maintain records which substantially meets the requirements of Section 4.7;
(b) make a report which substantially meets the requirements of Section 4.5; or
(c) permit an audit pursuant to Section 4.7; and

if LICENSEE does not cure such breach within sixty (60) days after mailing of written notice from *IBM* to LICENSEE specifying the nature of such breach; unless such breach is the subject of a good faith dispute between *IBM* and LICENSEE. *IBM's* termination of this Agreement or of the license shall be effective upon written notice.

5.4 No termination of this Agreement or the license granted hereunder shall relieve LICENSEE of any obligation or liability accrued hereunder prior to such termination.

Section 6. *Option Granted*

6.1 LICENSEE grants to *IBM*, the right to obtain a license to make, use, import, offer to sell, sell and otherwise transfer any information handling system product. Said license shall be on terms, including royalty rates, no less favorable than those granted to LICENSEE herein or in any amendment hereto. Said right shall bewith respect to any patent under which LICENSEE or any of its Subsidiaries has the right to grant licenses to unaffiliated third parties at any time on or before the Effective Date and shall be limited to a number equivalent to the number of Licensed Patents licensed hereunder.

Section 7. *Means of Payment and Communication*

7.1 Payment shall be made by electronic funds transfer. Payments shall be deemed to be made on the date credited to the following account:

IBM, Director of Licensing
The Bank of New York
48 Wall Street
New York, New York 10286
United States of America
Credit Account No.890-0209-674
ABA No. 0210-0001-8

7.2 Notices and other communications shall be sent by facsimile or by registered or certified mail to the following address and shall be effective upon mailing:

For *IBM*:	For LICENSEE:
Director of Licensing	Director, Intellectual Property
IBM Corporation	Uniphase Corporation
500 Columbus Avenue	163 Baypointe Parkway
Thornwood, New York 10594	San Jose, CA 95134
Facsimile: (914) 742-6737	(408) 954-0540

Section 8.   *Miscellaneous*

8.1 LICENSEE shall not assign this Agreement, assign or sublicense any rights under it, nor delegate any of its obligations. Any attempt to do so shall be void.

8.2 Both parties agree not to use or refer to this Agreement or any of its provisions in any promotional activity.

8.3 *IBM* shall not have any obligation hereunder to institute any action or suit against third parties for infringement of any Licensed Patents or to defend any action or suit brought by a third party which challenges or concerns the validity of Licensed Patents. LICENSEE shall not have any right to institute any action or suit against third parties for infringement of any Licensed Patents.

8.4 *IBM* represents and warrants that it has the full right and power to grant the license set forth in Section 2. *IBM* MAKES NO REPRESENTATIONS OR WARRANTIES, EXPRESS OR IMPLIED, NOR SHALL *IBM* HAVE ANY LIABILITY, IN RESPECT OF ANY INFRINGEMENT OF PATENTS OR OTHER RIGHTS OF THIRD PARTIES DUE TO LICENSEE'S OPERATION UNDER THE LICENSE HEREIN GRANTED.

8.5 This Agreement shall not be binding upon the parties until it has been signed hereinbelow by or on behalf of each party. No amendment or modification hereof shall be valid or binding upon the parties unless made in writing and signed as aforesaid.

8.6 If any section of this Agreement is found by competent authority to be invalid, illegal or unenforceable in any respect for any reason, the validity, legality and enforceability of any such section in every other respect and the remainder of this Agreement shall continue in effect so long as the Agreement still expresses the intent of the parties. However, if the intent of the parties cannot be preserved, this Agreement shall be either renegotiated or terminated.

8.7 This Agreement shall be construed, and the legal relations between the parties hereto shall be determined, in accordance with the law of the State of New York, USA, as such law applies to contracts signed and fully performed in such State.

8.8 The headings of sections are inserted for convenience of reference only and are not intended to be part of or to affect the meaning or interpretation of this Agreement.

This Agreement, including its Exhibit, and the Technology License Agreement of even date herewith, embody the entire understanding of the parties with respect to the Licensed Patents, and replaces any prior oral or written communications between them.

Agreed to: Agreed to:

UNIPHASE CORPORATION   INTERNATIONAL BUSINESS MACHINES
                                    CORPORATION

By: Danny E. Pettit   By: Suzanne C. Lewis
Name: Danny E. Pettit   Name: Suzanne C. Lewis
Title: Vice President,   Title: Business Development Consultant
       Finance and CFO

Exhibit 1

"Licensed Patents" shall mean the following patents, patents issuing from the following applications, and all patents which are reissues, divisions, continuations, or extensions of any of the following patents:

Patent/Application Number	Issue or File Date (DD/MM/YY)
4,246,548	20/01/81
4,805,179	14/02/89
4,901,329	13/02/90
4,917,453	17/04/90
4,971,927	20/11/90
5,029,555	09/07/91
5,032,219	16/07/91
5,032,879	16/07/91
5,0377,76	06/08/91
5,059,552	22/10/91
5,060,233	22/10/91
5,100,220	31/03/92
5,103,493	07/04/92
5,111,468	05/05/92
5,153,890	06/10/92
5,172,365	15/12/92
5,177,031	05/01/93
5,185,289	09/02/93
5,247,597	21/09/93
5,259,049	02/11/93
5,280,535	18/01/94
5,284,792	08/02/94
5,287,001	15/02/94
5,307,357	26/04/94
5,309,465	03/05/94
5,311,539	10/05/94
5,319,725	07/06/94
5,327,415	05/07/94
5,331,655	19/07/94
5,344,746	06/09/94
5,373,166	13/12/94
5,376,582	27/12/94
5,376,587	27/12/94
5,414,293	09/05/95
5,463,705	31/10/95
5,498,973	12/03/96
5,516,727	14/05/96
5,594,749	14/01/97
Appl.721072	26/09/96
PCT/IB97/00055	27/01/97

Agreement for the Exchange of Confidential Information[26]

Uniphase Corporation	International Business Machines Corporation
163 Baypointe Parkway	c/o Research Division
San Jose, CA 95134	Zurich Research Laboratory
	CH-8803 Ruschlikon

Uniphase Laser Enterprise AG
c/o Treuhand von Flue AG,
Grienbackstrasse 17
CH-6301 Zug

Uniphase Corporation and *Uniphase Laser Enterprise AG* collectively (*Uniphase*) and *International Business Machines Corporation* (*IBM*) agree that the following terms and conditions apply when one of the parties (Discloser) discloses Confidential Information (Information) to the other (Recipient) under this Agreement.

Uniphase and *IBM* agree that our mutual objective under this Agreement is to provide appropriate protection for Information while maintaining our ability to conduct our respective business activities.

Information means any and all information disclosed to, or obtained through observation on other perception at the jointly occupied facility located at Ruschlikon, Saumerstrasse 4, by either party pertaining to the other party (Disclosing Party) which is marked with a restrictive legend, or which, in the reasonable judgement of an ordinary person, would appear to be of a proprietary nature and, therefore, in his judgement, should not be disclosed to a third party without the Discloser's consent; including business, financial, customer, supplier, and technical data.

1. DISCLOSURE

The Discloser's and the Recipient's Point of Contact will coordinate and document as necessary the disclosure. The initial Point of Contact for *Uniphase* will be Volkar Graf and for *IBM* will be Peter Buttner. Either party may change its Point of Contact by notifying the other party in writing. Information will be disclosed either:

a) in writing;
b) by delivery of items;
c) by initiation of access to Information, such as may be containned in a data base; or
d) by oral and/or visual presentation;
e) by accidental observation.

---

[26] *Source: http://cobrands.contracts.findlaw.com/agreements/uniphase/ibm.confid. 1997.03.10. html (18.11.2004).*

Information should be marked with a restrictive legend of the Discloser. If Information is not marked with such legend or is disclosed orally or observed accidentally, 1) the Information will be identified as confidential at the time of disclosure or within ten (10) working days and 2) the Discloser will promptly provide the Recipient's Point of Contact with a written summary including the date disclosed and a brief non-confidential description of the Information.

2. OBLIGATIONS

The Recipient agrees to use the same care and discretion to avoid disclosure, publication or dissemination of the Discloser's Information as it uses with its own similar Information that it does not wish to disclose, publish or disseminate. The Recipient may use the Discloser's Information for any purpose which does not violate such obligation, but will not disclose Information to third parties without the permission of the Discloser.

3. CONFIDENTIALITY PERIOD / TERM

Information disclosed pursuant to this Agreement will be subject to the terms of this Agreement for three years from the date of disclosure. The Term of this Agreement will begin on March 10, 1997 and will expire upon the termination or expiration date of the Laboratory Real Estate Lease Agreement entered into by Uniphase and *IBM* (the "Lease Agreement") or June 30, 1999 which ever is earlier.

4. EXCEPTIONS TO OBLIGATIONS

The Recipient may disclose, publish, disseminate, and use Information that is

1) already in its possession without obligation of confidentiality;
2) developed independently;
3) obtained from a source other than the Discloser without obligation of confidentiality;
4) publicly available when received, or thereafter becomes publicly available through no fault of the Recipient; or
5) disclosed by the Discloser to another party without obligation of confidentiality.

5. RESIDUAL INFORMATION

The Recipient may disclose, publish, disseminate, and use the ideas, concepts, know-how and techniques, related to the Recipient's business activities, which are contained in the Discloser's Information and retained in the memories of Recipient's employees who have had access to the Information pursuant to this Agreement (Residual Information).

Nothing contained in this Section gives the Recipient the right to disclose, publish, or disseminate, except as set forth elsewhere in this Agreement:

1) the source of Residual Information;

2) any financial, statistical or personnel data of the Discloser; or

3) the business plans of the Discloser.

6. DISCLAIMERS

THE DISCLOSER PROVIDES INFORMATION SOLELY ON AN "AS IS" BASIS.

The Discloser will not be liable for any damages arising out of the use of Information disclosed hereunder. Neither this Agreement nor any disclosure of Information hereunder grants the Recipient any right or license under any trademark, copyright or patent now or hereafter owned or controlled by the Discloser. The receipt of Information pursuant to this Agreement will not preclude, or in any way limit, the Recipient from:

1) providing to others products or services which may be competitive with products or services of the Discloser;

2) providing products or services to others who compete with the Discloser; or

3) assigning its employees in any way it may choose.

7. GENERAL

This Agreement does not require either party to disclose or to receive Information. Neither party may assign, or otherwise transfer, its rights or delegate its duties or obligations under this Agreement without prior written consent. Any attempt to do so is void. This Agreement may only be modified by a written agreement signed by authorized representatives of both parties. Neither party may terminate this Agreement unless the Lease Agreement expires or is terminated. Any provisions of this Agreement which by their nature extend beyond its termination remain in effect until fulfilled and apply to both parties' successors and assigns. Waiver of any breach of this Agreement shall not be a waiver of any subsequent breach nor shall it be a waiver of the underlying obligations. The Laws of State of New York, without regard to its principles of conflicts of lows govern this Agreement.

The parties acknowledge that they have read this Agreement, understand it, and agree to be bound by its terms and conditions. This Agreement is the complete and exclusive agreement between the parties regarding disclosures of Information and replaces any prior oral or written communications between the parties. Once signed, any reproduction of this Agreement made by reliable means (for example, photocopy or facsimile) is considered an original.

Agreed to: Agreed to:

Uniphase Corporation   INTERNATIONAL BUSINESS MACHINES
163 Baypointe Parkway   CORPORATION
San Jose, CA 95134   Research Division
                                        Zurich Research Laboratory
                                        CH-8803 Ruschlikon

By: Danny E. Pettit
Name: Danny E. Pettit
Title: Vice President,
        Finance and CFO
Date: 3/10/97

By: Suzanne C. Lewis
Name: Suzanne C. Lewis
Title: Business Development Consultant

Date: 3/10/97

Uniphase Laser Enterprise AG, Zug
By: Danny E. Pettit
Name: Danny E. Pettit
Title: Vice President, Finance and CFO
Date: 3/10/97

References

Abraham, B.P.; Moitra, S.D. (2001): Innovation assessment through patent analysis. *Technovation*, Vol. 21, No. 4, pp. 245-252.

AIPLA (2001): *Economic Report 2001*. AIPLA American Intellectual Property Law Association: Arlington, Virginia.

Aitken, M.; Baskaran, S.; Lamarre, E.; Silber, M.; Waters, S. (2000): A license to cure. *McKinsey Quarterly*, No. 1, pp. 80-89.

Anand, B.N.; Khanna, T. (2000): *Do Firms Learn to Create Value? The Case of Alliances*. Strategic Management Journal, Vol. 21, pp. 295-315.

Anderson, E.; Weitz, B. (1989): Determinants of continuity in conventional industrial channel dyads. *Marketing Science*, Vol. 8, pp. 310-323.

Anderson, J.C.; Narus, J.A. (1995): Capturing the value of supplementary services. *Harvard Business Review*, Vol. 73, No. 3, pp. 75-83.

Arora, A. (1997): Patents, licensing, and market structure in the chemical industry. *Research Policy*, Vol. 26, No. 4-5, pp. 391-403.

Arundel, A. (2001): The relative effectiveness of patents and secrecy for appropriation. *Research Policy*, Vol. 30, No. 4, pp. 611-624.

Arundel, A.; Kabla, I. (1998): What percentage of innovations are patented? Empirical estimates for European firms. *Research Policy*, Vol. 27, No. 2, pp. 127-141.

Askar, K. (2005): *Intellectual Property Management in R&D Collaborations*. Bachelor Thesis at Institute of Technology Management (ITEM) of University of St.Gallen (HSG): St. Gallen.

Athreye, S. and Cantwell, J. (2005): Royalty and Licensing Fees, World 1950-2003. In: Gambardella, A. (2005): *Assessing the Market for Technology in Europe*. Presentation on the occasion of the European Patent Academy conference: Berlin.

Atrua (2005): *Swisscom Mobile, Sicap and Atrua improve usability of GSM mobile data services*. Februare 15th, 2005, http://www.atrua.com/news/news_15feb05_a.html

Austin, D.H. (1993): An event-study approach to measuring innovative output: The case of biotechnology. *American Economic Review*, Vol. 83, No. 2, pp. 253-258.

Axelrod, R.; Mitchell, W.; Thomas, R.E.; Bennet S.D.; Bruderer, E. (1995): Coalition formation in standard-setting alliances. *Management Science*, Vol. 41, No. 9, pp. 1493-1508.

Bader, M.A. (2006a): *Managing Intellectual Property in Inter-firm R&D Collaborations. The Case of the Service Industry Sector.* Dissertation at University of St.Gallen (HSG): St. Gallen, No. 3150.

Bader, M.A. (2006b): Risikominimierung durch Intellectual Property Management. In: Gassmann, O.; Kobe, C. (eds.): *Management von Innovation und Risiko – Quantensprünge in der Entwicklung erfolgreich managen.* Springer: Berlin, 2nd ed.

Bader, M.A. (2006c): Von den Grundlagen des gewerblichen Rechtsschutzes zum strategischen Umgang. In: *Intellectual Property – Recht und Management.* Management Circle: Eschborn.

Bader, M.A. (2006d): Outsourcing des Patentanmeldeprozesses. *Mitteilungen der Deutschen Patentanwälte,* (forthcoming).

Bader, M.A. (2006e): Managing intellectual property in a collaborative environment: learning from IBM. *International Journal of Intellectual Property Management,* (forthcoming).

Bader, M.A. (2006f): Managing intellectual property in the financial services industry sector: learning from Swiss Re. *International Journal of Services Technology and Management,* (forthcoming).

Bader, M.A.; Bischof, D. (2005): Intellectual Property Management in der Finanzdienstleistungsbranche. In: Gassmann, O.; Albers, S. (eds.): *Handbuch Technologie- und Innovationsmanagement.* Gabler: Wiesbaden.

Bader, M.A.; Cuypers, F. (2006): Swiss Re: Global Intellectual Property Management in the Financial Services Industry. In: Boutellier, R.; Gassmann, O.; von Zedtwitz, M. (eds.): *Managing Global Innovation.* Springer: Berlin, 3rd ed. (forthcoming).

Balakrishnan, S.; Koza, M.P. (1993): Information asymmetry, adverse selection and joint-ventures: Theory and evidence. *Journal of Economic Behavior & Organization,* Vol. 20, No. 1, pp. 99-117.

Barkema, H.; Shenkar, O.; Vermeulen, F., Bell, J.H.J. (1997): Working abroad, working with others: how firms learn to operate international joint ventures. *Academy of Management Journal,* Vol. 40, pp. 426-442.

Beamish, P.J. (1987): Joint ventures in LDCs: Partner selection and performance. *Management International Review,* Vol. 27, pp. 23-37.

Beck, D. (2005) *Webpage of Didier Beck.* June 6, 2005, http://www.didierbeck .com/2005_05_01_blogs.php.

Beckenbauer, A. (2005a): *Intellectual Property Management in the early stage of R&D inter-firm cooperations.* Projet de Fin d'Etudes à l'Ecole Nationale Supérieure de Génie Industriel INP Grenoble: Grenoble.

Beckenbauer, A. (2005b): *Intellectual Property Management in the early stage of R&D inter-firm cooperations.* Master Recherche 2ième année, Management Stratégique et Génie des Organisations spécialité «Génie Industriel». Ecole Nationale Supérieure de Génie Industriel INP Grenoble: Grenoble.

Becker, W.; Dietz, J. (2004): R&D cooperation and innovation activities of firms - evidence for the German manufacturing industry. *Research Policy,* Vol. 33, No. 2, pp. 209-223.

Becker, W.; Peters, J. (1998): R&D-competition between vertical corporate networks: structure, efficiency and R&D spillovers. *Economics of Innovation and New Technology*, Vol. 6, pp. 51-71.

Behrmann, N. (1998): *Technisches Wissen aus Patenten*. Dissertation at University of St.Gallen (HSG): St. Gallen, No. 2104.

Bekkers, R.; Duysters, G.; Verspagen, B. (2002): Intellectual property rights, strategic technology agreements and market structure: The case of GSM. *Research Policy*, Vol. 31, No. 7, pp. 1141-1161.

Belderbos, R.; Carree, M.; Lokshin B. (2004): Cooperative R&D and firm performance. *Research Policy*, Vol. 33, No. 10.; 1477-1492.

Belz, C. (1998): *Akzente im innovativen Marketing*. Thexis/Ueberreuter: St. Gallen/Wien.

Belz, C., Schuh, G., Groos, A.; Reinecke, S. (1997): *Industrie als Dienstleister*. Thexis, St. Gallen.

Berkowitz, J. (2000): *Patenting the new business model: building fences in cyberspace*, New York.

Bessen, J.; Maskin E. (1999): *Sequential Innovation, Patents, and Imitation*. Working Paper. Harvard University and Massachusetts Institute of Technology, Department of Economics.

Betschart, A.O. (2004): *Patentmanagement in China*. Bachelor Thesis at Institute of Technology Management (ITEM) of University of St.Gallen (HSG): St. Gallen.

Bleeke, J.; Ernst D. (1993): *Collaborating to Compete: Using Strategic Alliances and Acquisitions in the Global Market Place*. John Wiley and Sons: New York.

Bleicher, K. (1991): *Das Konzept Integriertes Management*, Frankfurt: Campus

Blind, K.; Thumm, N. (2004): Interrelation between patenting and standardisation strategies: empirical evidence and policy implications. *Research Policy*, Vol. 33, No. 10, pp. 1583-1598.

Borg, E.A. (2001): Knowledge, information and intellectual property: implications for marketing relationships. *Technovation*, Vol. 21, No. 8, pp. 515-524.

Boss, M.A. (2000): The Beneficial Cycle of Innovation and Commercialization. *les Nouvelles – Journal of the Licensing Executives Society*, Vol. XXXV, No. 3, pp. 149-151.

Boutellier, R.; Behrmann, N. (1997): Quellen technischen Wissens. Ansätze für eine inhaltsorientierte Betrachtung von Patentdokumenten. *Wissenschaftsmanagement*, No. 3, pp.123-129.

Boutellier, R.; Behrmann, N.; Bratzler, M. (1998): Patentsystem als Wissensfundus. *Wissenschaftsmanagement*, No. 1, pp. 50-60.

Boutellier, R.; Gassmann, O.; von Zedtwitz, M. (2000): *Managing Global Innovation*. Springer: Berlin, 2nd ed.

Bouty, I. (2000): Interpersonal and interaction influences on informal resource exchanges between R&D researches across organizational boundaries. *Academy of Management Journal*, Vol. 43, No. 1, pp. 50-56.

Boyt, T.; Harvey, M. (1997): Classification of Industrial Service: A Model with Strategic Implications. *Industrial Marketing Management*, Vol. 26, No. 6, pp. 291-300.

Bramson, R.S. (2000): Mining the Patent Portfolio for Licensing Opportunities and Revenues. *les Nouvelles – Journal of the Licensing Executives Society*, Vol. XXXV, No. 3, pp. 109-115.

Brandenburger, A.; Nalebuff, B.J. (1996): *Coopetition*. Doubleday Books: New York.

Breese, P. (2002): Valuation Of Technological Intangible Assets. *les Nouvelles – Journal of the Licensing Executives Society*, Vol. XXXVII, No. 2, pp. 54-57.

Breitzman, A.; Thomas, P.; Cheney, M. (2002): Technological powerhouse or diluted competence: Techniques for assessing mergers via patent analysis. *R&D Management*, Vol. 32, No. 1, pp. 1-10.

Brockhoff, K.K. (1999): *Forschung und Entwicklung: Planung und Kontrolle*. Oldenburg: Munich, 5th ed.

Brockhoff, K.K.; Ernst, H.; Hundhausen, E. (1999): Gains and pains from licensing - patent-portfolios as strategic weapons in the cardiac rhythm management industry. *Technovation*, Vol. 19, No. 10, pp. 605-614.

Brouwer, E.; Kleinknecht, A. (1999): Innovative output, and a firm's propensity to patent.: An exploration of CIS micro data. *Research Policy*, Vol. 28, No. 6, pp. 615-624.

Brown, J. (2000): Allocations of ownership of inventions in joint development agreements – the united kingdom perspective. *Les Nouvelles – Journal of the Licensing Executives Society,* Vol. XXXV, No. 4, pp. 173-175.

Camagni, R. (1993): Inter-firm industrial network: the cost and benefits of cooperative behavior. *Journal of Industry Studies*, Vol. 1, No. 1, pp. 1-15.

Casagranda, M. (1994): *Industrielles Service-Management: Grundlagen, Instrumente, Perspektiven*. Gabler: Wiesbaden.

Chesbrough, H. (2001): Old dogs can learn new tricks. *MIT Technology Review Online*, July, 2001.

Chesbrough, H. (2003a): *Open Innovation: The New Imperative for Creating and Profiting from Technology*. Harvard Business School Press: Boston.

Chesbrough, H. (2003b): The Era of Open Innovation. *MIT Sloan Management Review*, Spring 2003, pp. 35-41.

Chiesa, V.; Manzini, R. (1998): Organizing for technological collaborations; A managerial perspective. *R&D Management*, Vol. 28, No. 3, pp. 199-212.

Chiesa, V.; Manzini, R.; Toletti, G. (2002): Standard-setting processes: evidence from two case studies. *R&D Management*, Vol. 32, No. 5, pp. 431-450.

Cohen, W.M.; Goto, A.; Nagata, A., Nelson, R.R.; Walsh, J.P. (2002): R&D spillovers, patents and the incentives to innovate in Japan and the United States. *Research Policy*, Vol. 31, No. 8-9, pp. 1349-1367.

Cohen, W.M.; Nelson, R.R.; Walsh, J.P. (2000): *Protecting Their Intellectual Assets: Approbability Conditions and Why US Manufacturing Firms Patent or Not*. NBER Working Paper, No. 7552.

Coriat, B.; Orsi, F. (2002): Establishing a new intellectual property rights regime in the United States: Origins, content and problems. *Research Policy*, Vol. 31, No. 8-9, pp. 1491-1507.

Corsten, H. (1990): *Betriebswirtschaftslehre der Dienstleistungsunternehmen*. Oldenburg: Munich, 2nd ed.

Culler, K.G. (2001): Out of the Lab and into the Marketplace: It's About a Business Plan. *les Nouvelles – Journal of the Licensing Executives Society*, Vol. XXXVI, No. 4, pp. 125-127.

Cuypers, F. (2003): *The path to knowledge is patently clear*. Swiss Reinsurance Company: Zurich.

Dacin, M.T.; Hitt, M.A.; Levitas, E. (1997): Selecting partners for successful international alliances: examination of U.S. and Korean firms. *Journal of World Business*, Vol. 32, No. 1, pp. 3-16.

Daft, R.L. (1998): *Organization theory and design*. South-Western College Publishing: Cincinnati, Ohio.

Dahan, E.; Hauser, J.R. (2001): Product Development – Managing a Dispersed Process. In: Weitz, B.A.; Wensley, R. (eds.): *Handbook of Marketing*. Sage: London, pp. 179-222.

Dahan, E.; Hauser, J.R. (2002): The virtual customer. *Journal of Product Innovation Management*, Vol. 19, No. 5, pp. 332-353.

Davenport, S.; Davies, J.; Miller, A. (1999): Framing of international research alliances: Influence on strategy. *R&D Management*, Vol. 29, No. 4, pp. 329-342.

Deng, Z.; Lev, B.; Narin, F. (1999): Science & technology as predictors of stock performance. *Financial Analysts Journal*, Vol. 55, No. 5, pp. 20-32.

Dillahunty, G.T. (2002): How to (and how not to) deal with inventorship in joint agreements. *Les Nouvelles – Journal of the Licensing Executives Society*, Vol. XXXVII, No. 1, pp. 1-6.

Dixi, A.K.; Nalebuff, J.N. (1990): *Spieltheorie für Einsteiger*. Schäffer-Poeschel: Stuttgart.

Doz, Y.; Hamel, G. (1998): *Alliance Advantage: The art of creating value through partnering*. Harvard Business School Press: Boston.

Duysters, G.; Kok, G.; Vaandrager, M. (1999): Crafting successful strategic technology partnerships. *R&D Management*, Vol. 29, No. 4, pp. 343-351.

Dyer, J.H.; Singh, H. (1998): The Relational View: Cooperative Strategy and Sources of Interorganizational Competitive Advantage. *Academy of Management Review*, Vol. 23, pp. 660-679.

Edler, J.; Meyer-Krahmer, F.; Reger, G. (2002): Changes in the strategic management of technology: results of a global benchmarking study. *R&D Management*, Vol. 32, No. 2, pp. 149-164.

Ehrat, M. (1997): *Kompetenzorientierte, analysegestützte Technologiestrategieerarbeitung*. Dissertation at University of St.Gallen (HSG): St. Gallen, No. 1981.

Ehrbar, T.J. (1993): *Business International's guide to international licensing: building a licensing strategy for 14 key markets around the world*. McGraw-Hill: New York.

Eisenhardt, K.M. (1989): Building theories from case study research. *Academy of Management Review*, Vol. 14, No. 4, pp. 532-550.

Elton, J.J.; Shah, B.R.; Voyzey, J.N. (2002): Patent profits. *McKinsey Quarterly*, No. 3, p. 19.

Engelhardt, W.; Kleinaltenkamp, M., Reckenfelderbäumer, M. (1992): *Dienstleistungen als Absatzobjekt*. Report No. 52 of Institut für Unternehmensführung und Unternehmensforschung at Ruhr-Universität Bochum: Bochum.

Engelhardt, W.; Reckenfelderbäumer, M. (1999): Industrielles Service Management. In: Kleinaltenkamp, M.; Plinke, W. (eds.): *Markt- und Produktmanagement*. Springer: Berlin, pp. 184-278.

Enkel, E. (2005): *Management von Wissensnetzwerken. Erfolgsfaktoren und Beispiele*. Deutscher Universitäts-Verlag: Wiesbaden.

Enkel, E.; Kausch, C.; Gassmann, O. (2005): Managing the Risk of Customer Integration. *European Management Journal*, Vol. 23, No. 2, pp. 203-213.

Erickson, S.G. (1996): Using patents to benchmark technological standing: international differences in citation patterns. Benchmarking for Quality. *Management & Technology*, Vol. 3, No. 1, pp. 5-18.

Ernst, H. (1995): Patenting strategies in the German mechanical engineering industry and their relationship to company performance. *Technovation*, Vol. 15, No. 4, pp. 225-240.

Ernst, H. (1996): *Patentinformationen für die strategische Planung von Forschung und Entwicklung*. Gabler: Wiesbaden.

Ernst, H. (1997): The Use of Patent Data for Technological Forecasting: The Diffusion of CNC-Technology in the Machine Tool Industry. *Small Business Economics*, No. 9, pp. 361-381.

Ernst, H. (1998a): Industrial research as a source of important patents. *Research Policy*, Vol. 27, No. 1, pp. 1-15.

Ernst, H. (1998b): Patent Portfolios for Strategic R&D Planning. *Journal of Engineering and Technology Management*, Vol. 15, No. 4, pp. 279-308.

Ernst, H. (2001): Patent applications and subsequent changes of performance: evidence from time-series cross-section analyses on the firm level. *Research Policy*, Vol. 30, pp. 143-157.

Ernst, H. (2002a): Patentmanagement. In: Specht, D.; Möhrle, M.G. (eds.): *Lexikon Technologiemanagement*. Gabler: Wiesbaden, pp. 214-218.

Ernst, H. (2002b): Strategisches IP-Management in schnell wachsenden Technologieunternehmen. In: Hommel, U.; Knecht, T. (eds.): *Wertorientiertes Start-Up Management. Grundlagen, Instrumente, Strategien*. Vahlen: Munich, pp. 292-319.

Ernst, H. (2002c): Success Factors of New Product Development: A Review of the Empirical Literature. *International Journal of Management Reviews*, Vol. 4, No. 1, pp. 1-40.

Ernst, H.; Leptien, C.; Vitt, J. (1999): Schlüsselerfinder in F&E: Implikationen für das F&E-Personalmanagement. *Zeitschrift für Betriebswirtschaft*, Erg.-H. 1, pp. 91-118.

Ernst, H.; Leptien, C.; Vitt, J. (2000): Inventors Are Not Alike: The Distribution of Patenting Output Among Industrial R&D Personnel. *IEEE Transactions on Engineering Management*, Vol. 47, No. 2, pp. 184-199.

Ernst, H.; Omland, N. (2003): Patentmanagement junger Technologieunternehmen. *Zeitschrift für Betriebswirtschaft*, Erg.-H. 2, pp. 95-113.

Ernst, H.; Soll, J.H. (2002): An integrated portfolio approach to support market-oriented R&D planning. *International Journal of Entrepreneurship and Innovation Management*, Vol. 26, No. 5/6, pp. 540-560.

Ernst, H.; Vitt, J. (2000): The Influence of Corporate Acquisitions on the Behavior of Key Inventors. *R&D Management*, Vol. 30, No. 2, pp. 105-119.

European Commission (2001): EUR 19456 – Working Paper: *Intellectual Property Rights aspects of Internet collaborations*. Office for Official Publications of the European Communities: Luxembourg.

European Commission (2002): EUR 20230 – Working Paper: *Expert group report on role and strategic use of intellectual property rights in international research collaborations*. Office for Official Publications of the European Communities: Luxembourg.

Faber, J; Hesen, A.B. (2004): Innovation capabilities of European nations, Cross-national analysis of patents and sales of product innovations. *Research Policy*, Vol. 33, No. 2, pp.193-207.

Faix, A. (1998): *Patente im strategischen Marketing. Sicherung der Wettbewerbsfähigkeit durch systematische Patentanalyse und Patentnutzung*. Erich Schmidt: Berlin.

Fassnacht, M.; Homburg, C. (2001): Deutschsprachige Dienstleistungsforschung im internationalen Vergleich. *Die Unternehmung*, Vol. 55, No. 4/5, pp. 279-293.

FAZ (2001): Der Nutzen von Softwarepatenten ist umstritten. *Frankfurter Allgemeine Zeitung*, May 2nd, 2001, No. 101, p. 31.

FhG (2003): *Patents in the Service Industries. Final Report*. Fraunhofer Institute Systems and Innovation Research: Karlsruhe.

Fontanari, M.L. (1995): Voraussetzungen für den Kooperationserfolg – eine empirische Analyse. In: Schertler, W. (ed.): *Management von Unternehmenskooperationen – branchenspezifische Analyse – neueste Forschungsergebnisse*. Ueberreuter: Wien.

Fontanari, M.L. (1996): *Kooperationsgestaltungsprozesse in Theorie und Praxis*. Duncker: Berlin.

Fox, S.P. (1999): How to Get the Patents Others Want. *les Nouvelles – Journal of the Licensing Executives Society*, Vol. XXXIV, No. 1, pp. 3-8.

Fradkin, H.E. (2000): Technology Mining at Ford Motor Company. *les Nouvelles – Journal of the Licensing Executives Society*, Vol. XXXV, No. 4, pp. 160-162.

Frambach, R.; Wels-Lips, I.; Gündlach, A. (1997): Pro-active product service strategies – an application to the European health market. *Industrial Marketing Management*, Vol. 26, pp. 341-352.

Fraunhofer ISI, Fraunhofer PST, Max-Planck-Institute MPI (2001): *Micro- an Macroeconomic Implications of the Patentability of Software Innovations. In-*

tellectual Property Rights in Information Technologies between Competition and Innovation. Fraunhofer Institute for Foreign and International Patent, Copyright and Competition Law: Munich.

Friese, M. (1998): *Kooperation als Wettbewerbsstrategie für Dienstleistungsunternehmen*. Gabler: Wiesbaden.

Gadiesh, O.; Gilbert, J. (1998): Profit Pools: A fresh look at strategy. *Harvard Business Review*, Vol. 76, No. 3, pp. 139-147.

Gassmann, O. (1999): Praxisnähe mit Fallstudienforschung, *Wissenschaftsmanagement*, Vol. 6, No. 3, pp. 11-16.

Gassmann, O. (2001): E-Technologien in dezentralen Innovationsprozessen. *Zeitschrift für Betriebswirtschaft*, Erg.-H. 3/2001, pp. 73-90.

Gassmann, O. (2003): Wege zum erfolgreichen Produkt: Management von Innovationsprozessen. In: Österle, H.; Winter, R. (eds.): *Business Engineering – Auf dem Weg zum Unternehmen des Informationszeitalters*. Springer: Berlin, pp. 249-263.

Gassmann, O.; Bader M.A. (2003): Erfolg durch Intellectual Property Management. *Technische Rundschau*, Vol. 95, No. 6, pp. 24-25.

Gassmann, O.; Bader, M.A. (2004a): Bodyguards für Ihre Ideen. *io new management*, No. 4, pp. 10-14.

Gassmann, O.; Bader, M.A. (2004b): Geschickter Einsatz von Patenten. Mit Schutz- und Störstrategien zu Wettbewerbsvorteilen. *Neue Zürcher Zeitung*, August 7/8th, 2004, Nr. 182, p. 29.

Gassmann, O.; Bader, M.A. (2004c): *Abschlussbericht des Arbeitskreises Intellectual Property Management*. Undisclosed workshop report. University of St.Gallen (HSG): St. Gallen, pp. 1-182.

Gassmann, O.; Bader, M.A. (2006a): *Patentmanagement. Innovationen erfolgreich nutzen und schützen*. Springer: Berlin.

Gassmann, O.; Bader, M.A. (2006b): Intellectual Property Management in Interfirm R&D Collaborations. *Taiwan Academy of Management Journal*, Vol. 6, No. 2, pp. 217-236.

Gassmann, O.; Fuchs, M. (2001): Multilaterale Kooperationen. *Zeitschrift Führung + Organisation*, Vol. 70, No. 6, pp. 346-353.

Gassmann, O.; Hipp, C. (2001): Hebeleffekte in der Wissensgenerierung: Die Rolle von technischen Dienstleistern als externe Wissensquelle. *Zeitschrift für Betriebswirtschaft*, Erg.-H. 1, pp. 141-159.

Gassmann, O.; Sandmeier, P.; Wecht, C.H. (2004): Innovationsprozesse – Öffnung statt Alleingang. *io new management*, No. 1/2, pp. 22-27.

Gassmann, O.; von Zedtwitz, M. (1996): *Internationales Innovationsmanagement, Gestaltung von Innovationsprozessen im globalen Wettbewerb*. Vahlen: Munich.

Gassmann, O.; von Zedtwitz, M. (1998): Organization of Industrial R&D on a Global Scale. *R&D Management*, Vol. 28, No. 3, pp. 147-161.

Gassmann, O.; von Zedtwitz, M. (1999): New Concepts and Trends in International R&D Organization. *Research Policy*, Vol. 28, pp. 231-250.

Gassmann, O.; von Zedtwitz, M. (2003): Organizing Virtual R&D Teams: Towards a Contingency Approach. *R&D Management*, Vol. 33, No. 3, pp. 243-262.

Gebauer, H. (2004): *Die Transformation vom Produzenten zum produzierenden Dienstleister*. Disstertation at University of St.Gallen (HSG): St. Gallen, No. 2873.

Gebauer, H.; Fleisch, E.; Friedli, T. (2005): Overcoming the Service Paradox in Manufacturing Companies. *European Management Journal*, Vol. 23, No. 1, pp. 14-26.

George, V.P.; Farris, G. (1999): Performance of alliances: formative stages and changing organizational and environmental influences. *R&D Management*. Vol. 29, No. 4, pp. 379-389.

Geringer, J. (1991): Strategic determinants of partner selection criteria in international joint ventures. *Journal of International Business Studies*, Vol. 22, pp. 41-62.

Gerpott, T.J. (1999): *Strategisches Technologie- und Innovationsmanagement*. Schäffer-Poeschel: Stuttgart.

Gerstenberger, W. (1992): Zur Wettbewerbsposition der deutschen Industrie im High-Tech Bereich. *Ifo-Schnelldienst*, Vol. 45, No. 13, pp. 14-23.

Gerybadze, A. (1995): *Strategic Alliances and Process Redesign – effective management and restructuring of cooperative projects and networks*. de Gruyter: Berlin.

Geschka, H. (1995): Methoden der Technologiefrühaufklärung und der Technologievorhersage. In: Zahn, E. (ed.): *Handbuch Technologiemanagement*, Schäffer-Poeschel: Stuttgart.

Glaister, K.W.; Buckley, P.J. (1999): Performance Relationships in UK International Alliances. *Management International Review (MIR)*, Vol. 39, No. 2, pp. 123-147.

Gomez, P. (1999): *Unternehmensorganisation: Profile, Dynamik, Methodik*. Campus: Frankfurt a.M., 4th ed.

Granstrand, O. (1998): Towards a theory of the technology-based firm. *Research Policy*, Vol. 27, No. 5, pp. 465-489.

Granstrand, O. (2000): Corporate management of intellectual property in Japan. *International Journal of Technology Management*, Vol. 19, No. 1/2, pp. 121-148.

Granstrand, O; Hakanson, L.; Sjolander, S. (1992): *Technology Management and International Business: Internationalization of R&D Technology*. John Wiley and Sons: New York.

Griliches, Z. (1990): Patent statistics as economic indicators: a survey. *Journal of Economic Literature*, Vol. 28, pp. 1661-1707.

Griliches, Z. (1998): *R&D and Productivity - The Economic Evidence*. The University of Chicago Press: Chicago.

Grindley, P.C.; Teece, D.J. (1997): Managing Intellectual Capital: Licensing and cross-licensing in semiconductors and electronics. *California Management Review*, Vol. 39, pp. 8-41.

Gruetzmacher, R.R.; Khoury, S.; Willey, T.F. (2000): License Pricing - The Role of Company and University Complementary Assets. *les Nouvelles – Journal of the Licensing Executives Society*, Vol. XXXV, No. 3, pp. 116-123.

Gu, F.; Lev, B. (2000): *Markets in Intangibles: Patent Licensing.* Working Paper. Boston/New York.

Guellec, D.; van Pottelsberghe de la Potterie, B. (2001): The internationalisation of technology analysed with patent data. *Research Policy*, Vol. 30, No. 8, pp. 1253-1266.

Gulati, R. (1995a): Does Familiarity Breed Trust? The Implications of Repeated Ties for Contractual Choice in Alliances. *Academy of Management Journal*, Vol. 38, pp. 85-112.

Gulati, R. (1995b): Social structure and alliance formation patterns: A longitudinal analysis. *Administrative Science Quarterly*, Vol. 40, pp. 619-652.

Hagedoorn, J. (1993): Understanding the rationale of strategic technology partnering: inter-organizational modes of cooperation and sectoral differences. *Strategic Management Journal*, Vol. 14, No. 5, pp. 371-385.

Hagedoorn, J. (2002): Inter-firm R&D partnerships: an overview of major trends and patterns since 1960. *Research Policy*, Vol. 31, pp. 477-492.

Hagedoorn, J. (2003): Sharing intellectual property rights - an exploratory study of joint patenting amongst companies. *Industrial and Corporate Change*, Vol. 12, No. 5, pp. 1035-1050.

Hagedoorn, J.; Carayannis, E.; Alexander, J. (2001): Strange bedfellows in the personal computer industry: technology alliances between IBM and Apple. *Research Policy*, Vol. 30, No. 5, pp. 837-849.

Hagedoorn, J.; Cloodt, D.; van Kranenburg, H. (2005): Intellectual property rights and the governance of international R&D partnerships. *Journal of International Business Studies*, Vol. 36, No. 2, pp. 175-186.

Hagedoorn, J.; Cloodt, M. (2003): Measuring innovative performance: is there an advantage in using multiple indicators? *Research Policy*, Vol. 32, No. 8, pp. 1365-1379.

Hagedoorn, J.; Narula, R. (1996): Choosing Organizational Modes of Strategic Technology Partnering: International and Sectoral Differences. *Journal of International Business Studies*, Vol. 27, No. 2, pp. 265-284.

Hagedoorn, J.; Schakenraad, J. (1994): The effect of strategic technology alliances on company performance. *Strategic Management Journal*, Vol. 15, No. 4, pp. 291-311.

Hagedoorn, J.; van Kranenburg, H.; Osborn, R.N. (2003): Joint Patenting Amongst Companies – Exploring the Effects of Inter-Firm R&D Partnering and Experience. *Managerial & Decision Economics*, Vol. 24, No. 2/3, pp. 71-84.

Hall, B.H.; Jaffe, A.B.; Traijtenberg, M. (2000): Market value and patent citations: a first look. *NBER Working Paper*, No. 7741.

Hall, B.H.; Ziedonis, R.M. (2001): The patent paradox revisited: an empirical study of patenting in the semiconductor industry. *RAND Journal of Economics*, Vol. 32, No. 1, pp. 101-128.

Hamel, G. (1996): Strategy as a Revolution. *Harvard Business Review*, Vol. 74, No. 4, pp. 69-82.

Hamel, G.; Prahalad, C.K. (1990): The core competence and the corporation. *Harvard Business Review*, Vol. 68, No. 3, pp. 79-91.

Hamel, G.; Prahalad, C.K. (1995): *Wettlauf um die Zukunft*. Ueberreuter: Wien.

Hargadon, A.; Sutton, R.I. (2000): Wie Innovationen systematisch erarbeitet werden. *Harvard Business Manager*, Vol. 22, No. 6, pp. 46-54.

Harhoff, D.; Reitzig, M. (2001): Strategien zur Gewinnmaximierung bei der Anmeldung von Patenten. *Zeitschrift für Betriebswirtschaft*, Vol. 71, No. 5, pp. 509-530.

Harhoff, D.; Reitzig, M. (2004): Determinants of opposition against EPO patent grants--the case of biotechnology and pharmaceuticals. *International Journal of Industrial Organization*, Vol. 22, No. 4, pp. 443-480.

Harhoff, D.; Scherer, F.M.; Vopel, K. (2003): Citations, family size, opposition and the value of patent rights. *Research Policy*, Vol. 32, No. 8, pp. 1343-1363.

Harmann, B.-G. (2003): *Patente als strategisches Instrument zum Management technologischer Diskontinuitäten*. Dissertation at University of St.Gallen (HSG): St. Gallen, No. 2808.

Harrigan, K.R. (1985): *Managing joint ventures success*. Praeger: New York.

Harrigan, K.R. (1988): Strategic alliances and partnership asymmetries. *Management International Review*, Vol. 28, pp. 53-72.

Heide, J.B.; Miner, S. (1992): The Shadow of the Future: Effects of Anticipated Interaction and Frequency of Contact on Buyer-Seller Cooperation. *Academy of Management Journal*, Vol. 35, pp. 265-291.

Helm, R; Kloyer, M. (2004): Controlling contractual exchange risks in R&D interfirm cooperation: an empirical study. *Research Policy*, Vol 33, No. 8, pp. 1103-1122.

Hennart, J. (1988): A transaction costs theory of equity joint ventures. *Strategic Management Journal*, Vol. 9, No. 14, pp. 361-374.

Heskett, J.L.; Sasser, W.E.; Schlesinger L.A. (1997): *The service profit chain: how leading companies link profit and growth to loyalty, satisfaction, and value*. Free Press: New York.

Heuser, L.; Bader, M.A. (2006): SAP: Global Intellectual Property Management in the Software Industry Sector. In: Boutellier, R.; Gassmann, O.; von Zedtwitz, M. (eds.): *Managing Global Innovation*. Springer: Berlin, 3rd ed. (forthcoming).

Hicks, D.; Narin, F. (2000): *Strategic research alliances and 360 degree bibliometric indicators*. NSF workshop on Strategic research partnerships B2 - NSF workshop on Strategic research partnerships.

Hipp, C. (2000): *Innovationsprozesse im Dienstleistungssektor. Eine theoretisch und empirisch basierte Innovationstypologie*. Physica: Heidelberg.

Homburg, C; Garbe, B. (1996): Industrielle Dienstleistungen – Bestandsaufnahme und Entwicklungsrichtungen. *Zeitschrift für Betriebswirtschaft*, Vol. 66, No. 3, pp. 253-282.

Homburg, C; Günther, C.; Fassnacht, M. (2002): Erfolgreiche Umsetzung dienst-leistungsorientierter Strategien von Industrieunternehmen. *Schmalenbachs Zeitschrift für betriebswirtschaftliche Forschung*, Vol. 54, No. 9, pp. 487-508.

IGE (2003): *Research and Patenting in Biotechnology. A Survey in Switzerland.* Eidgenössisches Institut für Geistiges Eigentum: Bern, Publication No. 1, 12/03.

IMF – World economic outlook (International Monetary Fund) (September, 2002): *World economic outlook: a survey by the staff of the International Monetary Fund.* The Fund, 1980: Washington D.C.

Informationweek Smallbizpipeline (2005). *Microsoft Pitches Technology-For-Equity Licensing to Small Businesses and Entrepreneurs.* May 9th, 2005, http://www.informationweek.smallbizpipeline.com.162101514.

ITEM (2004a): *Strategic Technology Management.* Eight months international benchmarking study based on 61 technology intensive, global companies of which 13 case studies were extracted and of which five companies in Switzerland, Germany, Great Britain and USA got visited for in-depth analysis. Institute of Technology Management (ITEM) of University of St.Gallen (HSG): St. Gallen.

ITEM (2004b): *Expert Workshop Series on Intellectual Property Management.* Seven in-depth workshops over a time frame of nine months on intellectual property management, based on nine participating plus six guest multinational companies. Institute of Technology Management (ITEM) of University of St.Gallen (HSG): St. Gallen.

ITEM (2005a): *Multiplication Opportunities of Intellectual Property.* Eight month study including benchmarking within software and business solutions industry. Institute of Technology Management (ITEM) of University of St.Gallen (HSG): St. Gallen.

ITEM (2005b): *Exploitation of Intellectual Property.* Four months international benchmarking study in the chemical, pharmaceutical and biotechnology industry. Institute of Technology Management (ITEM) of University of St. Gallen (HSG): St. Gallen.

Iwasaki, Y. (2001): Licensing: A Tool to Expand Business. *les Nouvelles – Journal of the Licensing Executives Society*, Vol. XXXVI, No. 1, pp. 5-8.

Jaffe, A.B. (2000): The U.S. patent system in transition: policy innovation and the innovation process. *Research Policy*, Vol. 29, No. 4-5, pp. 531-557.

Jennewein, K. (2005): *Intellectual Property Management. The Role of Technology-Brands in the Appropriation of Technological Innovation.* Physica: Heidelberg.

Jones, O. (2000): Innovation management as a post-modern phenomenon: The outsourcing of pharmaceutical R&D. *British Journal of Management*, Vol. 11, pp. 341-356.

Jones, O.; Conway, S.; Steward, F. (2000): Introduction: Social interaction and organisation change. In: Jones, O; Conway, S; Steward, F. (eds.): *Social interaction and organisational change: Aston perspectives on innovation networks.* Imperial College Press: London.

Jorde, T.M.; Teece D.J. (1990): Innovation and cooperation: Implications for competition and antitrust. *Journal of Economic Perspectives. American Economic Association*, Vol. 4, No. 3, pp. 75-96.

Kahin, B. (2002): *Competition and intellectual property law and policy in the knowledge-based economy.* FTC/DOJ: Washington D.C.

Kale, P.; Singh, H. (1999): *Building alliance capabilities: a knowledge-based approach.* Academy of Management Best Paper Proceedings.

Kale, P.; Singh, H.; Perlmutter, H. (2000): Learning and protection of proprietary assets in strategic alliances: Building relational capital. Philadelphia. *Strategic Management Journal*, Vol. 21, No. 3, pp. 217-237.

Kanter, R.M. (1994): Collaborative Advantage: the Art of Alliances. *Harvard Business Review*, Vol. 72, No. 4, pp. 96-108.

Katz, M.L.; Ordover, J.A. (1990): R&D cooperation and competition. *Brooking Papers on Economic Activity: Microeconomics,* pp. 137-203.

Kelly, M.; Schaan, J.; Joncas, H. (2002): Managing alliance relationships: key challenges in the early stages of collaboration. *R&D Management,* Vol. 32, No. 1, pp. 11-22.

Khurana, A.; Rosenthal, S.R. (1997): Integrating the Fuzzy Front End of New Product Development. *Sloan Management Review*, Vol. 38, No. 2, pp. 103-120.

Kim, J.; Wilemon, D. (2002a): Focusing the fuzzy front-end in new product development. *R&D Management*, Vol. 32, No. 4, pp. 269-279.

Kim, J.; Wilemon, D. (2002b): Strategic issues in managing innovation's fuzzy front-end. *European Journal of Innovation Management*, Vol. 5, No. 1, pp. 27-39.

Kline, D. (2003): Sharing the Corporate Crown Jewels. *MIT Sloan Management Review*, Vol. 44, pp. 89-93.

Klinger, R. (2003): *Schutz von Dienstleistungsinnovationen gegen Imitation.* Peter Lang: Frankfurt a.M.

Knecht, T.; Leszinki, R.; Weber, F. (1993): Memo to the CEO. *McKinsey Quarterly*, Vol. 4, pp. 79-86.

Koen, P.; Ajamian, G.; Burkart, R.; Clamen, A.; Davidson, J.; D'Amore, R.; Elkins, C.; Herald, K.; Incorvia, M.; Johnson, A.; Karol, R.; Seibert, R.; Slavejkov, A.; Wagner, K. (2001): Providing Clarity and a Common Language to the 'Fuzzy Front End'. *Research Technology Management*, Vol. 44, No. 2, pp. 46-55.

Koen, P.; McDermott, R.; Olsen, R.; Prather, C. (2002): Enhancing Organizational Knowledge Creation for Breakthrough Innovation: Tools and Techniques. In: Belliveau, P.; Griffin, A.; Somermeyer, S. (eds.): *PDMA Toolbook for New Product Development.* John Wiley and Sons: New York.

Kogut, B. (1988): A study of the life cycle of joint ventures. In: Contractor, F.K.; Lorange, P. (eds.): Cooperative strategies in international business. *Management International Review*, special issue.

Kogut, B. (1989): The stability of joint ventures: Reciprocity and competitive rivalry. *Journal of Industrial Economics*, Vol. 38, pp. 183-198.

Kollmer, H.; Dowling, M. (2004): Licensing as a commercialisation strategy for new technology-based firms. *Research Policy*, Vol. 33, No. 8, pp. 1141-1151.

Kondo, M. (1999): R&D dynamics of creating patents in the Japanese industry. *Research Policy*, Vol. 28, No. 6, pp. 587-600.

Kortum, S.; Lerner, J. (1999): What is behind the recent surge in patenting? *Research Policy*, Vol. 28, No. 1, pp. 1-22.

Kromrey, H. (2002): *Empirische Sozialforschung – Modelle und Methoden der Datenerhebung und Auswertung*. VS Verlag für Sozialwissenschaften: Wiesbaden, 10th ed.

Kubicek, H. (1977): *Heuri*stische Bezugsrahmen und heuristisch angelegte Forschungsdesigns als Elemente einer Konstruktionsstrategie empirischer Forschung. In: Köhler, R. (ed.): *Empirische und handlungstheoretische Forschungskonzeptionen in der Betriebswirtschaftslehre*. Bericht über die Tagung des Verbandes der Hochschullehrer für Betriebswirtschaft e.V.: Stuttgart, pp. 5-36.

Lamnek, S. (1995): *Qualitative Sozialforschung: Methoden und Techniken*. Beltz PVU: Weinheim, 3rd ed.

Leonard, D. and Rayport, J.F. (1997) Spark innovation through empathic design. *Harvard Business Review*, Vol. 75, No. 6, pp. 102-114.

Leonard-Barton, D. (1995): *Wellsprings of Knowledge*. Harvard Business School Press: Boston.

Leptien, C. (1996): *Anreizsysteme in Forschung und Entwicklung unter besonderer Berücksichtigung des Arbeitnehmererfindergesetzes*. Wiesbaden.

Lerner, J. (1994): The importance of patent scope: an empirical analysis. *RAND Journal of Economics*, Vol. 25, No. 2, pp. 319-332.

Levin, R.C.; Klevorick, A.K.; Nelson, R.R.; Winter, S.G. (1987): *Appropriating the Returns from Industrial Research and Development*. Brookings Papers on Economic Activity, Brookings Institution: Washington D.C.

Levinthal, D.; Fichman, M. (1988): Dynamics of interoganizational attachments: Auditor-client relationship. *Administrative Science Quarterly*, Vol. 33, pp. 345-369.

Linder, J.C.; Jarvenpaa, S.; Davenport, T.H. (2003): Toward an Innovation Sourcing Strategy. *MIT Sloan Management Review*, Vol. 44, No. 4, pp. 43-49.

Lowe, J.; Taylor, P. (1998): R&D and technology purchase through license agreements. *R&D Management*, Vol. 28, No. 4, pp. 263-278.

Luukkonen, T. (1998). The difficulties in assessing the impact of EU framework programmes. *Research Policy*, Vol. 27, pp. 599-610.

Lynn, G.S.; Morone, J.G.; Paulson, A.S. (1996): Wie echte Produktinnovationen entstehen. *Harvard Business Manager*, Vol. 18, No. 4, pp. 80-91.

Mansfield, E. (1986): Patents and Innovation: An Empirical Study. *Management Science*, Vol. 32, pp. 173-181.

Markwith, M. (2003): *How to protect ip before entering into new relationships. Interview in Supplier Selection & Managment Report*. Institute of Management & Administration: New York, April 2003, pp. 2-4.

Masurel, E. (2002): Patenting behavior by SMEs. *International Journal of Entrepreneurship and Innovation Management*, Vol. 2, No. 6, pp. 574-583.

Mathe, H.; Shapiro, R.D. (1993): *Integrating service strategy in the manufacturing company.* Chapman & Hall: London.

Mathieu, V. (2001): Product services: from a service supporting the product to a service supporting the client. *Journal of Business & Industrial Marketing,* Vol. 16, No. 1, pp. 39-58.

Mazzoleni, R.; Nelson, R.R. (1998): The benefits and costs of strong patent protection: a contribution to the current debate. *Research Policy,* Vol. 27, No. 3, pp. 273-284.

McQueen, D.H.; Olsson, H. (2003): Growth of embedded software related patents. *Technovation,* Vol. 23, No. 6, pp. 533-544.

Meckl, R. (1995): Zur Planung internationaler Unternehmenskooperationen. *Zeitschrift für Planung.*

Meffert, H.; Bruhn, M. (2003): *Dienstleistungsmarketing.* Gabler: Wiesbaden, 4th ed.

Merchant, H. (1997): International joint venture performance of firms in the nonmanufacturing sector. In: Beamish, P.; Inkpen, A. (eds.): *Cooperative Strategies.* Lexington Books: Lexington.

Miles, I.; Andersen, B.; Boden, M.; Howells, J. (2000): Service production and intellectual property. *International Journal of Technology Management,* Vol. 20, No. 1/2, pp. 95-115.

Miotti, L.; Sachwald, F. (2003): Co-operative R&D: why and with whom?: An integrated framework of analysis. *Research Policy,* Vol. 32, No. 8, pp. 1481-1499.

Mobley, J.W. (1999): Licensing Is Key To Success at U.S. Federal Labs. *les Nouvelles – Journal of the Licensing Executives Society,* Vol. XXXIV, No. 1, pp. 30-34.

Mogee, M.E. (1997): Patents and Technology Intelligence. In: Ashton, W.B.; Klavans, R.A. (eds.), *Keeping Abreast of Science and Technology.* Battelle Press: Ohio.

Mogee, M.E.; Kolar R. (1994): International Patent Analysis as a Tool for Corporate Technology Analysis and Planning. *Technology Analysis and Strategic Management,* Vol. 6, pp. 485-503.

More, E.; McGrath, G.M. (1996): *Cooperative Corporate Strategies in Australia's Telecommunication Sector – The Nature of Strategic Alliances.* Department of Industrie, Science and Tourism: Canberra.

Mowery, D. (1988): *International Collaborative Ventures in US Manufacturing.* Ballinger: Cambridge.

Mowery, D. (1989): Collaborative ventures between U.S. and foreign manufacturing firms. *Research Policy,* Vol. 18, No. 1, pp. 19-32.

Much, D. (1997): Harmonisierung von technischer Auftragsabwicklung und Produktionsplanung und -steuerung bei Unternehmenszusammenschlüssen. In: *Berichte des Forschungsinstitutes für Rationalisierung und des Instituts für Arbeitswissenschaft Aachen.* Shaker: Aachen, Vol. 9.

Mühlbauer, P. (2001): *Die Resozialisierung des Giganten,* Heinz Heise: Hannover, October 8th, 2003, http://www.heise.de/tp/deutsch/inhalt/co/8778/1.html.

Müller, L. (2004): *Kooperationen für Innovationen. Erfolgsfaktoren in der Setup-Phase unter besonderer Berücksichtigung von Intellectual Property.* Bachelor Thesis at Institute of Technology Management (ITEM) of University of St. Gallen (HSG): St. Gallen.

Müller, R. (1998): *Kommerzialisierung industrieller Dienstleistungen.* Disstertation at University of St.Gallen (HSG): St. Gallen, No. 2144.

Müller-Stewens, G.; Lechner, C. (2003): *Strategisches Management.* Schäffer-Poeschel: Stuttgart, 2nd ed.

Murtha, E.J.; Myers, R.A. (2000): Increasing the Value of a Patent Portfolio. *les Nouvelles – Journal of the Licensing Executives Society*, Vol. XXXV, No. 4, pp. 153-155.

Mytelka, L.K. (1991): *Strategic Partnerships and the World Economy.* Pinter: London.

National Science Foundation (2000): *Science and Engineering Indicators 2000.* Arlington, Virginia.

Nakano, K. (2000): Allocations of ownership of inventions in joint development agreements – the Japanese perspective. *Les Nouvelles – Journal of the Licensing Executives Society*, Vol. XXXV, No. 4, pp. 181-182.

Negasse, S. (2004): R&D co-operation and innovation a microeconometric study on French firms. *Research Policy*, Vol. 33, No. 3, pp. 365-384.

Nooteboom, B. (1999): Innovation and inter-firm linkages: new implications for policy. *Research Policy*, Vol. 28, No. 8, pp. 793-805.

Nooteboom, B. (2004): *Inter-firm collaboration, learning & networks. An integrated approach.* Routledge: London and New York.

Nooteboom, B.; Berger, H.; Noorderhaven, N. (1997): Effects of trust and governance on relational risk. *Academy of Management Journal*, Vol. 40, pp. 308-338.

O'Reilley, D.P. (2000): Allocations of ownership of inventions in joint development agreements – the united states perspective. *Les Nouvelles – Journal of the Licensing Executives Society*, Vol. XXXV, No. 4, pp. 168-172.

OECD (2002a): *OECD Science, Technology and Industry Outlook.* OECD: Paris.

OECD (2002b): *OECD/BIAC Survey on Business Patenting and Licensing: Preliminary Results.* OECD DSTI: Paris, June 20th, 2002.

OECD (2003a): *Turning Science into Business: Patenting and Licensing at Public Research Organisations*: OECD: Paris.

OECD (2003b), *Genetic Inventions, IPRs and Licensing Practices: Evidence and Policies.* OECD: Paris.

OECD (2004a): *Patents, Innovation and Economic Performance.* OECD Conference Proceedings: Paris.

OECD (2004b): *Science and Innovation Policy. Key Challenges and Opportunities.* OECD: Paris.

OECD (2004c): *Science, Technology and Industry Outlook.* OECD: Paris.

Ohly, A. (2001): Software und Geschäftsmethoden im Patentrecht. *Computerrecht*, No. 12, pp. 809-817.

Olemotz, T. (1995): *Strategische Wettbewerbsvorteile durch industrielle Dienstleistungen.* Europäischer Verlag der Wissenschaften: Frankfurt a.M.

Oliva, R.; Kallenberg R. (2003): *Managing the transition from products to services*. International Journal of Service Industry Management, Vol. 14, No. 2, pp. 160-172.

Olsson, H.; McQueen, D.H. (2000): Factors influencing patenting in small computer software producing companies. *Technovation*, Vol. 20, No. 10, pp. 563-576.

Osborn, R.N.; Baughn, C.C. (1990): Forms of Intel-organizational governance for multinational alliances. *Academy of Management Journal*, Vol. 33, pp. 503-519.

Oster, S.M. (1992). *Modern Competitive Analysis*. Oxford University Press: New York.

Österle, H. (2000): Auf dem Weg zum Service-Portal. In: Belz, C.; Bieger, T. (eds.): *Dienstleistungskompetenz und innovative Geschäftsmodelle*. Thexis: St. Gallen, pp. 168-177.

Park, S.; Ungson, G. (1997): The effect of national culture, organizational complementarity and economic motivation on joint venture dissolution. *Academy of Management Journal*, Vol. 40, pp. 279-307.

Parkhe, A. (1998a): Building trust in international alliances. *Journal of World Business*, Vol. 33, pp. 417-437.

Parkhe, A. (1998b): Understanding trust in international alliances. *Journal of World Business*, Vol. 33, pp. 219-240.

Pavitt, K. (1982): R&D, patenting and innovative activities: A statistical exploration. *Research Policy*, Vol. 11, No. 1, pp. 33-51.

Pavitt, K. (1985): Patent statistics as indicators of innovative activities: possibilities and problems. *Scientometrics*, Vol. 7, pp. 77-99.

Pavitt, K. (1988): Uses and abuses of patent statistics. In: van Raan, A.F.J. (ed.): *Handbook of quantitative studies of science and technology*. Elsevier: Amsterdam, pp. 509-536.

Pavitt, K.; Patel, P. (1988): The international distribution and determinants of technological activities. *Oxford Review of Economic Policy*, Vol. 4, pp. 35-55.

Pearson, A.W.; Nixon, W.A. (2000): R&D as a business – what are the implications for performance measurement? *R&D Management*, Vol. 30, Vol. 4, pp. 355-366.

Penner-Hahn, J.; Myles Shaver, J. (2005): Does international research and development increase patent output? An analysis of japanese pharmaceutical firms. *Strategic Management Journal*, Vol. 26, pp. 121-140.

Pisano, G.P. (1990): The R&D boundaries of the firm: an empirical analysis. *Administrative Science Quarterly*, Vol. 35, pp. 177-207.

Pitkethly, R.H. (2001): Intellectual property strategy in Japanese and UK companies: patent licensing decisions and learning opportunities. *Research Policy*, Vol. 30, No. 3, pp. 425-442.

Plunket, A.; Voisin, C.; Bellon, B. (2001): *The Dynamics of Industrial Collaboration*. Cheltenham: Northampton.

Porter, M. (1980): *Competitive Strategy: techniques for analysing industries and competitors*. Free Press: New York.

Porter, M.E. (1997): Nur Strategie sichert auf Dauer hohe Erträge. *Harvard Business Manager*, Vol. 19, No. 3, pp. 42-58.

Potts, G. (1988): Exploiting your product service life cycle. *Harvard Business Review*, Vol. 66, No. 5, pp. 32-35.

Powell, W.W.; Koput, K.W.; Smith-Doerr, L. (1996): Interorganizational Collaboration and the Locus of Innovation: Networks of Learning in Biotechnology. *Administrative Science Quarterly*, Vol. 41, pp. 116-145.

Prahalad, C.K.; Hamel, G. (1990): The Core Competence of the Corporation. *Harvard Business Review*, Vol. 68, No. 3, pp. 79-91.

Quinn, J.B. (1992): *Intelligent Enterprise*. Free Press: New York.

Rahnasto, I. (2003): *Intellectual Property Rights, External Effects, and Anti-trust Law*. Oxford University Press: New York.

Razgaitis, R. (2003a): *Dealmaking Using Monte Carlo and Real Options Analysis*. John Wiley & Sons: Chichester.

Razgaitis, R. (2003b): *Valuation and Pricing of Technology-Based Intellectual Property*. John Wiley & Sons: Chichester.

Reger, G. (2001): Risikoreduktion durch Technologie-Früherkennung. In: Gassmann, O.; Kobe, C.; Voit, E. (eds.): *High-Risk-Projekte – Quantensprünge in der Entwicklung erfolgreich managen*. Springer: Berlin.

Reitzig, M. (2003): What determines patent value?: Insights from the semiconductor industry. *Research Policy*, Vol. 32, pp. 13-26.

Reitzig, M. (2004): Strategic Management of Intellectual Property. *MIT Sloan Management Review*, Spring 2004, pp. 35-40.

Rice, M.; Kelley, D.; Peters, L.; O'Connor, G.C. (2001): Radical innovation: triggering initiation of opportunity recognition and evaluation. *R&D Management*, Vol. 31, No. 4, pp. 409-420.

Ring, P.S.; van de Ven, A.H. (1992): Structuring cooperative relationships between organizations. *Strategic Management Journal*, Vol. 13, pp. 483-498.

Rivette, K.G.; Kline, D. (2000a): Discovering New Value in Intellectual Property. *Harvard Business Review*, Vol. 78, No. 1, pp. 54-66.

Rivette, K.G.; Kline, D. (2000b): *Rembrandts in the attic: unlocking the hidden value of patents*. Harvard Business School Press: Boston.

Robertson, P.L.; Langlois, R.N. (1995): Innovation, networks, and vertical integration. *Research Policy*, Vol. 24, No. 4, pp. 543-562.

Rogers, E.M.; Carayannis, E.G.; Kurihara, K.; Allbritton, M.M. (1998): Cooperative Research and Development Agreements (CRADAs) as technology transfer mechanisms. *R&D Management*, Vol. 28, No. 2, pp. 79-88.

Rohner, N. (2004): *Möglichkeiten und Grenzen von Patenten als Instrumente der strategischen Frühaufklärung*. Diploma Thesis at Institute of Technology Management (ITEM) of University of St.Gallen (HSG): St. Gallen.

Rühl, J. (2001): *Vertragliche Gestaltung von Innovationskooperationen: Optimierung bei Informationsasymmetrie*. Deutscher Universitäts-Verlag: Wiesbaden.

Sanche, N. (2002): *Strategische Erfolgsposition industrieller Service: Eine empirische Untersuchung zur Entwicklung industrieller Dienstleistungsstrategien*. Dissertation at University of St.Gallen (HSG): St. Gallen, No. 2655.

Santangelo, G.D. (2000): Corporate strategic technological partnerships in the European information and communications technology industry. *Research Policy*, Vol. 29, No. 9, pp. 1015-1031.

Saxton, T. (1997): *The Effects of Partner and Relationship Characteristics on Alliance Outcomes*. Academy of Management Journal, Vol. 40, pp. 443-461.

Schmenner, R.W. (1986): How can service businesses survive and prosper. *Sloan Management Review*, Vol. 27, No. 3, pp. 21-32.

Schmid, B.F. (1999): Elektronische Märkte – Merkmale, Organisation und Potentiale. In: Hermanns, A.; Sauter, M. (eds.): *Management-Handbuch Electronic Commerce*. Vahlen: Munich, pp. 31-48.

Schmid, B.F. (2000a): Informatik verändert Dienstleistungsprozesse – Einleitung. In: Belz, C.; Bieger, T. (eds.): *Dienstleistungskompetenz und innovative Geschäftsmodelle*. Thexis: St. Gallen, pp. 144-145.

Schmid, B.F. (2000b): Was ist neu an der digitalen Ökonomie? In: Belz, C.; Bieger, T. (eds.): *Dienstleistungskompetenz und innovative Geschäftsmodelle*. Thexis: St. Gallen, pp. 178-196.

Schögel, M. (1999): *Kooperative Leistungssysteme: Eigenschaften, Herausforderungen und Lösungsansätze*. Thexis: St. Gallen.

Segrestin, B. (2005): Partnering to explore: The Renault-Nissan Alliance as a forerunner of new cooperative patterns. *Research Policy*, Vol. 34, No. 5, pp. 657-672.

Shane, S. (2001): Technological opportunities and new firm creation. *Management Science*, Vol. 47, No. 2, pp. 205-220.

Shapiro, C. (2002): *Competition Policy and Innovation*. OECD STI Working Papers, 2002/11.

Sherman, S. (1992): Are strategic alliances working? *Fortune*, September 21st, pp. 77-78.

Sherry, E.F.; Teece, D.J. (2004): Royalties, evolving patent rights, and the value of innovation. *Research Policy*, Vol. 33, No. 2, pp. 179-191.

Siaw, T. (2000): Allocations of ownership of inventions in joint development agreements – the Malaysian perspective. *Les Nouvelles – Journal of the Licensing Executives Society*, Vol. XXXV, No. 4, p. 176.

Siemens (2004): Coverstory Patente: Die harte Siemens-Währung. *SiemensWelt*, No. 7/2004, pp. 38-41.

Simon, H. (1993): *Industrielle Dienstleistungen*. Schäffer-Poeschel, Stuttgart.

Smith, M.; Hansen, F. (2002): Managing intellectual property: a strategic point of view. *Journal of Intellectual Capital*, Vol. 3, No. 4, pp. 366-374.

Somaya, D. (2002): *Theoretical Perspectives on Patent Strategy*. Working Paper. University of Maryland.

Somaya, D. (2003): Strategic determinants of decisions not to settle patent litigation. *Strategic Management Journal*, Vol. 24, No. 1, pp. 17-38.

Somaya, D.; Teece, D. (2001): *Combining Patented Inventions in Multi-invention Products. Transactional Challenges and Organizational Choices*. Working Paper. University of Maryland, University of California at Berkeley.

Specht, D.; Beckmann, C. (1996): *F&E-Management*. Schäffer-Poeschel: Stuttgart.

Spekman, R.E.; Lynn, A.I.; MacAvoy, T.C.; Forbes III, T. (1996): Creating strategic alliances which endure. *Long Range Planning*, Vol. 29, No. 3, pp. 346-357.

Stolpe, M. (2002): Determinants of knowledge diffusion as evidenced in patent data: the case of liquid crystal display technology. *Research Policy*, Vol. 31, No. 7, pp. 1181-1198.

Sudia, F.W. (2001): An Overview of Structured Licensing. *les Nouvelles – Journal of the Licensing Executives Society*, Vol. XXXVI, No. 4, pp. 128-131.

Sullivan, P.H. (2001): *Profiting From Intellectual Capital.* John Wiley & Sons: New York.

Sutter, R. (2003): *Intellectual Property Management in Cooperative Innovation Processes.* Diploma Thesis at Institute of Technology Management (ITEM) of University of St.Gallen (HSG): St. Gallen.

Swiss Re (2004a): *Intellectual Property Report 2003.* Bischof, D.; Cuypers, F.; Swiss Reinsurance Company: Zurich.

Swiss Re (2004b): *Geschäftsbericht 2003.* Swiss Reinsurance Company: Zurich.

Sydow, J. (1992): *Strategische Netzwerke: Evolution und Organisation.* Gabler: Wiesbaden.

Täger, U.C. (1989): Entwicklungstendenzen im Patentverhalten deutscher Erfinder und Unternehmen. *Ifo-Schnelldienst*, Vol. 42, No. 23, pp. 14-26.

Tapon, F.; Thong, M. (1999): Research collaborations by multi-national research oriented pharmaceutical firms: 1988-1997. *R&D Management*, Vol. 29, No. 3, pp. 219-231.

Teece, D.J. (1977): Technology transfer by multinational firms: the resource cost of transferring technologic know-how. *Economic Journal*, Vol. 87, pp. 242-261.

Teece, D.J. (1988): Capturing Value from Technological Innovation: Integration, Strategic Partnering, and Licensing Decisions. *Interfaces*, Vol. 18, No. 3, pp. 46-61.

Tether, B.S. (2002): Who co-operates for innovation, and why: An empirical analysis. *Research Policy*, Vol. 31, No. 6, pp. 947-967.

Teufel, F. (2003): *Praxisbeitrag – Verwertungspraxis in der Informations- und Telekommunikationsindustrie.* Presentation on the occasion of conference "Patente 2003". Management Circle: Stuttgart, October 9th, 2003.

Teufel, F. (2004): *IBM – IP-Management bei IBM.* Presentation on the occasion of conference "Patentmanagement". VPP: Stuttgart, May 14th, 2004.

Thumm, N. (2000): *Intellectual Property Rights. National Systems and Harmonisation in Europe.* Physica: Heidelberg.

Thumm, N. (2001): Management of intellectual property rights in European biotechnology firms. *Technological Forecasting and Social Change*, Vol. 67, pp. 259-272.

Thumm, N. (2004): Strategic Patenting in Biotechnology. *Technology Analysis & Strategic Management*, Vol. 16, No. 4, pp. 529-538.

Tidd, J. (1997): Complexity, networks and learning: Integrative themes for research on the management of innovation. *International Journal of Innovation Management*, Vol. 1, No. 1, pp. 1-19.

Tijssen, R.J.W. (2002): Science dependence of technologies: evidence from inventions and their inventors. *Research Policy*, Vol. 31, No. 4, pp. 509-526.

Tomczak, T. (1992): Forschungsmethoden in der Marketingwissenschaft. *Marketing ZFP*, No. 2, pp. 77-78

Torres, A. (1999): Unlocking the value of intellectual assets. *McKinsey Quarterly*, No. 4, pp. 28-37.

Trilateral Statistical Report (2004): *Trilateral Statistical Report 2003*. European Patent Office, Japan Patent Office, United States Patent and Trademark Office: Munich, Tokyo, Alexandria.

Tsuji, Y.S. (2002): Organizational behavior in the R&D process based on patent analysis: Strategic R&D management in a Japanese electronics firm. *Technovation*, Vol. 22, No. 7, pp. 417-425.

Ulrich, H. (1981): Die Betriebswirtschaftslehre als anwendungsorientierte Sozialwissenschaft. In: Geist, M.; Köhler, R. (eds.): *Die Führung des Betriebes*. Poeschel: Stuttgart, pp. 1-26.

Ulrich, H.; Krieg, W. (1974): *St. Galler Management Modell*. Paul Haupt: Bern, 3rd ed.

United States Patent and Trademark Office, USPTO (2002): *The 21st century strategic plan*. USPTO: Washington D.C.

Upstill, G.; Symington, D. (2002): Technology transfer and the creation of companies: the CSIRO experience. *R&D Management*, Vol. 32, No. 3, pp. 233-239.

Urban, G.L. and von Hippel, E. (1988): Lead user analyses for the development of new industrial products. *Management Science*, Vol. 34, No. 5, pp.569-582.

van Dijk, T.; Duysters, G. (1998): Passing the European Patent Office: evidence from the data-processing industry. *Research Policy*, Vol. 27, No. 9, pp. 937-946.

Verma, R. (2000): An empirical analysis or management challenges in service factories, service shops, mass services and professional services. *International Journal of Service Industry Management*, Vol. 11, No. 1, pp. 8-25.

Veugelers, R. (1997): Internal R & D expenditures and external technology sourcing. *Research Policy*, Vol. 26, No. 3, pp. 303-315.

von Braun, C.-F. (1994): *Der Innovations-Krieg. Ziele und Grenzen der industriellen Forschung und Entwicklung*. Hanser: Munich.

von Hippel, E. (1986): Lead users: a source of novel product concepts. *Management Science*, Vol. 32, pp. 791-805.

von Hippel, E. (1988): *The Sources of Innovation*. Oxford University Press: New York.

Walls, G. (2002): Defuzzing the Fuzzy Front End. In: Walls, G.: *Creating Breakthrough Ideas: The Collaboration of Anthropologists and Designers in the Product Development Industry*. Greenwood Publishers: Westport.

Watts, R.J.; Porter, A.L.; Newmann, N.C. (1998): Innovation Forecasting Using Bibliometrics, *Competence Intelligence Review*, Vol. 9, No. 4, pp. 11-19.

Wehling, A. (2002): *Schutz innovativer Versicherungsdienstleistungen*. Peter Lang: Frankfurt a.M.

Weiss, M.B.H.; Sirbu, M. (1990): Technological choice in voluntary standards committees: an empirical analysis. *Economics of Innovation and New Technology*, Vol. 1, pp. 111-133.

Welt (2004): Microsoft kommt in Patentstreit ungeschoren davon. *Die Welt*, August 24th, 2004, p. 13.

Wessel, V.W. (1993). Technology transfer and intellectual property: An analysis of the NASA approach. *Technovation*, Vol. 13, No.3, pp.133-146.

Whittaker, E.; Bower, D.J. (1994): A Shift to External Alliances for Product Development in the Pharmaceutical Industry. *R&D Management*, Vol. 24, No. 3, pp. 249-260.

Williamson, O.E. (1985): *The Economic Institutions of Capitalism*. Free Press: New York.

Williamson, O.E. (1989): Transaction cost economics. In: Schmalensee, R.; Willig, R. (eds.): *Handbook of Industrial Organization*. Elsevier: Amsterdam, Vol. 1, pp. 135-182.

Williamson, O.E. (1996): *The Mechanisms of Governance*. Oxford University Press: Oxford.

Wise, R.; Baumgartner, P. (1999): Going Downstream: The new imperative in manufacturing. *Harvard Business Review*, Vol. 77, No. 5, pp. 133-141.

Wohlgemuth, A.C. (1989): Führung im Dienstleistungsbereich. Interaktionsintensität und Produktionsstandardisierung als Basis einer neuen Typologie. *Führung und Organisation*, Vol. 58, No. 5, pp. 339-345.

Wyatt, S.; Bertin, G.; Pavitt, K. (1985): Patents and multinational corporations: Results from questionnaires. *World Patent Information*, Vol. 7, No. 3, pp. 196-212.

Yahoo News (2005). *Microsoft to Offer Technology Licensing*. May 9th, 2005, http://dailynews.yahoo.com/s/ap/20050506/ap_on_hi_te/ microsoft_licensing/ nc:1209.

Yin, R.K. (1994): *Case Study Research: Design and Methods*. Sage: Thousand Oaks, 2nd ed.

Yoon, B.; Yoon, C.; Park, Y. (2002): On the development and application of a self-organizing feature map-based patent map. *R&D Management*, Vol. 32, No. 4, pp. 291-300.

Yoshino, M.; Rangan, U. (1995): *Strategic Alliances: An Entrepreneurial Approach to Globalization*. Harvard Business School Press: Boston.

Zaheer, A.; McEvily, B.; Perrone, V. (1998): Does trust matter? Exploring the effects of interorganizational and interpersonal trust on performance. *Organization Science*, Vol. 9, pp. 141-159.

List of Figures

List of Tables

List of Abbreviations

API	Application Program Interface
ATM	Asynchronous Transfer Mode
BCS	IBM Business Consulting Services
BU	Business Unit
CA	Canada
CDP	Customer Development Project (SAP)
CIB	Collective Intelligent Bricks
CEO	Chief Executive Officer
CMU	Carnegie Mellon University
COME	Communication, Media and Events (SAP)
CORE	Corporate Engagement (SAP)
CRIM	Centre de transfert de technologies et de connaissances (liaison and transfer centre whose primary financial partner is the Ministère du Développement Économique, de l'Innovation et de l'Exportation of Québec, Canada)
CSEM	Centre Suisse d'Electronique et de Microtechnique (Swiss Center for Electronics and Microtechnology)
CTO	Chief Technical Officer
CURE	Centre for Usability Research and Engineering, Austria
DE	Germany
DIPO	Divisional Intellectual Property Officer (Swiss Re)
DPMA	Deutsches Patent- und Markenamt (German Patent and Trademark Office)
DRM	Digital Rights Management
E3C	European Coordination Committee for Certification (ECCC)
ECLA	European Classification System, s.a. IPC, WPIDS
EICTA	European Information, Communications and Consumer Electronics Technology Industry Associations
EMEA	Europe, Middle East and Africa
EP	Europe
EPC	European Patent Convention
EPFL	École Polytechnique Fédérale de Lausanne, Switzerland
EPO	European Patent Office
ESA	Entertainment Software Association
ETH	Eidgenössische Technische Hochschule (Swiss Federal Institute of Technology)

ETHZ	Eidgenössische Technische Hochschule Zürich (Swiss Federal Institute of Technology Zurich)
EU	European Union
FOAK	First Of A Kind Research Projects (IBM)
FP5/6	5th/6th Framework Program of the European Union
FR	France
FTE	Full Time Equivalent
GIP	Global Intellectual Property Department (Swiss Re)
GOAL	Governmental Organizations and Alliances (SAP)
GPRS	General Package Radio Service (mobile Internet access)
GPS	Global Positioning System
GSM	Global System for Mobile Communication
HPCS	High Productivity Computing System
HSG	Hochschule St. Gallen (University of St.Gallen)
HTML	Hypertext Markup Language
IC	Integrated Circuit
ICT	Information and Communication Technology
ID	Identification
IP	Intellectual Property
IP&L	Intellectual Property and Legal Department (IBM)
IPC	International Patent Classification, s.a. ECLA, WPIDS
IPM	Intellectual Property Management
IPR	Intellectual Property Rights
ISL	Industry Solutions Labs (IBM)
IT	Information Technology
JPO	Japanese Patent Office
KTI	The Innovation Promotion Agency of the Swiss Federal Office for Professional Education and Technology
M&A	Mergers and Acquisitions
NCR	National Cash Register
NDA	Non Disclosure Agreement
ODIS	On Demand Innovation Services (IBM)
OECD	Organisation for Economic Co-operation and Development
OEM	Original Equipment Manufacturer
OSS	Open Source Software
OTC-Drug	Over-the-Counter Drug
PC	Personal Computer
PCT	Patent Cooperation Treaty
PDA	Personal Digital Assistant
PERCS	Reliable Computing System
PIN	Personal Identification Number
PMO	Project Management Office (SAP)
PPM	Patent Portfolio Management
PVT	Patent Value Tool (IBM)
QoS	Quality of Service (Swisscom)
R&D	Research and Development

RAND	Reasonable And Non-Discriminatory
RFID	Radio Frequency Identification
ROI	Return on Investment
S&D	Sales and Distribution
SCDP	Strategic Customer Development Project (SAP)
SDP	Strategic Development Project (SAP)
SDRAM	Synchronous Dynamic Random Access Memory
SIM	Subscriber Identity Module
SLA	Service Level Agreement (Swisscom)
SLAM	Service Level Agreement Management (Swisscom)
SME	Small and Medium Enterprise
STB	Set-Top-Box
SW	Software
T&C	Terms and Conditions
TDB	IBM Technical Disclosure Bulletin
TRIPS	Trade-Related Aspects of Intellectual Property Rights
TV	Television
UK	United Kingdom
UMTS	Universal Mobile Telecommunication System
US	United States of America
USPTO	United States Patent and Trademark Office
VAR	Value-Added Resellers (SAP)
W3C	World Wide Web Consortium
WAP	Wireless Application Protocol
WIPO	World Intellectual Property Organization
WLAN	Wireless Local Area Network
WPIDS	Derwent World Patents Index, s.a. IPC, ECLA
WPTS	Worldwide Patent Tracking System (IBM)
WTO	World Trade Organization

Index

Company Index

Author

Dr. Martin A. Bader is Managing Partner of the innovation and intellectual property management advisory group BGW AG, St. Gallen, Switzerland and Vienna, Austria. He is registered as Swiss and European Patent Attorney and holds a Master's degree in Electrical Engineering.

Martin Bader started his professional career at Siemens and then joined Infineon Technologies in Munich, Germany, as Vice President and Chief Intellectual Property Counsel being responsible for patents and trademarks, licensing and transactions as well as for knowledge and idea management.

From 2002 to 2005 he followed the PhD program at the Institute of Technology Management at the University of St.Gallen, Switzerland. His research focused on intellectual property management in the service industry sector with special interest in research and development collaborations.

He has been key speaker in numerous expert groups and conferences on innovation and intellectual property management and has published two books and several articles so far.